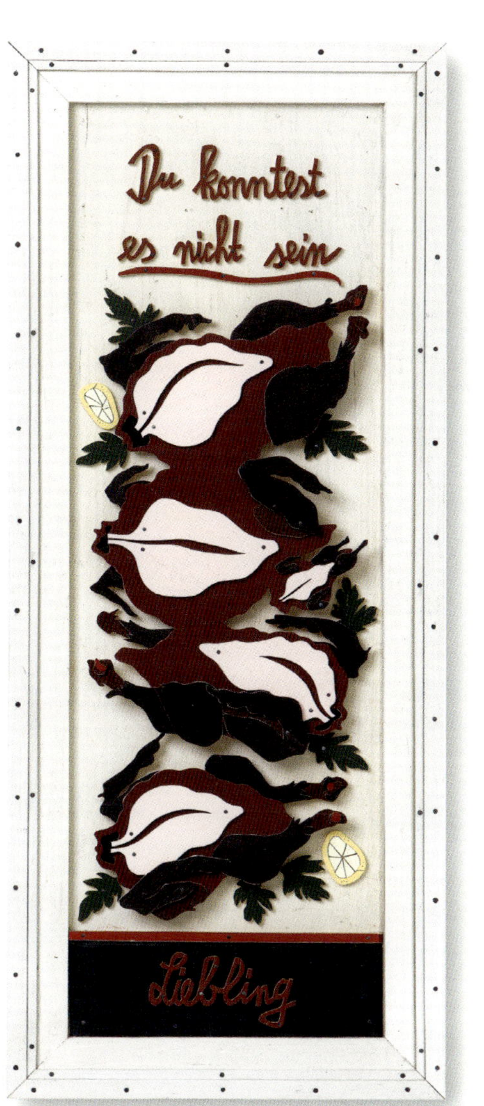

Du konntest
es nicht sein
Liebling

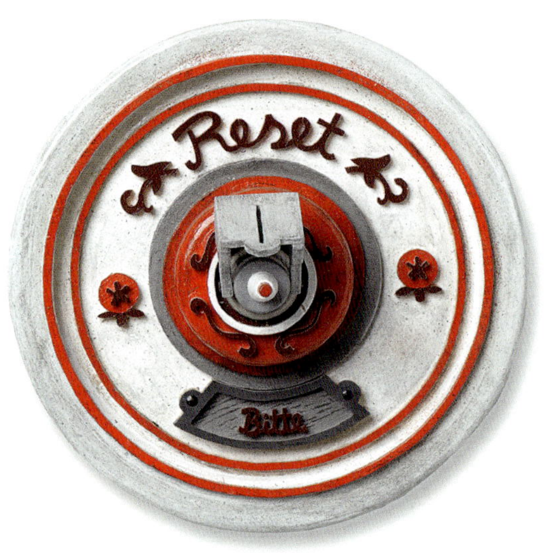
Reset
Bitte

Thorsten Passfeld

Ich bin zurück
It's me again

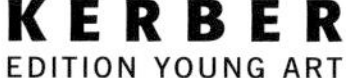

KERBER
EDITION YOUNG ART

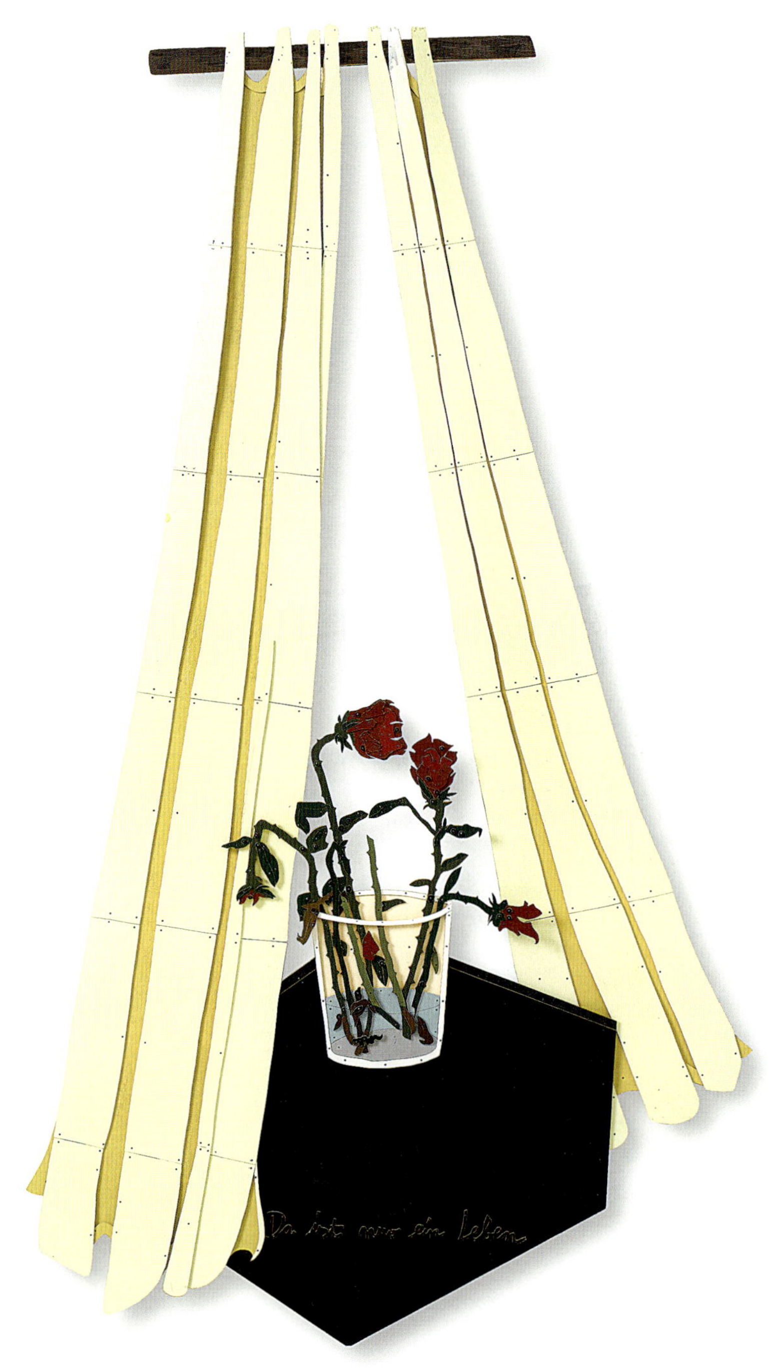

Das ist nur ein Leben

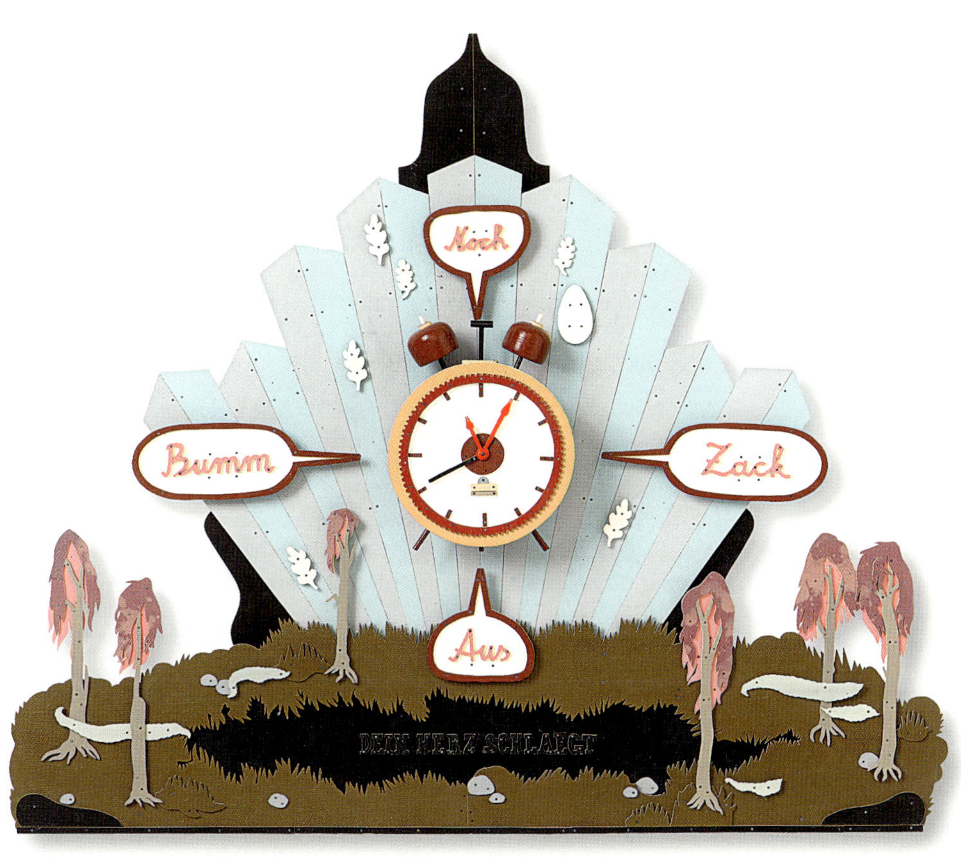

Noch
Bumm
Zack
Aus
DEIN HERZ SCHLAEGT

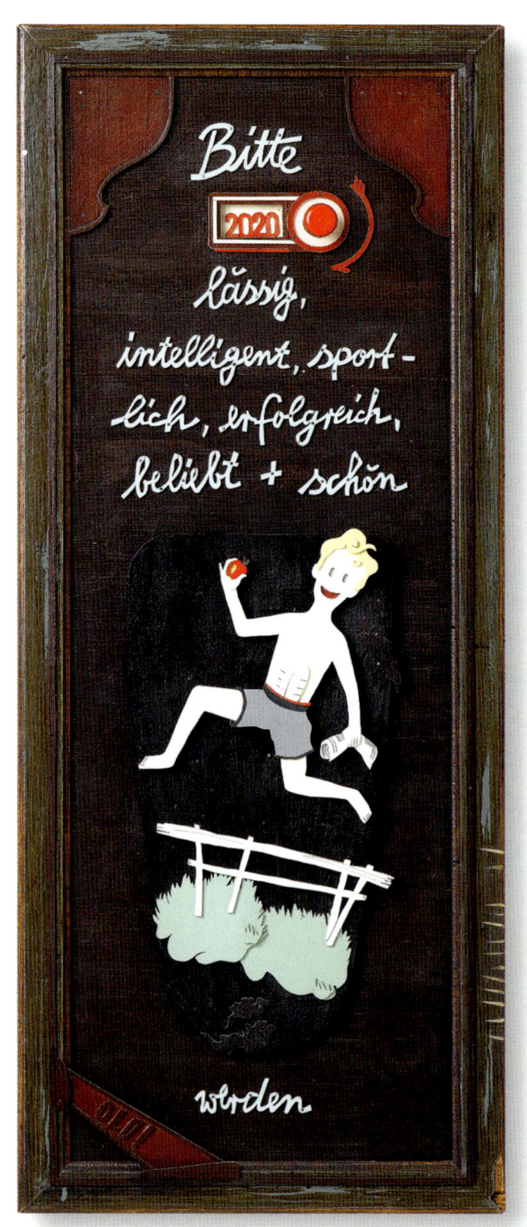
Bitte
2020
lässig,
intelligent, sport-
lich, erfolgreich,
beliebt + schön
werden.

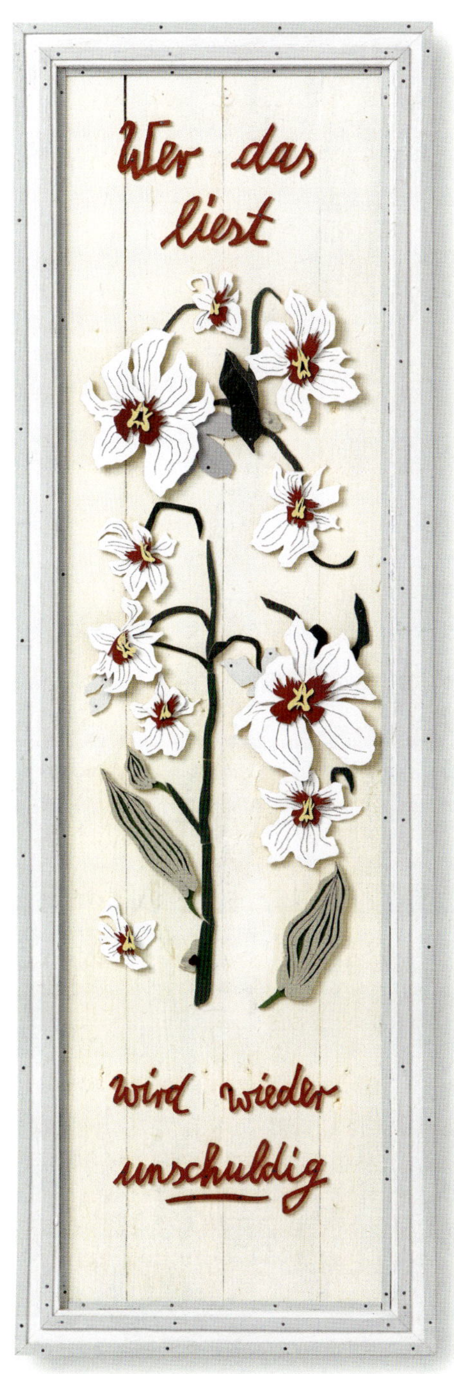
Wer das
liest
wird wieder
unschuldig

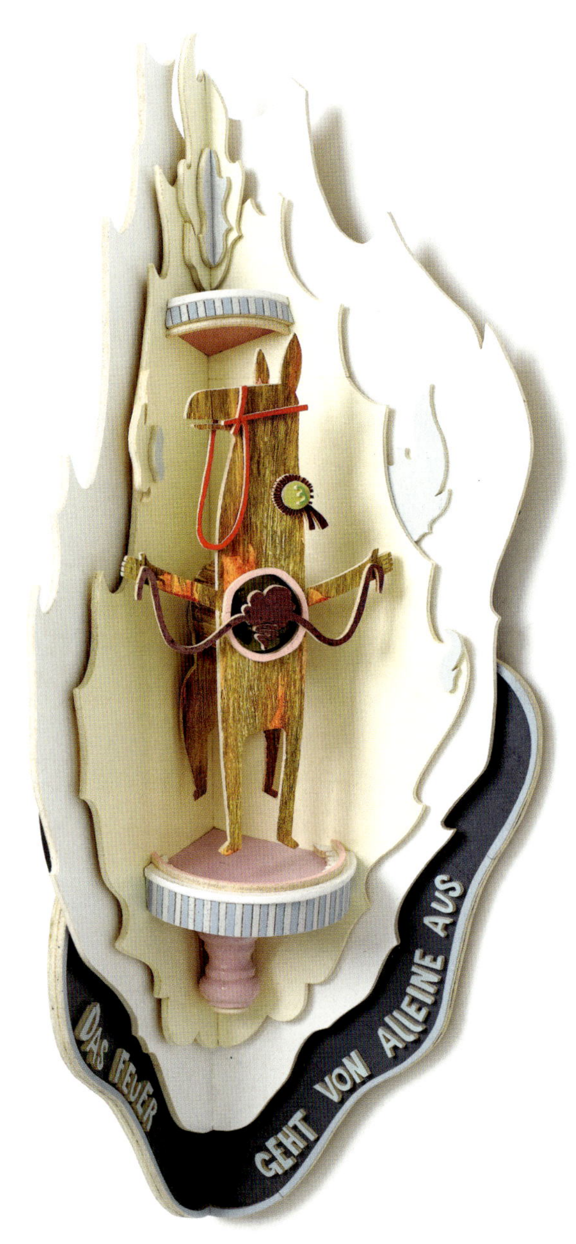

DAS FEUER
GEHT VON ALLEINE AUS

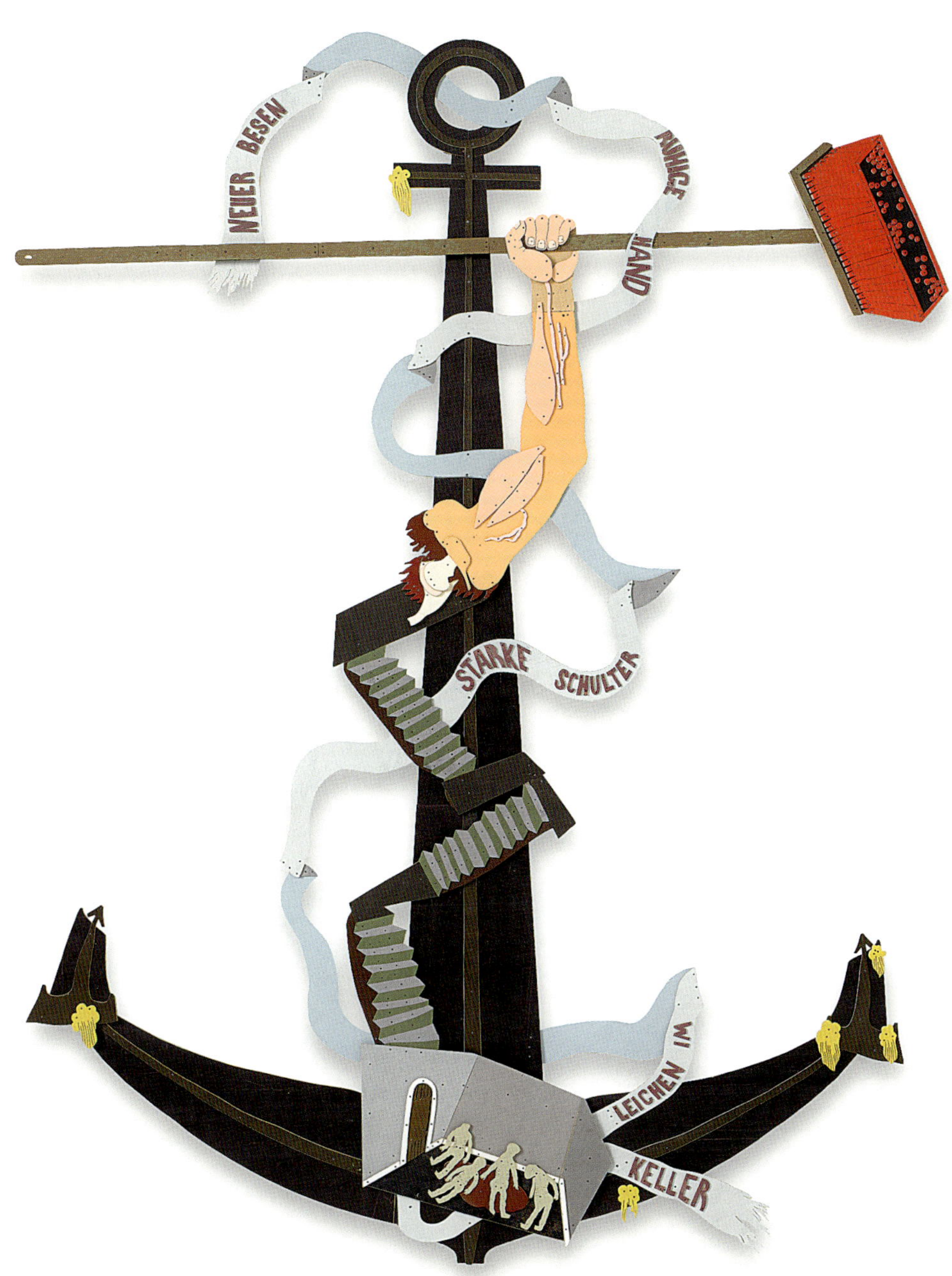

NEUER BESEN
RUHIGE HAND
STARKE SCHULTER
LEICHEN IM KELLER

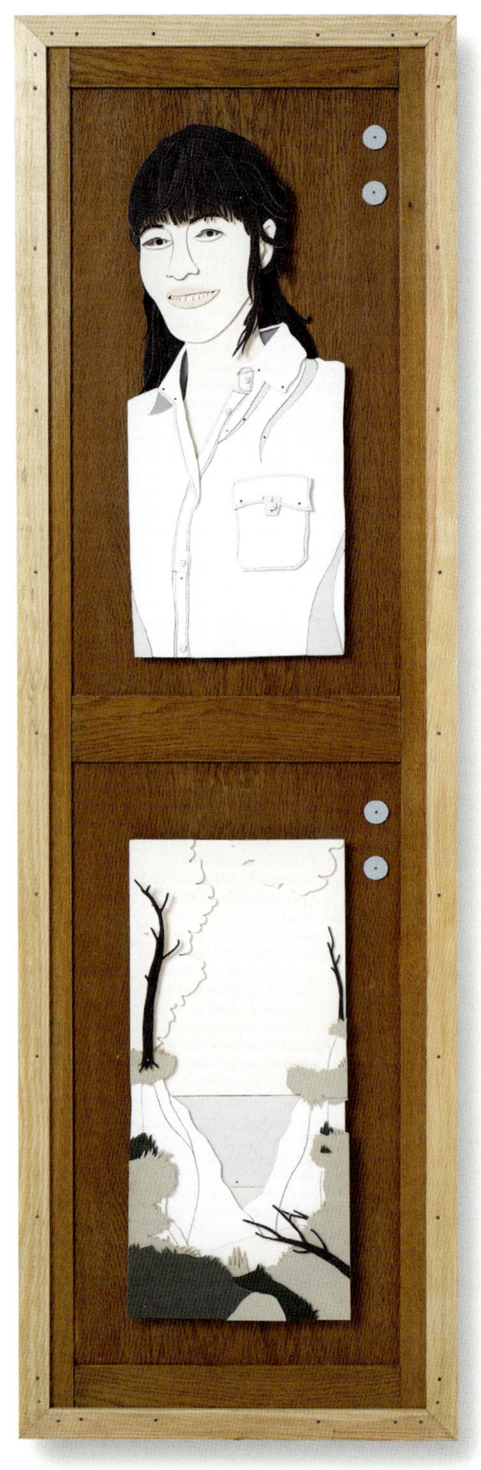

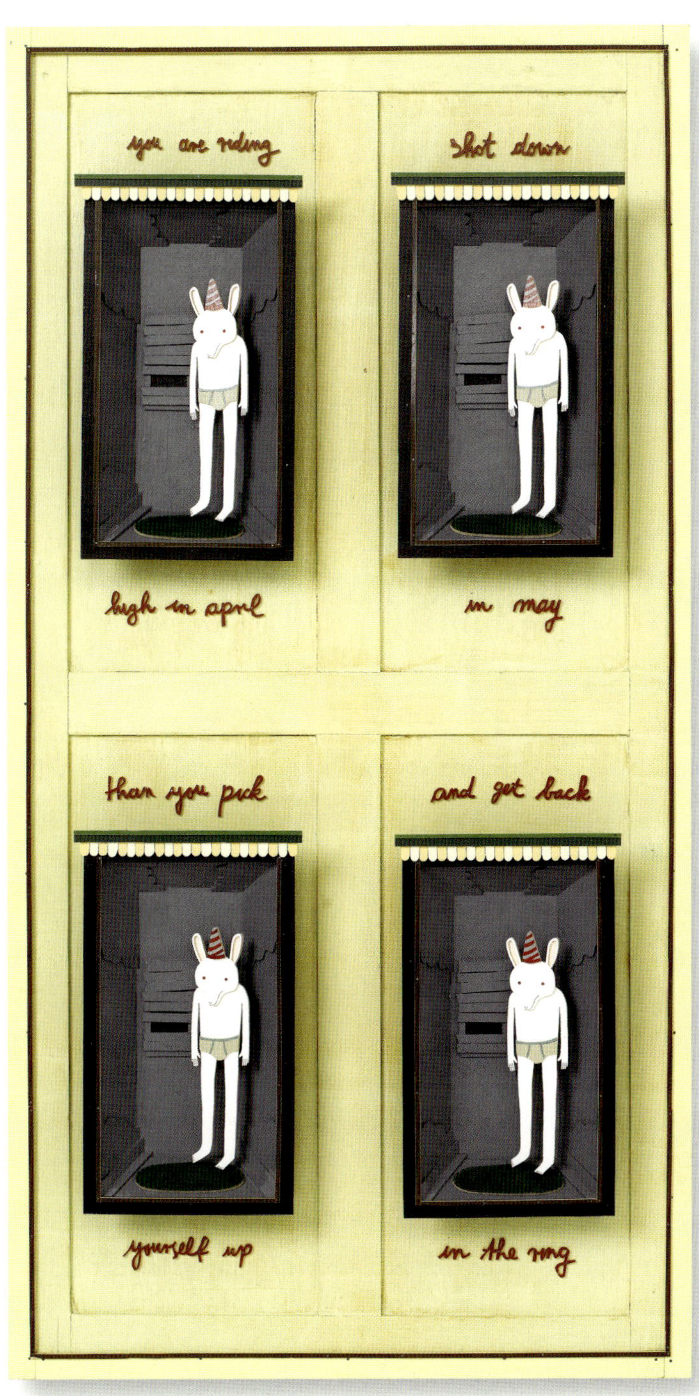
you are riding
shot down
high in april
in may
than you pick
and get back
yourself up
in the ring

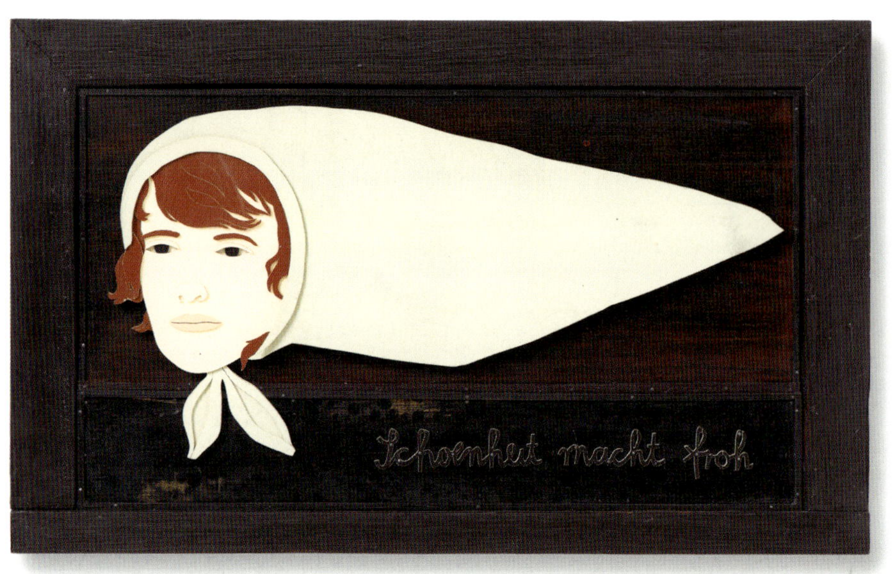

Schoenheit macht froh

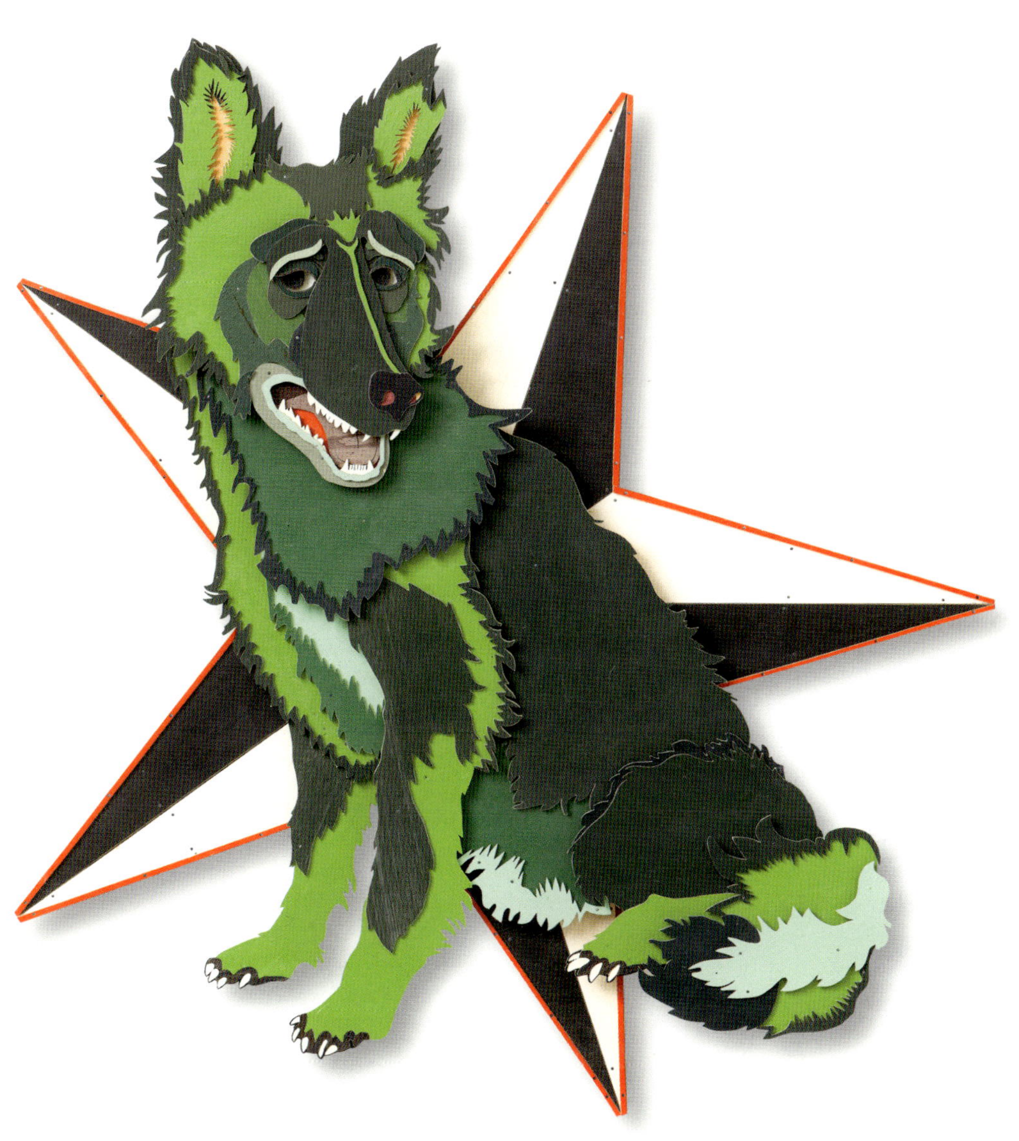

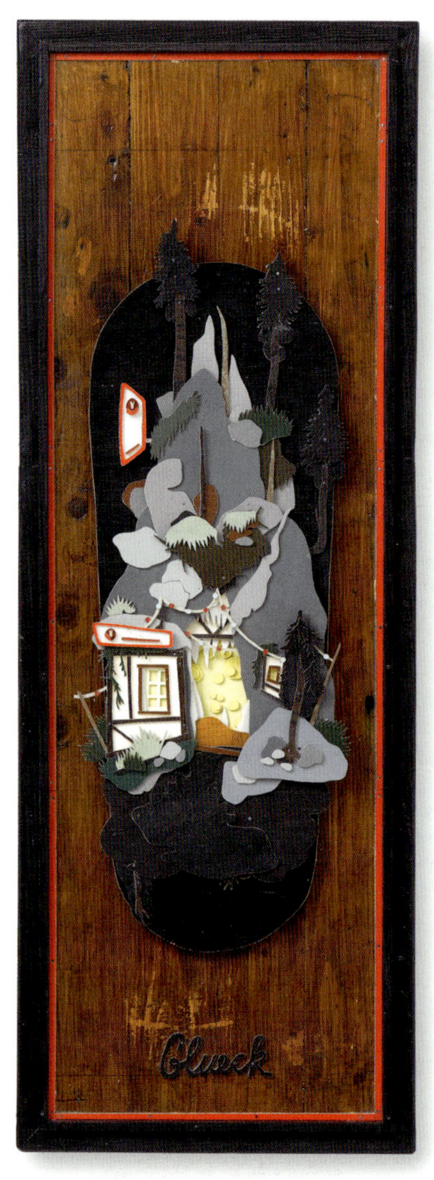
Glueck

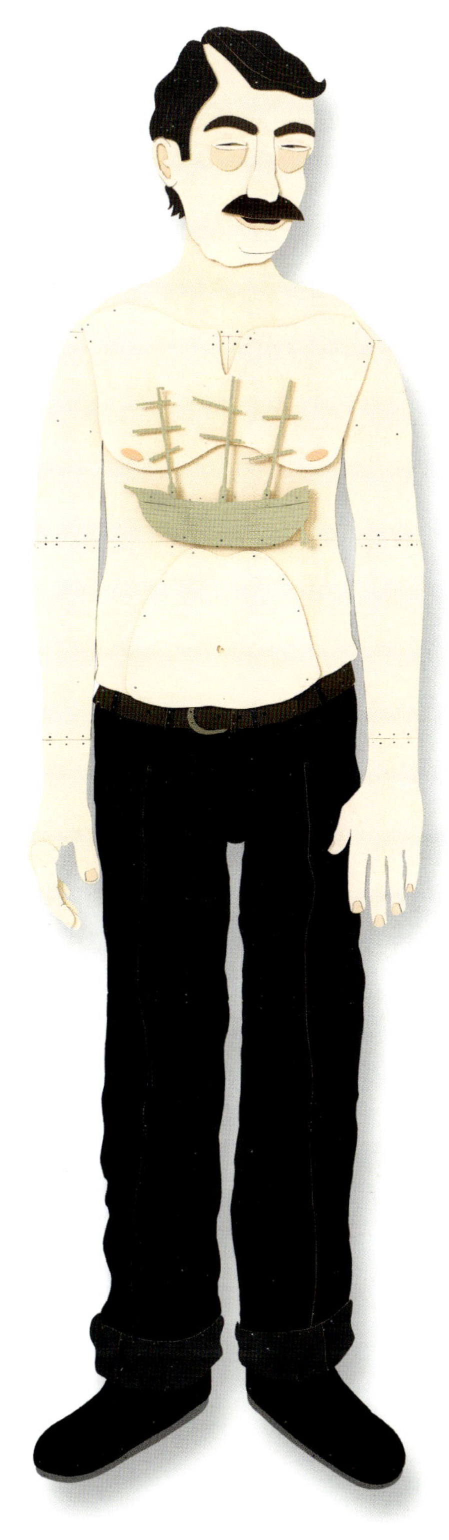

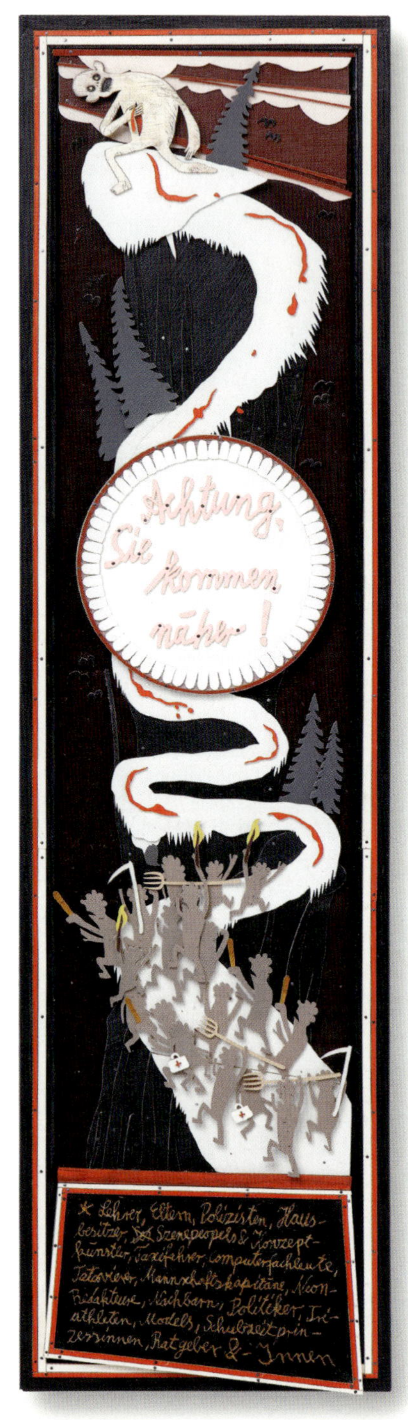

Achtung, Sie kommen näher!
* Lehrer, Eltern, Polizisten, Haus-
besitzer, Szenepeopels & Konzept-
künstler, Taxifahrer, Computerfachleute,
Tätowierer, Mannschaftskapitäne, Neon-
Redakteure, Nachbarn, Politiker, Tri-
athleten, Models, Schulzeitprin-
zessinnen, Ratgeber & -Innen

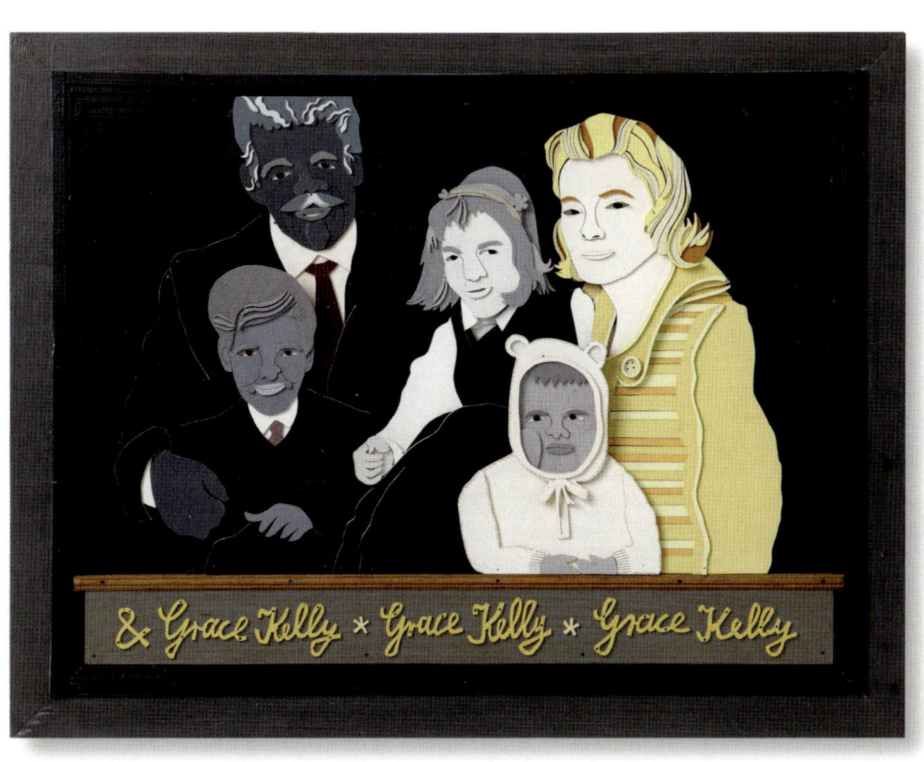

& Grace Kelly * Grace Kelly * Grace Kelly

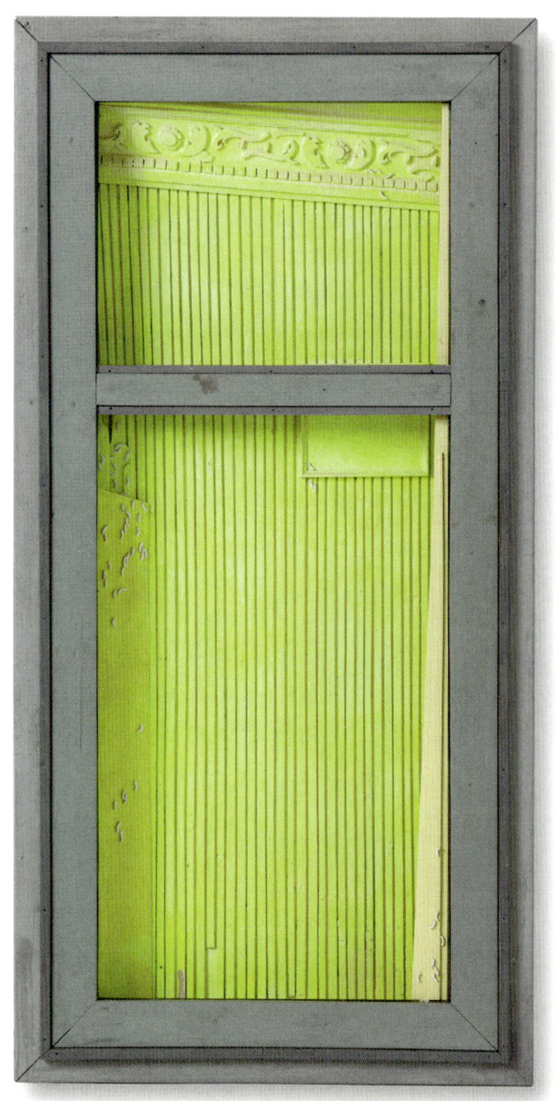

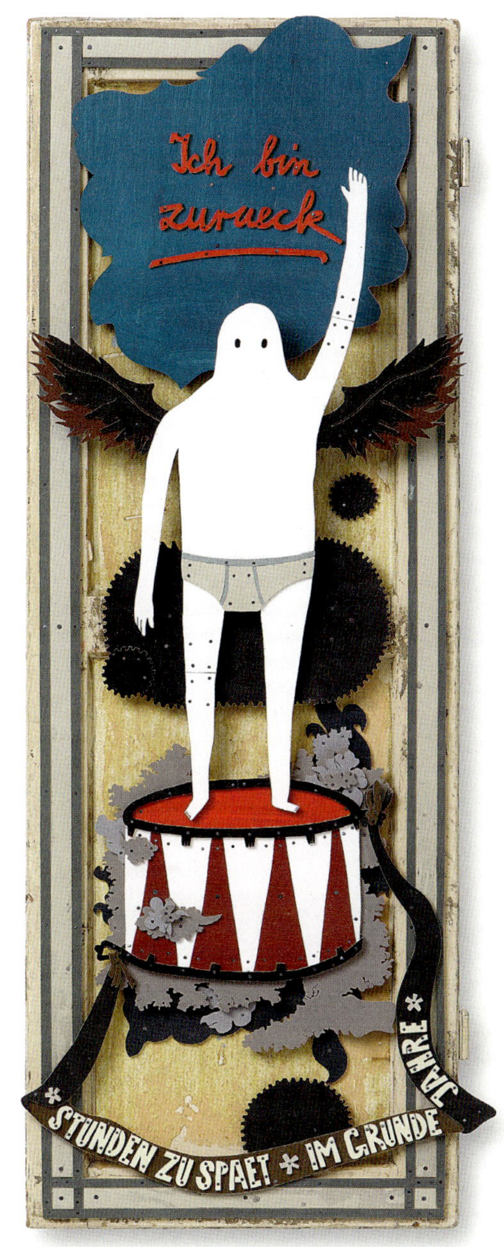

Ich bin zurueck
* STUNDEN ZU SPAET * IM GRUNDE JAHRE *

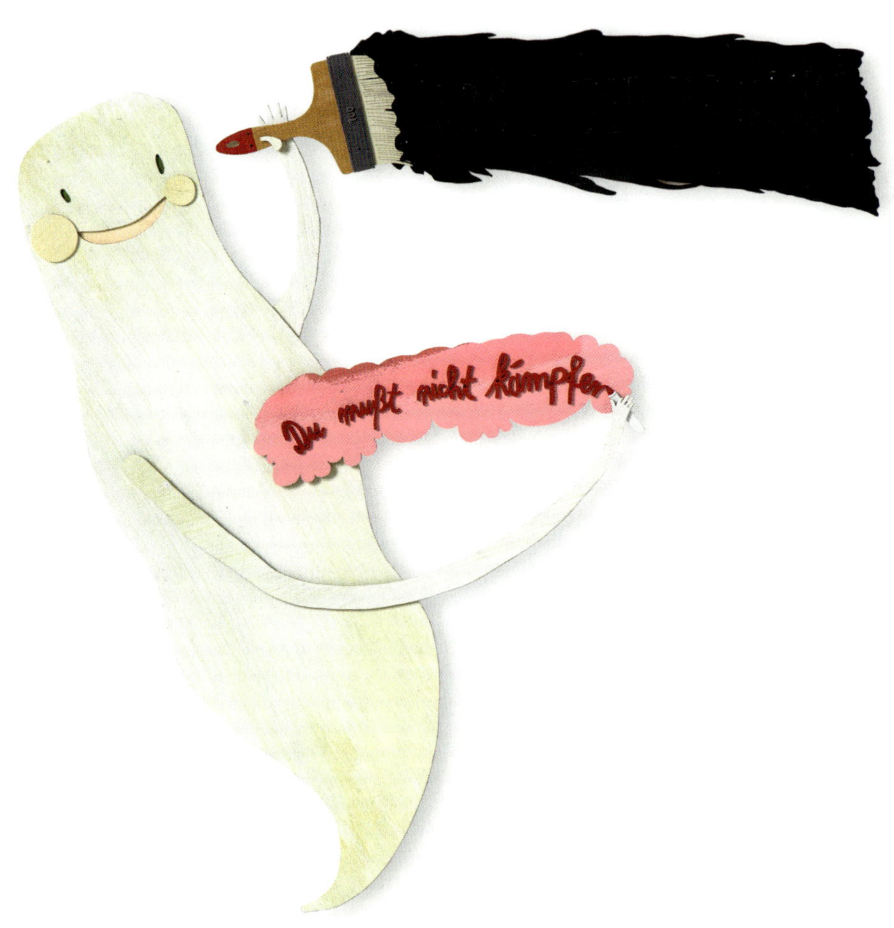

Du mußt nicht kämpfen

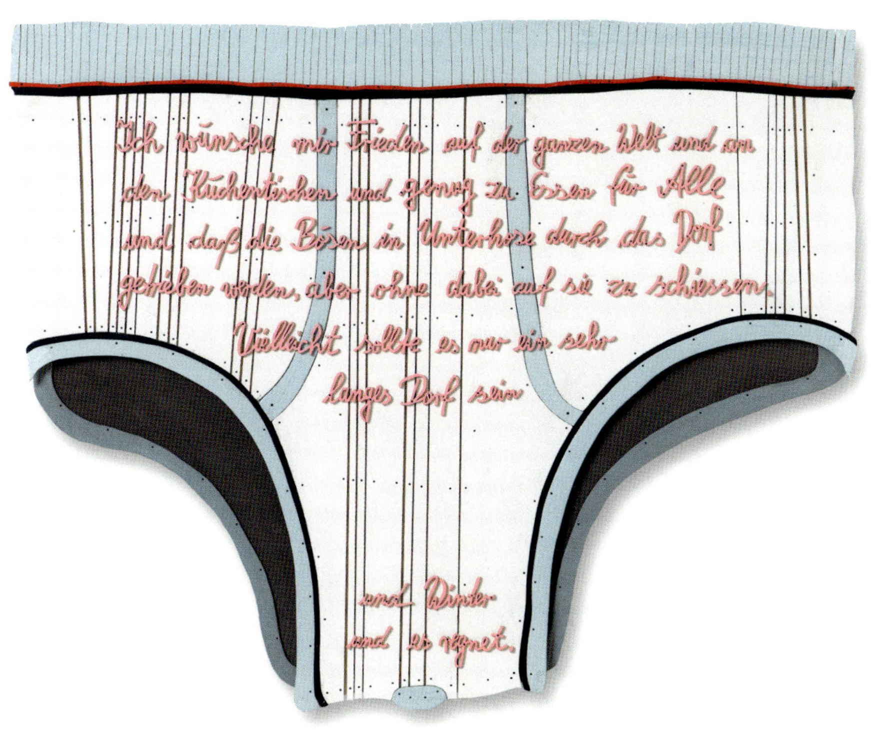

Ich wünsche mir Frieden auf der ganzen Welt und an
den Küchentischen und genug zu Essen für Alle
und daß die Bösen in Unterhose durch das Dorf
getrieben werden, aber ohne dabei auf sie zu schiessen.
Vielleicht sollte es nur ein sehr
langes Dorf sein
und Winter
und es regnet.

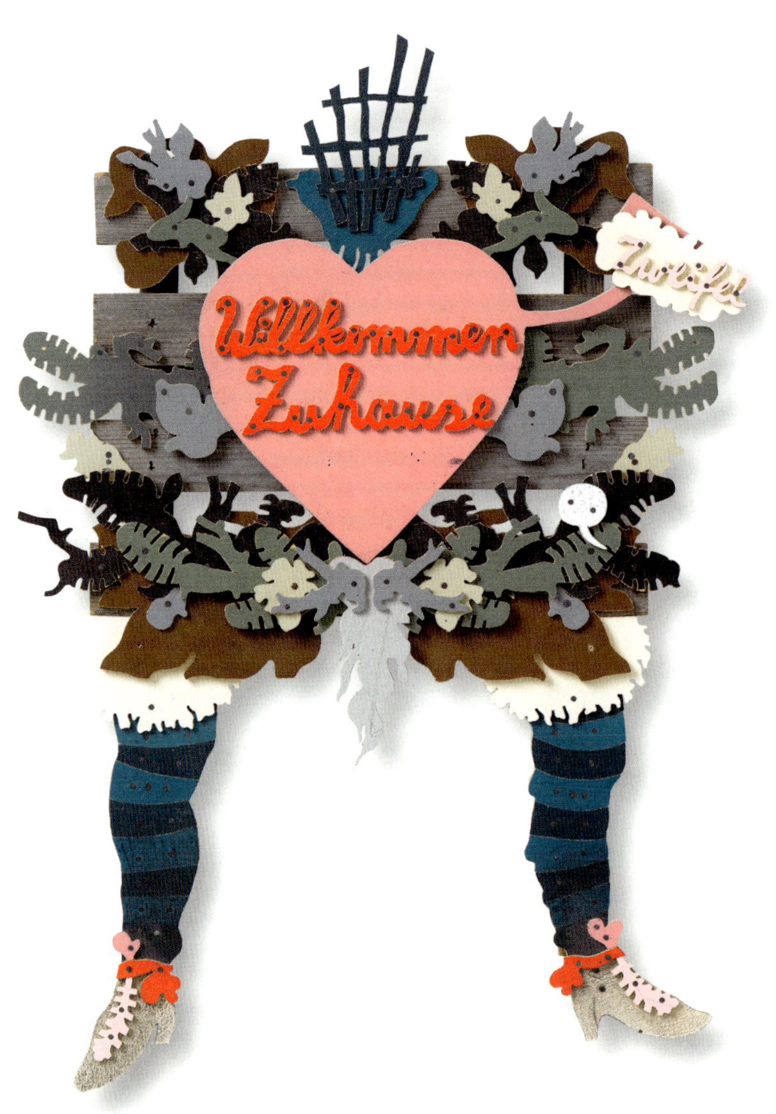
Willkommen Zuhause
Zweifel

spezialisiert auf regionale Hausmannskost. Den Auftrag bekam Passfeld vom heutigen Besitzer der Oberhafenkantine, dem Hamburger Kulturinvestor Klausmartin Kretschmer, der den hölzernen Nachbau als eine Art Kulturbotschafter Hamburgs um die Welt reisen lassen will.

Anders als sonst, wo Passfeld höchstens pro forma ein paar Zeichnungen macht und die Häuser sozusagen aus dem Kopf heraus errichtet, ging er hier streng nach den Bauplänen des Originals vor.

Die künstlerische Freiheit, die bei Auftragsarbeiten doch etwas zurücktritt, lebt er in den letzten Jahren verstärkt in den zahlreichen reliefhaft aus einzelnen Holzteilen zusammengesetzten, farbigen Wandobjekten aus. Der skulpturale Umgang mit dem Holz kommt dabei wieder mit seiner ursprünglichen Neigung zur Malerei zusammen. Aus der gestalterischen Vielfalt der Einzelteile entfaltet sich eine dekorative Qualität, die auch in der Ausgestaltung der Häuser an vielen Stellen zu finden ist, hier aber in die massive Gesamtwirkung des Gebauten eingebunden bleibt.

»Willkommen zuhause« steht auf einem rosa Herz, und hinter vielerlei wurmartigem Getier, das verkleinert an die Außenausstattung des *Erholungsheims für schuldbewusste Großstädter* erinnert, hängen zwei Beine wie bei einem Hampelmann herab. Vom Rest der Figur, sofern überhaupt vorhanden, sieht man nichts. Die kleinbürgerliche Welt hölzerner Spruchbilder wird surreal dekonstruiert, und die Maximen idyllischer Biederkeit finden sich bisweilen ersetzt durch Imperative, deren Befolgung die soziale Akzeptanz in anderen Milieus verspricht: *Bitte lässig, sportlich, erfolgreich, beliebt + schön werden.*

Die ironische Verbindung von Holzobjekt und Sprache ist dem oben erwähnten Vorgehen Georg Herolds nicht ganz unähnlich, auch was den Einsatz einer die herrschenden Kriterien des Kunstbetriebs bewusst unterlaufenden Materialästhetik betrifft. Beide Künstler stellen die Frage, ob der wahre Kleingeist nicht dort zu finden ist, wo man auf Ästhetiken und Materialien respektlos herabblickt, weil sie nicht dem entsprechen, was man cool findet oder zu finden hat. Doch manche Menschen finden Holz cool, weil es ihrem Bedürfnis nach Öko-Hipness entspricht.

Das Holz kann sowohl schwer und erdverbunden als auch schwebend leicht sein. Beides verkörpert sich in Passfelds Skulptur des *Fliegers*, die ein panzerartiges Militärfahrzeug sein könnte, aber auch an den Sonnenwagen des Apoll erinnert. Die kompakte, massive Form wird von der Leichtigkeit der Bauweise konterkariert. Wird das Gefährt sich gewaltsam den Weg bahnen oder leicht wie ein Vogel in den Himmel fliegen? Oder ist es nicht doch wieder ein Haus, das wir – zumindest in Gedanken – bewohnen können? So wird immer deutlicher, dass die gebauten Häuser Thorsten Passfelds, bei aller zumindest temporärer physischer Präsenz, auch und vielleicht vor allem Denkräume sind. Sie fordern zum Nachdenken darüber auf, ob nicht alles ganz anders sein könnte, angefangen mit dem Bau eines vollständigen Hauses ganz mit den eigenen Händen. Und eine Maxime, die Thorsten Passfelds Kunst durchgängig charakterisiert, könnte lauten: nichts aus der Hand geben.

Ludwig Seyfarth

1)   Monika Wagner, Das Material der Kunst. Eine andere Geschichte der Moderne, München 2001, S. 241 ff.
2)   Jean Baudrillard, Das System der Dinge. Über unser Verhältnis zu den alltäglichen Gegenständen, 3. Auflage, Frankfurt/New York 2007, S. 50.
3)   Ebd, S. 51.
4)   Ebd., S. 52.

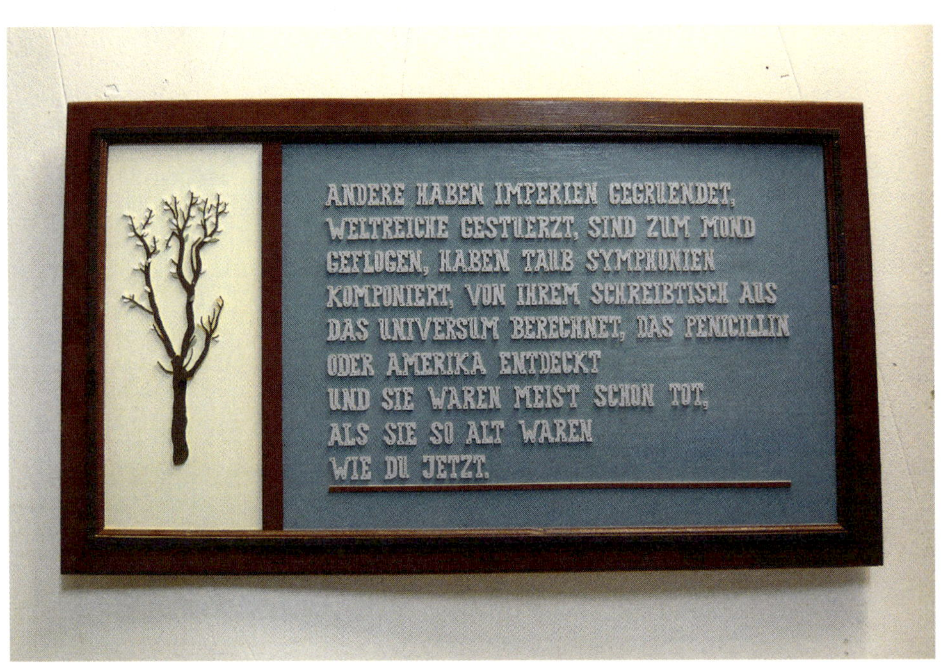

ANDERE HABEN IMPERIEN GEGRUENDET,
WELTREICHE GESTUERZT, SIND ZUM MOND
GEFLOGEN, HABEN TAUB SYMPHONIEN
KOMPONIERT, VON IHREM SCHREIBTISCH AUS
DAS UNIVERSUM BERECHNET, DAS PENICILLIN
ODER AMERIKA ENTDECKT
UND SIE WAREN MEIST SCHON TOT,
ALS SIE SO ALT WAREN
WIE DU JETZT.

The tenuous reputation that wood has as a material in the art world today is paradigmatically reflected by its categorization in Monika Wagner's book "The material of art", the standard work on the iconography of materials in Modernism. Here, wood appears above all in combination with fire, there where it is damaged or destroyed.[1] Wood is somehow out of fashion. Warmth, earthiness, naturalness: The qualities that are traditionally ascribed to it, have increasingly taken on an anachronistic note in the course of the industrialization of the living environment. In his early work, published in 1968 "The system of objects", Jean Baudrillard describes the affect scale which ensures that wood is "… so sought after today for nostalgic reasons. Wood draws its substance from the earth, it lives and breathes and 'labours' (…), it is a material that has being."[2] "… while wood, stone and metal are giving way to concrete and polystyrene."[3] Baudrillard comes to the classical 'postmodernist' conclusion that the differentiation between natural/artificial can no longer be met on the material substance level but has shifted completely to the area of social codification. "Which means that wood is no longer a primary natural material, dense and warm, but, rather, a mere cultural sign of such warmth."[4]

The postmodernist reaction against what is authentic found its art counterpart in the emphasis on Joseph Beuys' or Anselm Kiefer's closeness to nature, while in the case of the cleanly-crafted plywood objects by Thomas Schütte or Ludger Gerdes in the 1980s it is rather an adaptation of the aesthetics of wood to the more abstract, less restricted relationship that occurs, free of naturalizing metaphors, a relationship that usually develops towards synthetic materials.

There are no rough edges or knotholes visible here, in contrast to the "Dachlattenchip", (roof laths) which Georg Herold cobbled together and applied labels to such as "Sehr gut" (very good), "Kleiner mieser Besserwisser" (mean little know-it-all) or "Dieser Mann ist gut zu seiner Frau" (this man is good to his wife). In terms of material there could scarcely be a greater difference to silicon, which is used to manufacture computer chips. Herold also parodies an aesthetic of materials, by which 'natural' wood is perceived to be merely rubbish.

Thorsten Passfeld uses material most other people would throw in the fire to make wall objects, sculptures, installations and even whole houses. Passfeld had already trained as a set designer before he began his painting studies at the University of Fine Arts Hamburg. However he always had the urge to go beyond the purely visual and choose a material that he could work on directly with his own hands and from which he could autonomously develop larger structures.

Passfeld was drawn to just the thing that none of his fellow students took an interest in, something that was neither cool nor hip. He already sensed during his studies that he would never really feel at home in the context of the art world and its value system. So he chose instead to build his own homes out of wood that he found near demolished houses, on building sites or in skips.

The first of these works, *Haus aus Holz* (wooden house) built in 2002, was his diploma project. The house was located in St. Pauli behind a building at the entrance to the Reeperbahn, in which Passfeld had a studio as a member of the artist association SKAM. Although only 60 sqm in size, it had its own entrance hall, kitchen, bathroom, bedroom, attic, toilet, stairs, and a balcony. It would have by all means been possible to live in it long-term but, like all of the other houses, it only stood for a short time.

Passfeld is not interested in permanence. Whether the effort of constructing these houses stands in any "appropriate" proportion to the length or rather the shortness of the existence of the finished building, was not of primary importance to him. He was first and foremost concerned with the act of construction itself, not with the function of the building. This did not come until later as a response to commissions.

Although the exterior of the *Haus aus Holz* (wooden house) was quite plain and simple, Passfeld's other houses, which also had more detailed designs on the facade,

People who build houses can think more clearly

were more strongly reminiscent of other temporary architectural structures such as fairground booths or film- and theatre buildings. In this sense, some passers-by in Hamburg-St. Georg in 2004 might have thought that a Western was going to be filmed here, and that the building on which Passfeld worked week after week was a saloon. But it was in fact a temporary venue for the Hamburg Schauspielhaus. The artistic director of the theatre, Tom Stromberg, had commissioned Passfeld to build the construction. And in this way the 18 by 15 metre high *Hoftheater Vierlinden* (Vierlinden Royal Theatre), was created, and was given this name by the artist because it was situated beneath two chestnut trees. It contained a stage, an auditorium with space for fifty spectators, two aisles, a cloakroom and a bar. Over a period of ten days, the building, which had taken three weeks to construct, was the venue for a busy programme with six premieres.

Only one of the buildings was set up more than once. The 15 sqm harbour bar *Zum Falschen Freund* (to a false friend), was erected in 2005 on invitation by the art association Kunstverein Buchholz, and in 2006 was set up once more for a month in the Hafencity Hamburg as an event location in the context of the Baltic Raw Tower Project. In this case, the simple nature of the material is combined with a "low" social class, which frequently served Passfeld as a source of inspiration. The work *Bahnhofsklo zum letzten Anfang* (station loo for the last beginning), cre-

ated in 2006 as part of the exhibition event sculpture@CityNord, raises the question of whether or not even the most dismal, run-down place – the very essence of a stranded existence – can be the beginning of something new or at least a place of productive contemplation.

Within the context of the Senseo Art Initiative, Passefeld set up the *Erholungsheim für schuldbewusste Großstädter* (rest home for conscience-stricken city-slickers) in the Frappant building in the Große Bergstraße in Altona. What initially looked like a sculpture that had mushroomed wildly into the room was in its essence nonetheless a small, compact house, in which, on entering, the visitor initially saw nothing for several minutes, before the dim lighting revealed the faint outline of the other visitors. Even when loud parties and performances took place around it, the rest home remained a silent place for retreat. And somehow Passfeld's buildings are also reminiscent of favourite childhood retreats such as self-made tree houses, in which one could be completely alone while in the family apartment one perhaps had to share a room with brothers and sisters.

Meanwhile, even the attention of the Art Basel Miami Beach management was drawn to Passfeld's original buildings and at the end of 2006 they invited him to extensively design the outdoor site including an open-air café. He created, among other things, a huge relief made of sawn-out wooden elements, which covered the entrance built using several

containers. The reliefs showed in particular animal motifs, an elephant in the centre, and numerous dogs running around, as well as the words "Play with the Big", in large letters, which was also a reference to the situation of the artist himself, who, as a do-it-yourself artist without a large crew was suddenly dealing directly with the organisation of one of the world's largest art fairs. This contract from oversees was until that point almost the only one that came from the art market itself. Otherwise the requests mostly came and still do come from outdoor projects and festivals. In this way the largest house to date was created for the IBA Kunst- und Kultursommer 2007 (International Building Exhibition Arts and Culture Summer) in Hamburg-Wilhelmsburg. The building encompassed a ground floor area of 18 by 15 metres and was more than five metres high. An extensive programme was held in this *Kirche des Guten Willens* (Church of Goodwill), which pursued the question: How can one be a better person?

Is Passfeld an idealist who believes in a better world? Or is he a pragmatist who simply does what he is able to accomplish within his physical scope and the given economic basic parameters? His most recent house is also a commission when it comes to the design particulars. While in Wilhelmsburg the place was crammed full for three whole weeks, not a single event has been held in this building, constructed in summer 2009 and still standing. It is the reconstruction, on a scale of 1:1, of a legendary Hamburg location, the

Oberhafenkantine (the Oberhafen canteen), which has stood on the quay wall in the Stockmeyerstraße in the Hamburg harbour area since 1925 and has meanwhile been blown askew by the wind. The harbour workers used to be catered for here, today it is a bar and restaurant for everyone, specializing in regional home cooking. Passfeld was commissioned by the current owner of the Oberhafenkantine, the Hamburg investor in culture Klausmartin Kretschmer, who wants to send the wooden reconstruction around the world as a kind of cultural ambassador for Hamburg.

Unlike the other works, for which Passfeld made a few pro forma sketches at the most and constructed the houses off the top of his head so to speak, he in this case kept strictly to the original building plans.

In recent years, he has increasingly expressed his artistic freedom, which is rather neglected in the commissioned work, in the numerous relief-like coloured wall objects made up of individual pieces of wood. The sculptural approach to his work with wood correlates with his original affinity to painting. A decorative quality unfolds from the artistic diversity of the individual parts, visible in many places in the design of the houses, although here they remain incorporated in the solid overall appearance of the buildings.

"Welcome home" is written on a pink heart, and behind all kinds of worm-like creatures, which, when scaled down are reminiscent of the outside fittings of the *Erholungsheim für schuld-* *bewusste Großstädter*, two legs dangle like a jumping jack. The rest of the figure, in as much as it exists at all, is not visible. The petit bourgeois world of wooden signs with sayings on them is deconstructed in a surreal manner and the maxims of idyllic respectability have since been replaced by imperatives, and hold the promise of being socially accepted in another milieu if they are followed: *Please become nonchalant, sporty, successful, popular + beautiful.*

The ironic connection between the object in wood and the language is not dissimilar to the above-mentioned approach taken by Georg Herold, also when it comes to using a material aesthetic that intentionally undermines the dominant criteria of the art world. Both artists pose the question as to whether or not the true small-mindedness can be found there where one disrespectfully looks down on aesthetics and materials because they do not correspond to what one finds or should find cool. However some people find wood cool, because it appeals to their desire for ecological hipness.

Wood can be heavy and earthy but also wonderfully light. Both these elements are embodied in Passfeld's sculpture, the *Flieger* (aircraft), which could be a tank-like military vehicle, but is also reminiscent of Apollo's sun car. The compact, solid form is counteracted by the lightness of the construction. Will the vehicle forcibly blaze a trail or fly in the air, light as a bird? Or is it not perhaps a house again, one which we – at least in our thoughts – could inhabit?

And so it becomes increasingly clear that Thorsten Passfeld's constructed houses, despite having at least a temporary physical presence, also and perhaps above all, provide room for thought. They challenge us to think about whether things could not be completely different, starting with building a complete house with one's own hands. And one maxim that has constantly characterised Thorsten Passfeld's art could be: don't ever lose your grip.

Ludwig Seyfarth

1) Monika Wagner, Das Material der Kunst. Eine andere Geschichte der Moderne, München 2001, p. 241 ff.
2) Jean Baudrillard, The system of objects, London/New York 2005, p. 38..
3) Ibid, p. 51.
4) Ibid., p. 52.

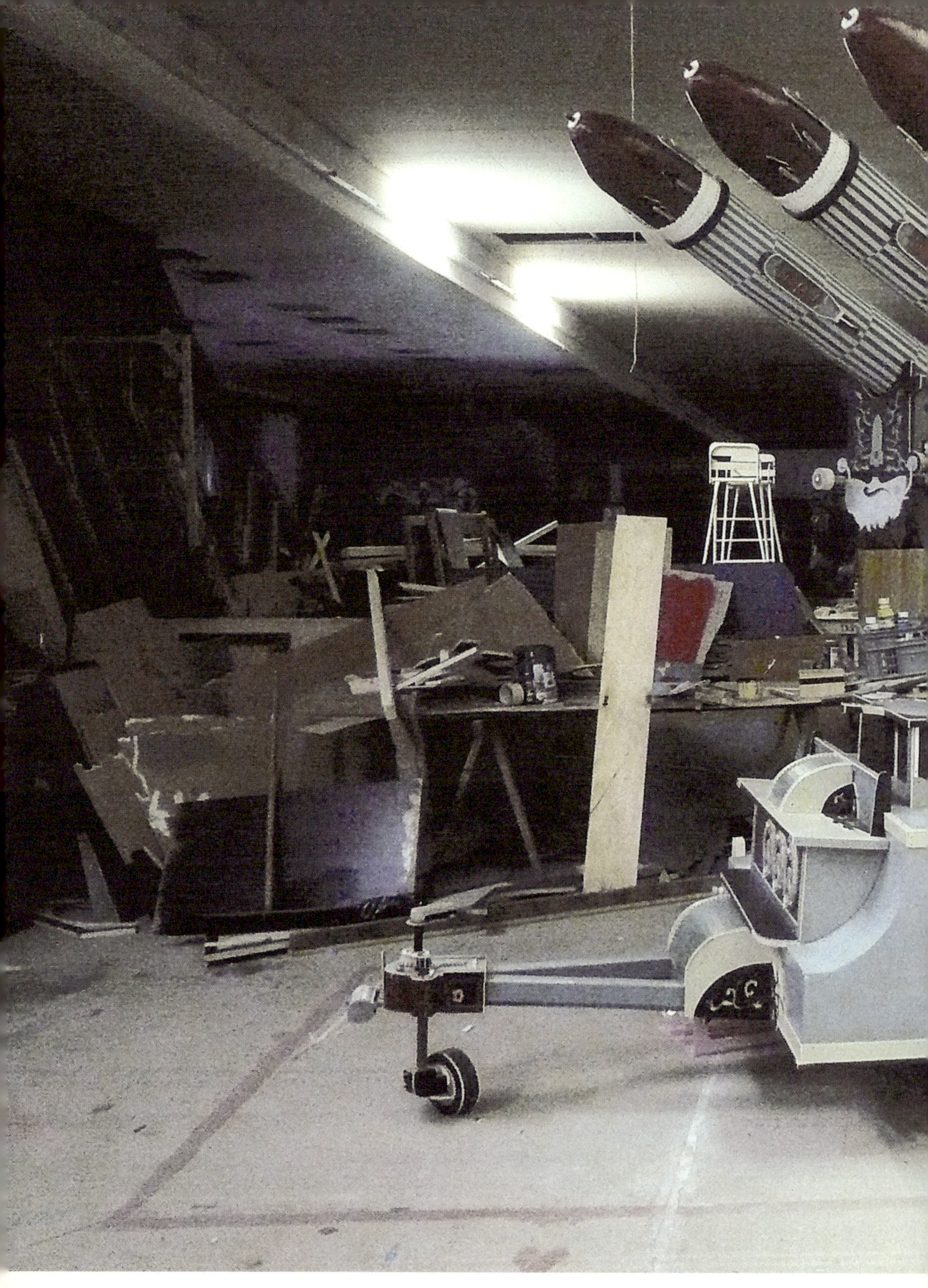

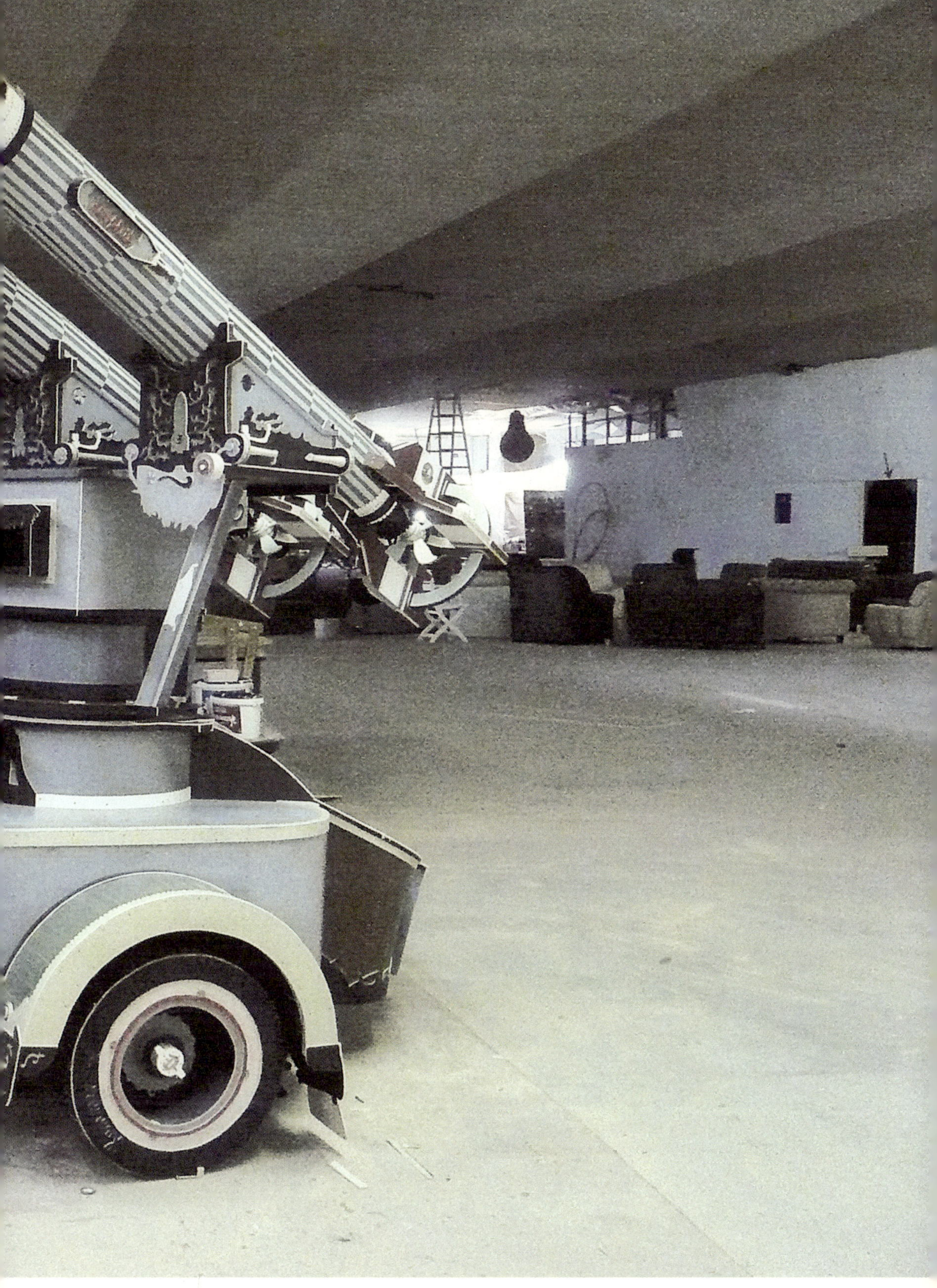

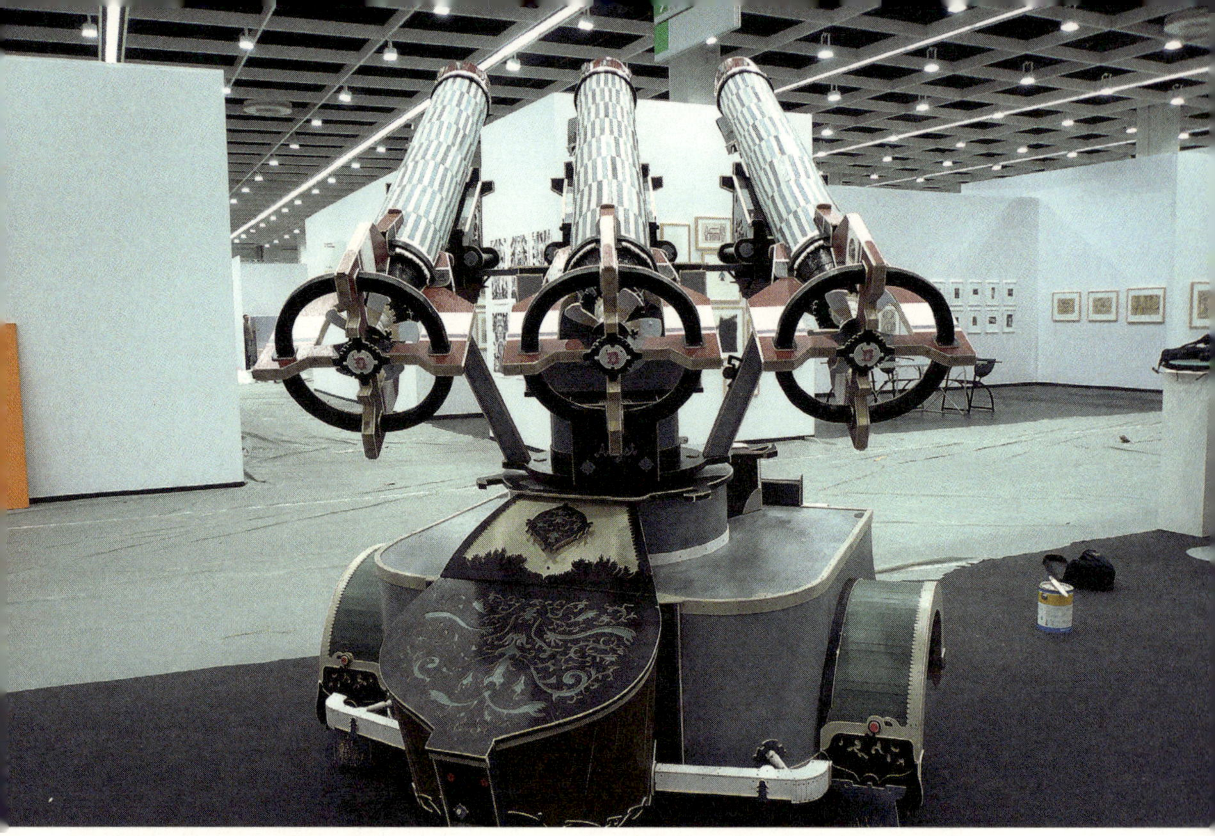

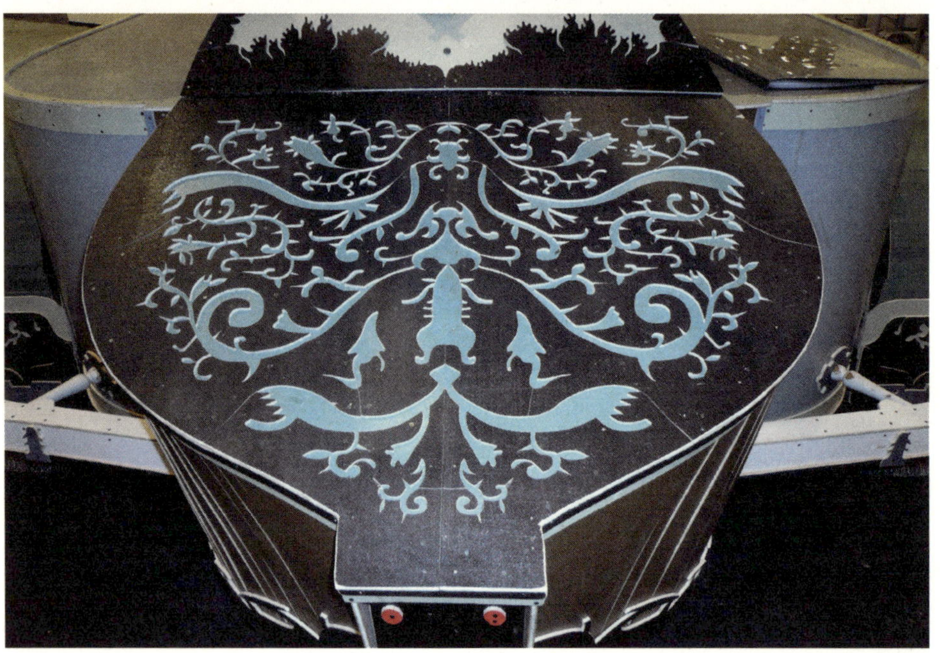

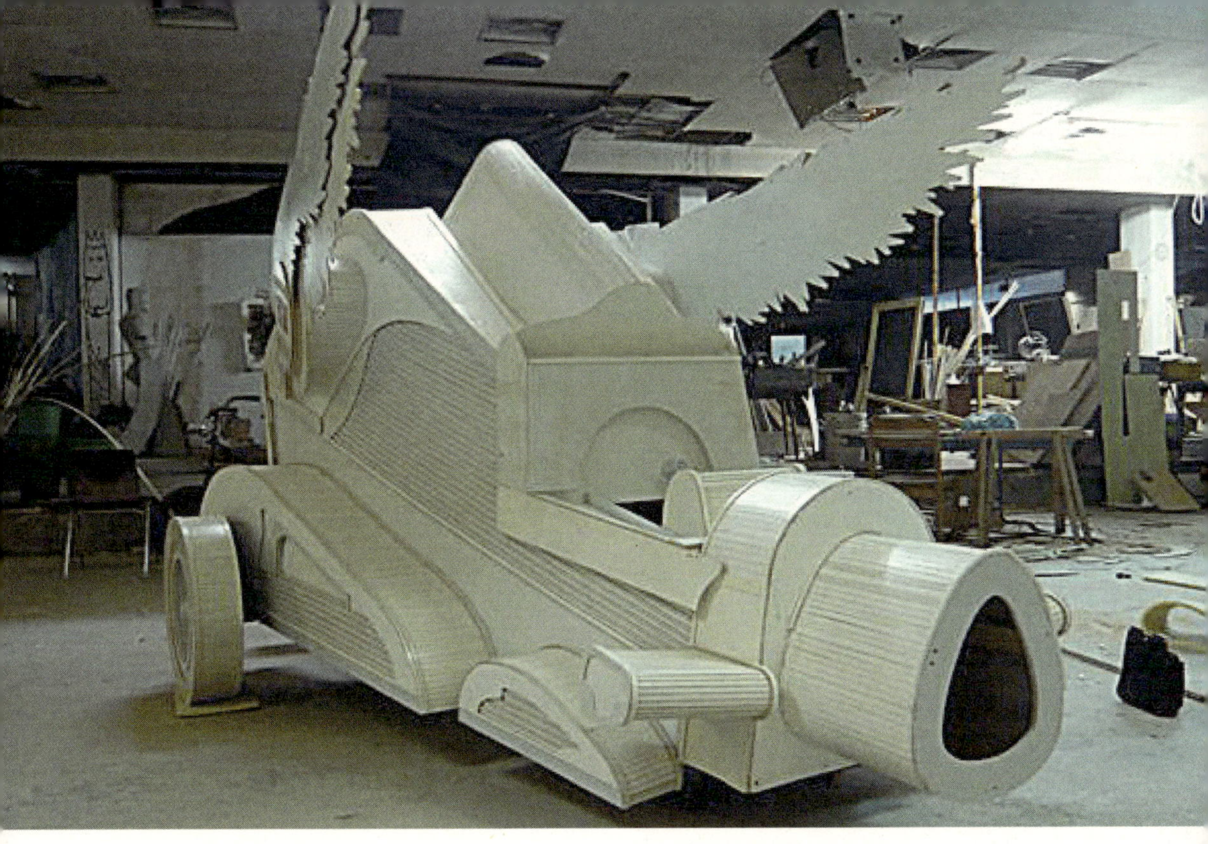

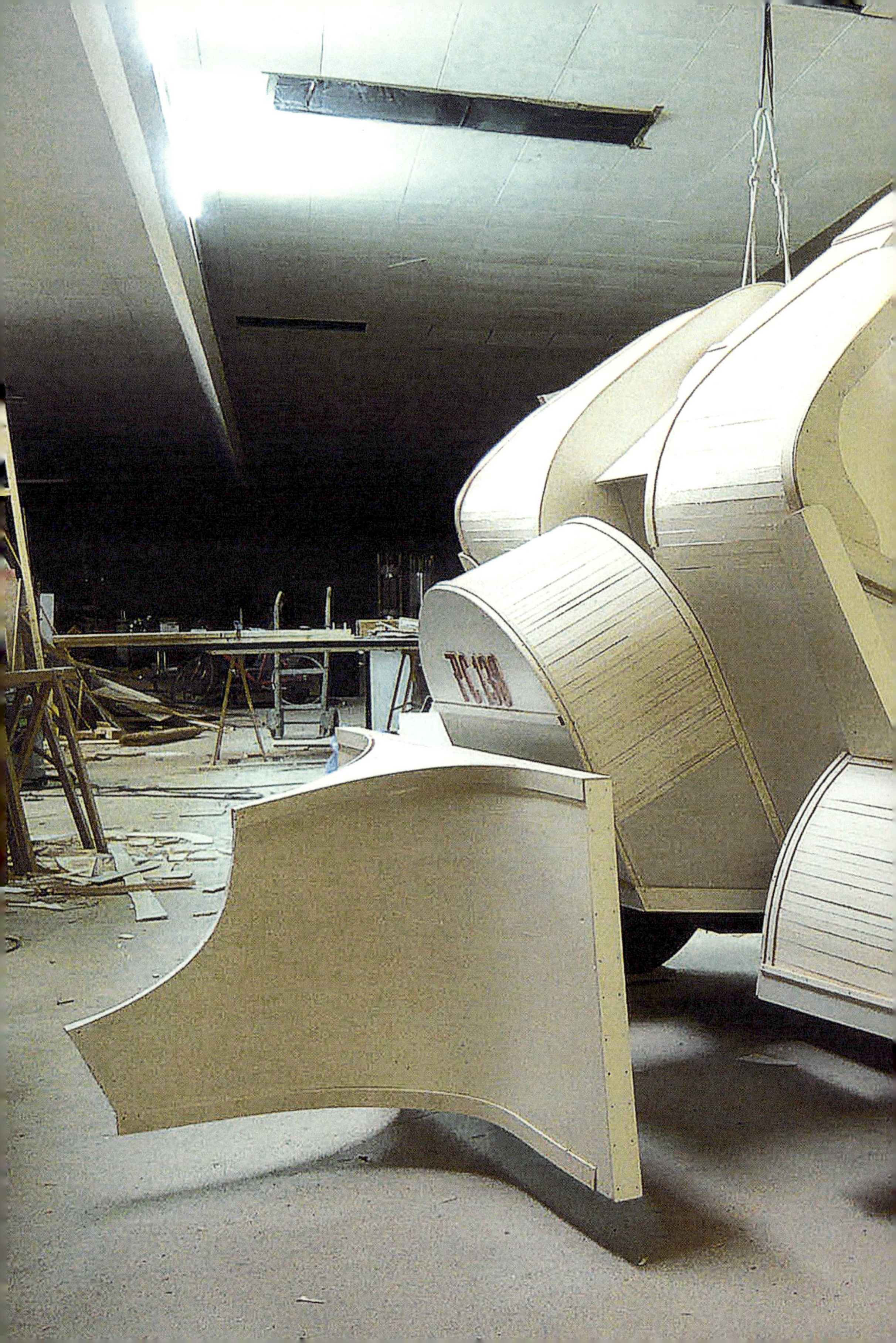
PC 138

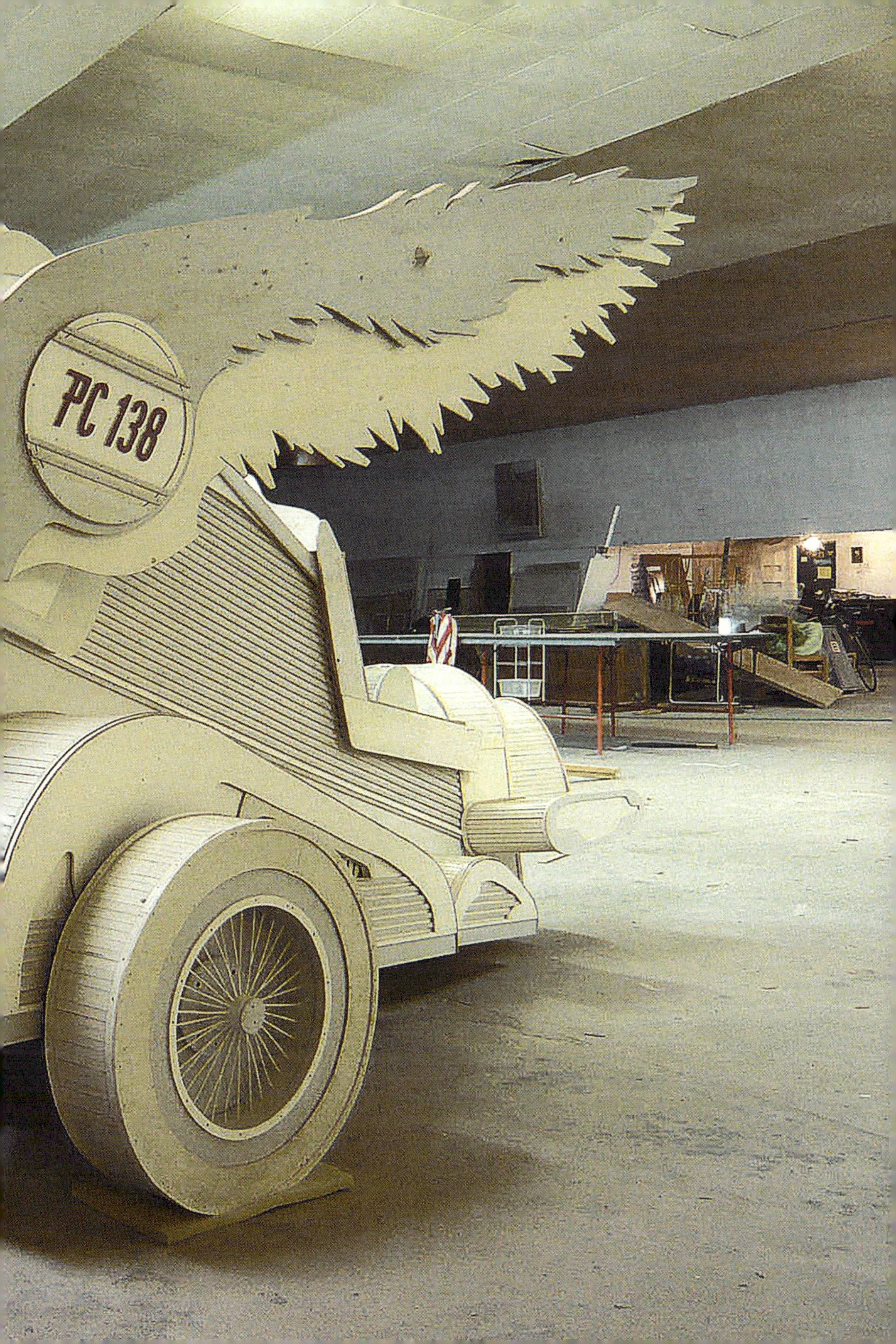

PC 138

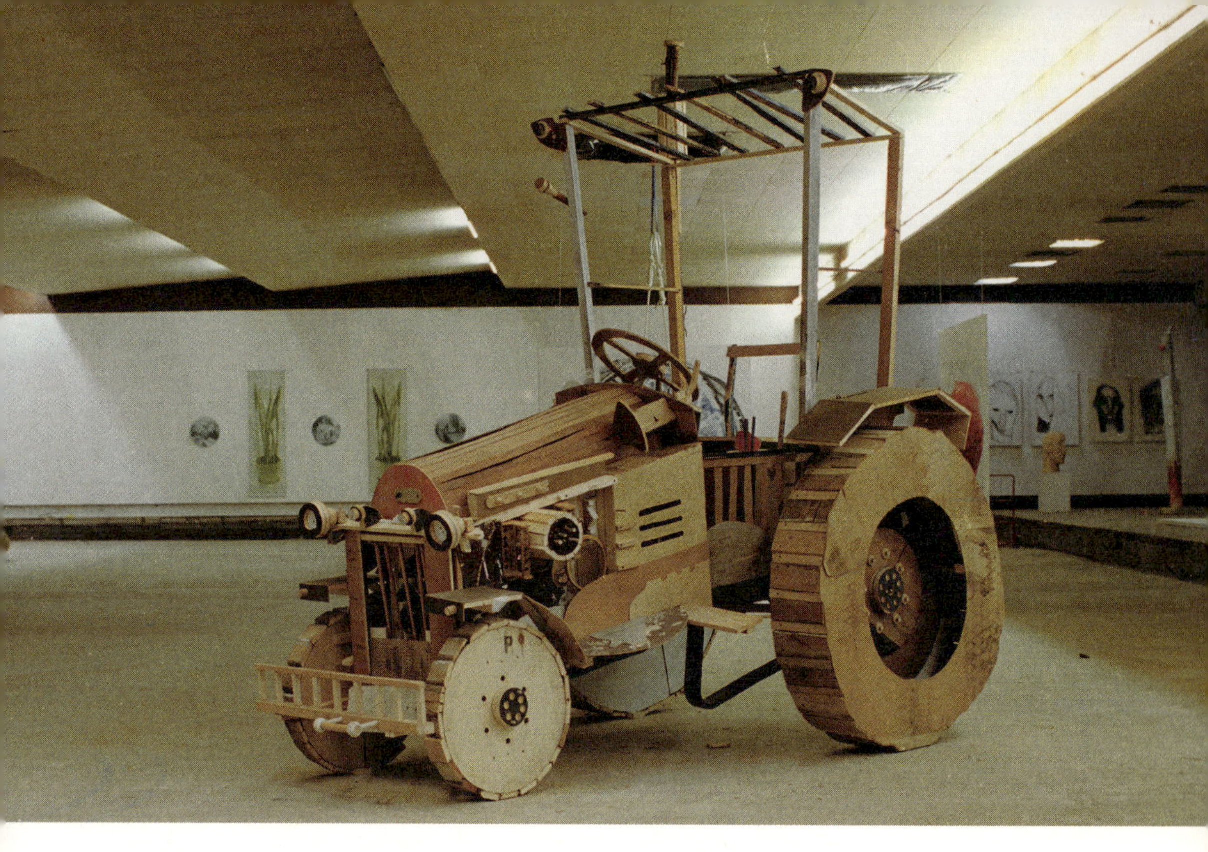

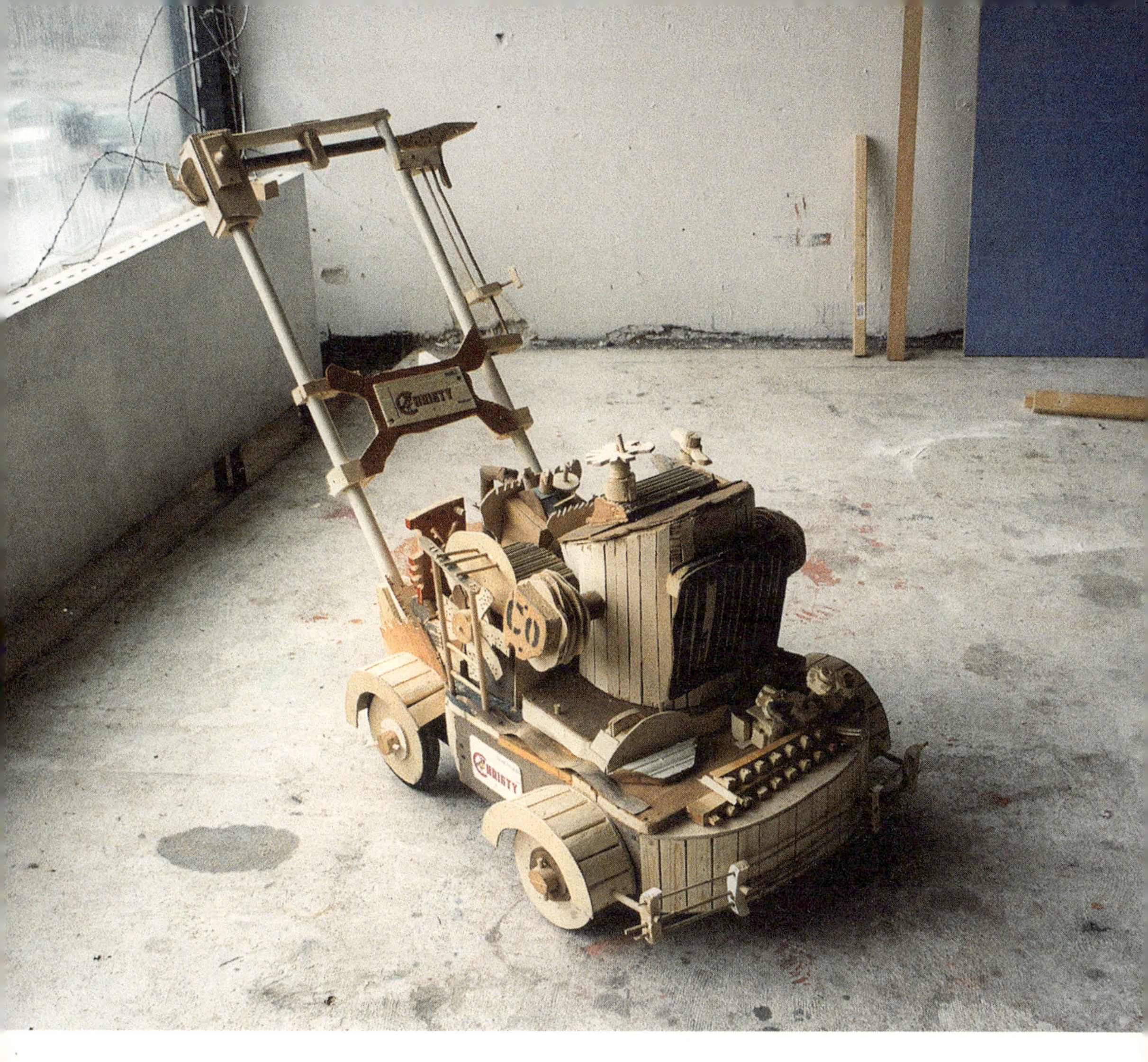

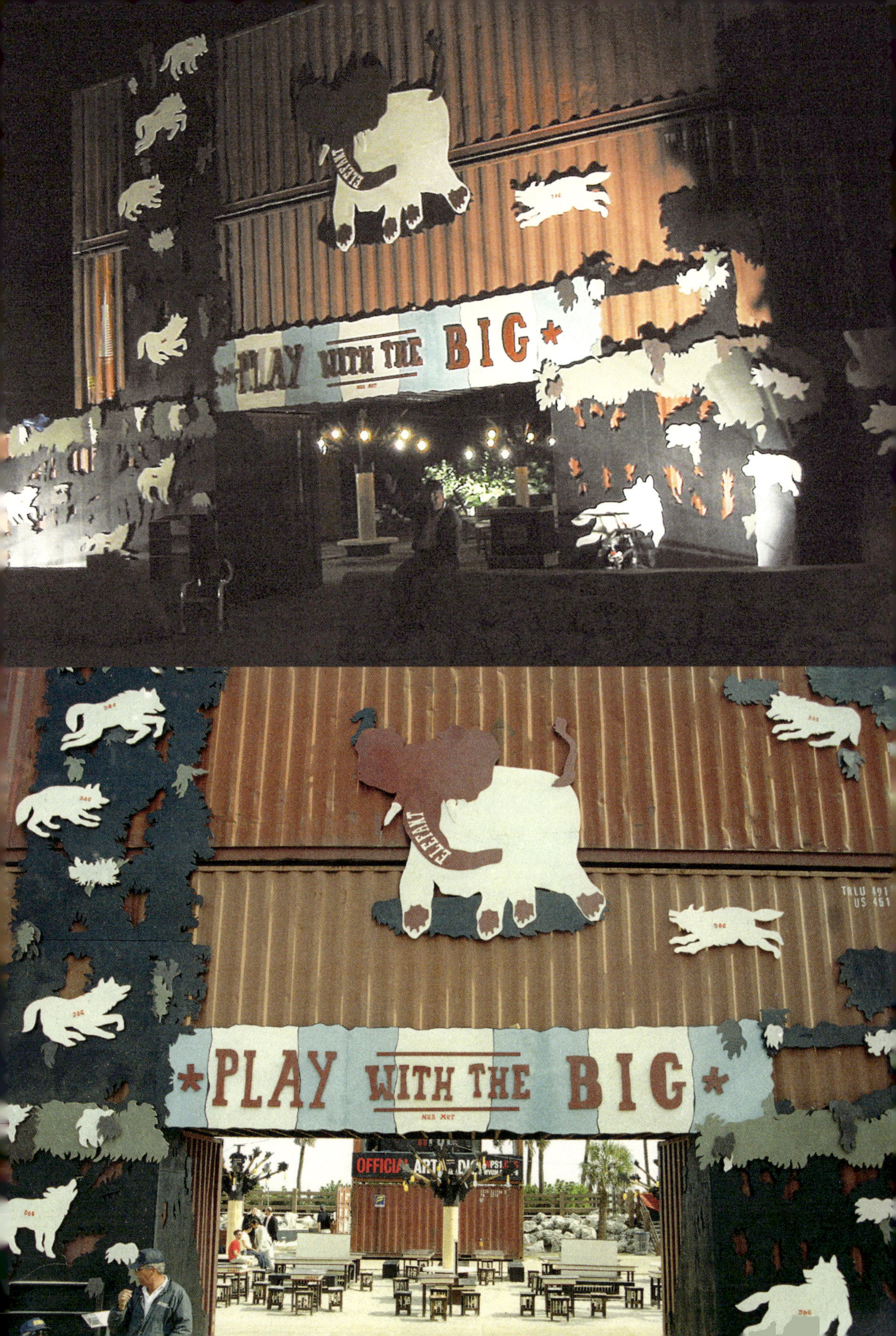
ELEPHANT
PLAY WITH THE BIG
NUB NUT
DOG
TRLU 491
US 461
OFFICIAL ART

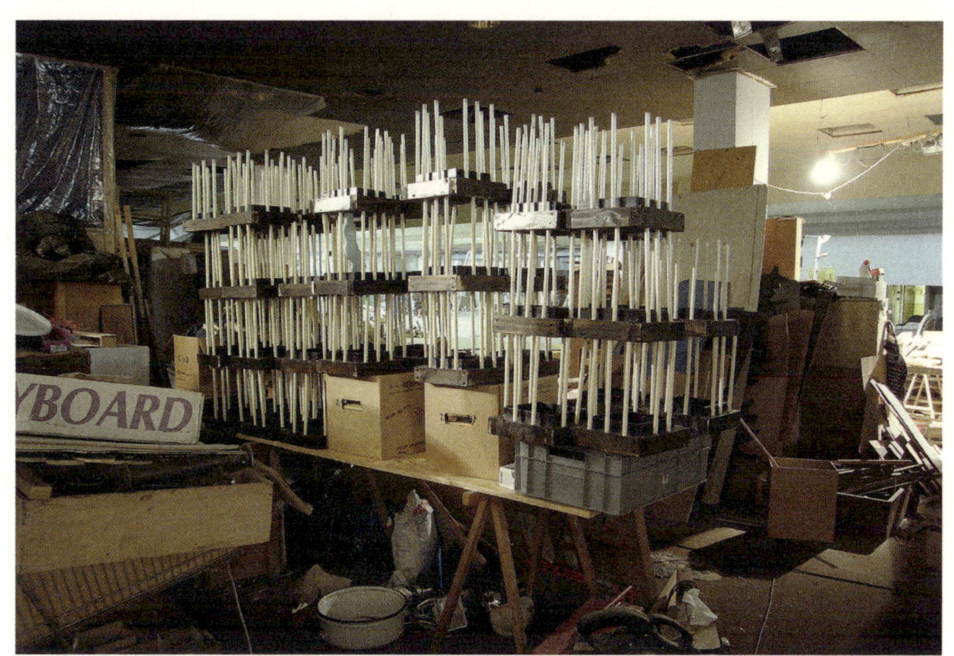
YBOARD

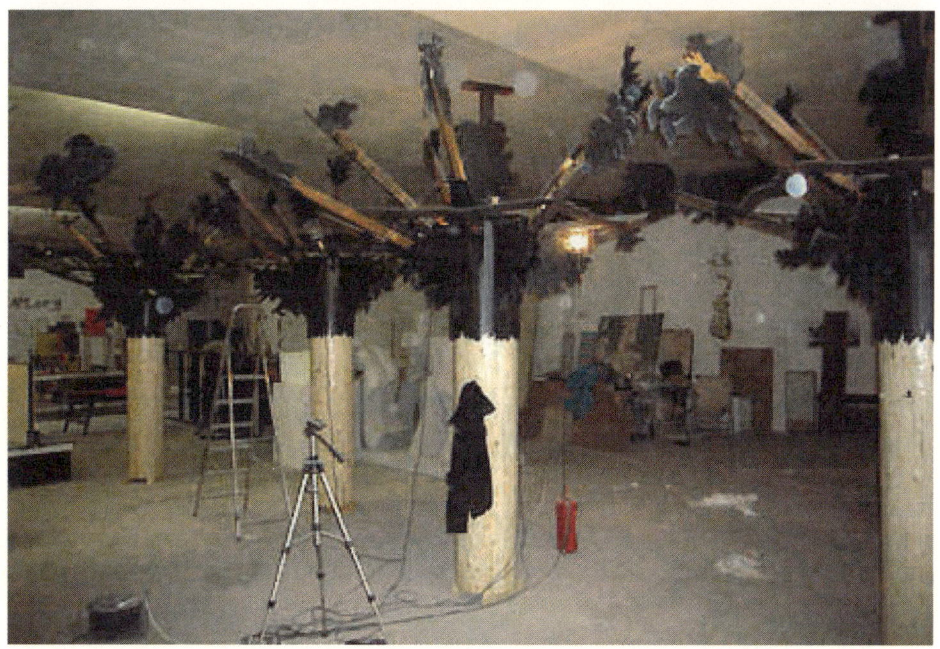

Um es gleich vorweg zu sagen: Ich habe im Grunde nicht die geringste Ahnung, wer Thorsten Passfeld eigentlich ist. Und das obwohl wir seit vielen Jahren befreundet sind. Doch was uns eint – ist neben vielem anderem – eben dieser Umstand. Er weiß es auch nicht, und manchmal sitzen wir dann da und überlegen. Schmeißen unsere Hände in die Luft und lassen sie wieder fallen. Das machen wir, wenn uns Stille nicht genug Ratlosigkeit ausdrückt.

»Ist doch eigentlich ganz gut so.

Immer gut, immer Nein![1]

Alles«, sage ich. Rede ich, rede auch ich oft komisch. »Vielleicht die braune Jacke weg«, sage ich. »Oder die Jeans kleiner.«

Doch Thorsten schüttelt den Kopf. »Nein«, sagt oder schreit er. Manchmal weiß man das bei ihm nicht so genau. »Es muss doch so gehen.«

Oft glaube ich, sein immenser Schaffensdrang ist Ausdruck einer Suche nach etwas. Nach einem Kosmos, in dem er so sein kann, wie er ist. Oder nach einem anderen Thorsten. Dann könnte die Welt so bleiben, wie sie ist.

In ihm steckt der Wunsch nach einer absolut heilen Welt, die ist wie die in einem Kinderbuch. Eine Welt, in der die Menschen rote Bäckchen vom Leben bekommen haben. Alles lächelt. Nicht nur die Menschen. Auch die Tiere. Die Blumen. Das vegetarische Essen. Alles sagt, »hey Kumpel«, und schlägt sich asexuell auf den Rücken. Seine früheren Bilder wirkten oft, als wollten sie genau

das festhalten. Bunte comicartige LSD-Kosmen, die nur durch ein paar flüchtig dahin gekritzelt wirkende Worte am Rand ins Schwanken gerieten. Durchhalteparolen für Depressive.

Irgendwann hörte er einfach auf, zu malen.

»Sieh mal, Sven«, sagte er, als ich ihn fragte warum, und schoss statt einer Antwort mit einem der Luftgewehre, die in letzter Zeit zu seinen Freunden geworden waren, auf eins seiner früheren Werke.

Ich nehme an, dass diese Bilder ihm einfach zu klein waren. Gaben ihm zu wenig Schutz. Metaebene, knickknack, aber auch ganz real. Unter uns Pastorentöchtern: Auch Größenwahn ist ein paar Schuhe, in dem Thorsten gerne ein paar Tanzschritte vollführt.

Mit einer harmlosen Schreibmaschine aus Holz fing es an. Dann kam ein Rasenmäher[2]. Ein Traktor. Ein Raketenwerfer. Später ganze Häuser. Städte. Man konnte das Gefühl bekommen, es ginge ihm gar nicht so sehr darum, was er da baute, sondern es musste nur groß sein. Gebaut aus Holzresten, die er draußen in der Stadt, vor der er sich versteckte, mehr oder weniger fand. Es war ein großer Teil des Prozesses. Nachts fuhr er nun übermüdet durch Hamburg und lud Holzreste ein, mochten sie noch so klein sein. Oft sah man ihn schon von Weitem, sein bleich glimmendes Gesicht in dem dunklen Passat.

Oft war der riesige Holzhaufen im *Skam*[3], seinem früheren Atelier über dem früheren Mojo, fast noch beeindruckender als die Kunstwerke, die Thorsten daraus schuf. Mit jedem Tag schien er weiter zu wachsen, ganz egal wie viel Thorsten davon auch verbaute. Als wäre es ein eigener Organismus, der Thorsten zu überwuchern begann, verpuppte, beschützte.

Anfangs waren es nur ein paar Bretter. Später dann wie ein Kokon aus Holz, der Thorsten umschloss, und Tage habe ich davor gesessen und auf den Holzschmetterling gewartet. Doch irgendwann krabbelte doch nur wieder Thorsten daraus hervor. Schmutzig. Bärtig. Bleich.

Stets war ein Hämmern und Sägen darin zu hören. Manchmal drang Licht daraus. Mittlerweile war er so groß, dass der Tag nicht mehr hineingekrochen kam.

Um ehrlich zu sein, ich habe den Verdacht, Thorsten saß oft nur dort und schlug wahllos auf irgendwelche Bretter ein. Genoss es einfach, allein zu sein. Nichts tun zu müssen. Auch das ist eine Sehnsucht in ihm: gar nichts zu tun. Unausgesprochen, wie so vieles. Ich glaube, es ist auch das Gefühl, dass er dem Leben etwas schuldet, das ihn antreibt.

Sie sehen: glauben, vermuten, annehmen – ich lüge nicht, ich habe wirklich keine Ahnung.

Thorsten sitzt nie irgendwo einfach rum. Ständig läuft er umher. Hebt Dinge an und stellt sie woanders hin. Zerbricht sie, um etwas Neues daraus zu machen. Manchmal zerbricht er sie auch nur. Immer scheint er in Bewegung. Selbst wenn wir irgendwo sitzen, und ich glaube, wir würden uns angeregt unterhalten. Hinter seinem Rücken schwirren seine suchenden Hände umher, tauchen hier auf, dann wieder dort. Sind auf der Suche nach etwas, das sie umklammern, zerbrechen oder einfach nur herumwirbeln können. Wie zwei dicke Vögel sind sie. Bewegen sich immer nur, wenn ich nicht hinsehe. Diese Unruhe!

Thorsten macht immer den Eindruck, als hätte er es eilig. Selbst wenn man nur zusammen in der Bar liegt und sich betrinkt. Bei Thorsten wirkt es wie Sport, und mit dem ersten leeren Bier tritt wieder sein Drang zutage, eine Grenze zwischen sich und das Leben zu bauen.

In der *Mutter* waren wir einmal so lange, dass ein richtiger Zaun aus Bierflaschen uns vor den anderen Gästen beschützte. Überall standen welche.

Immerhin baute er sie um uns beide. Vielleicht die rührendste Geste, die mir je von seiner Seite aus zu teil wurde.

Später lief er mit Stolz geschwellter Brust durch die Bar, schrie, zeigte auf Dinge. Brüllte: »Das baue ich aus Holz nach! Das baue ich aus Holz!«

Irgendwann zeigte er dabei auf Gäste. »Dich baue ich auch aus Holz! Und dich! Und dich! Besser. Viel besser.«

Gerade in letzter Zeit habe ich den Verdacht, er könne auch sich selbst längst schon aus Holz nachgebaut haben. Bin ich bei ihm, in seinem neuen Atelier, schicke ich ihn Bier holen. In der Hafencity dauert das Bierholen wesentlich länger als in St. Pauli. In seiner Abwesenheit durchsuche ich das Atelier.

Irgendwo werde ich ihn finden, einen Thorsten komplett aus Holz. Ein Ideal seiner selbst. *Immer gut, immer dein!* Ein lächelnder Thorsten in einem weißen Paillettenanzug. Ein wenig aufrechter als der richtige. Ein bisschen größer. Die Hände filigran und stets zum Winken gehoben. Mit Schuhen mit kleinen Absätzen daran. Die Arme so lang, dass man vieles damit umarmen könnte. Die Haare ordentlich gescheitelt. Ein kleiner Schnurrbart als Zeichen der Seriosität. Eine kleine Abdeckplatte, die man von seinem Kopf nehmen kann, um hineinzusehen. Es ist ordentlich darin. Verschiedene Zimmer. Türen, auf denen *Schuld* oder *Sühne* steht. Aber auch *Vergangenheit*. Dahinter ein Zimmer mit Regalsystemen. Zwei Reihen nur Regale, über denen *Dinslaken* steht. Darin kleine Bilder aus Holz, auf

denen man Thorsten mit seinen Freunden herumtollen sieht. Mit seinem Bruder Holger an einem Tisch, wie dieser ihm erklärt, wie ein Frosch funktioniert. Oder wie er mit seinem Vater einen elektrischen Zaun aus Holz baut.

Irgendwo wird es ihn geben, diesen Thorsten. Irgendwo wird er liegen und herauskommen, sind die beiden allein. Er wird neben Thorsten stehen mit seinen scheiß schönen Schuhen und ihn immer überragen. Stiefväterlich wird er seine vom Winken schweren Hände auf seine Schultern legen und ihm sagen: »Sieh mal, Thorsten, das ist völlig falsch, was du da tust. Und, mein Freund, es ist nicht nur falsch, sondern es ist auch noch sehr, sehr schlecht. Es muss besser sein. Nicht nur etwas, sondern viel. Sonst taugt es nicht. Verstehst du? Sonst taugst *du* nicht! Kunst ist im Grunde wie Katholizismus. Eine harte Angelegenheit, an die man fest glauben muss, damit sie Spaß macht. Kunst kann Strafe sein, aber eben auch Buße. Du hast es in der Hand, mein Freund.«

Und mit diesen Worten zerstört er, was Thorsten aufgebaut hat, damit dieser es neu erschafft. Immer wieder. Immer neu.

Sven Amtsberg

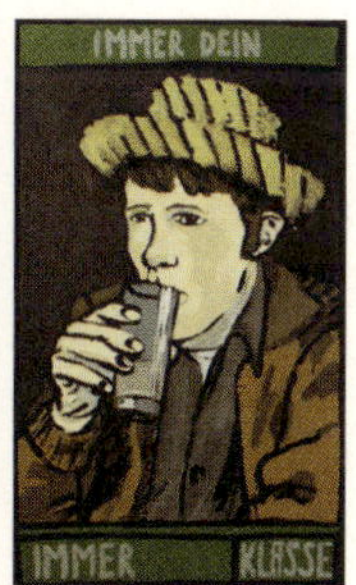

1)

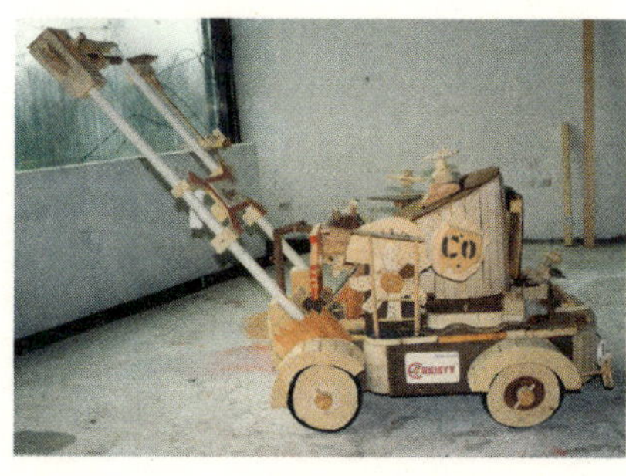

2)

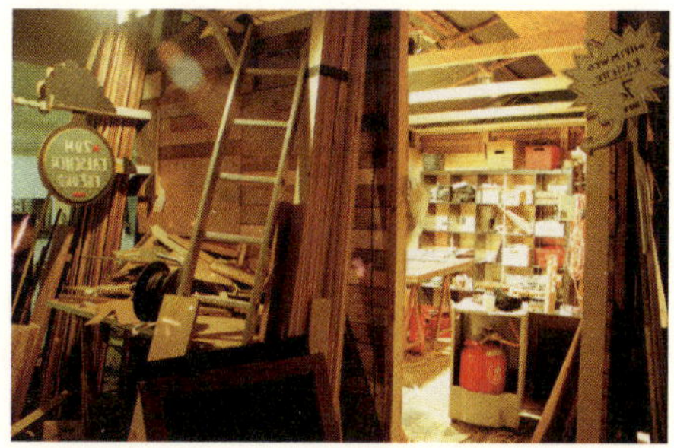

3)

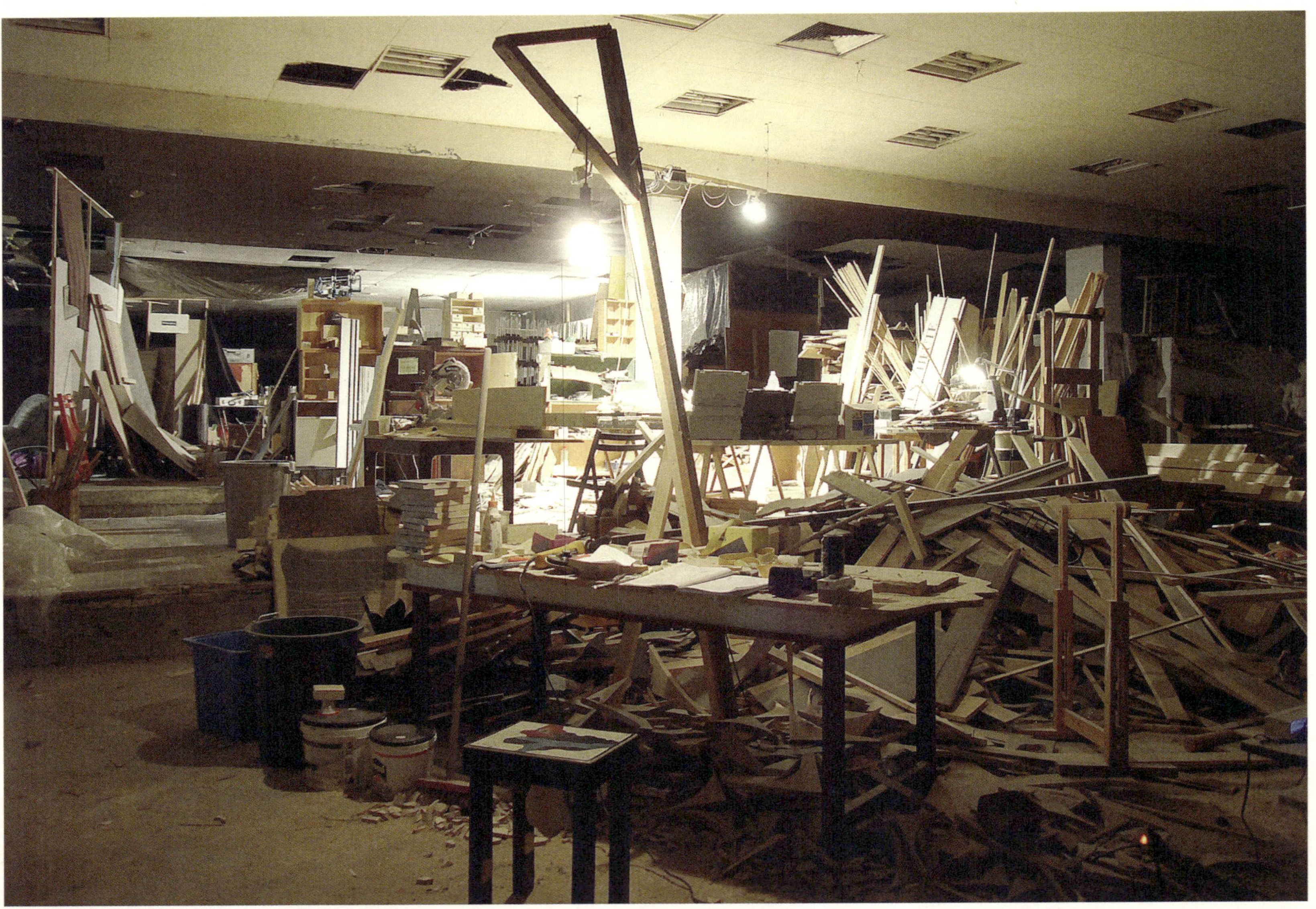

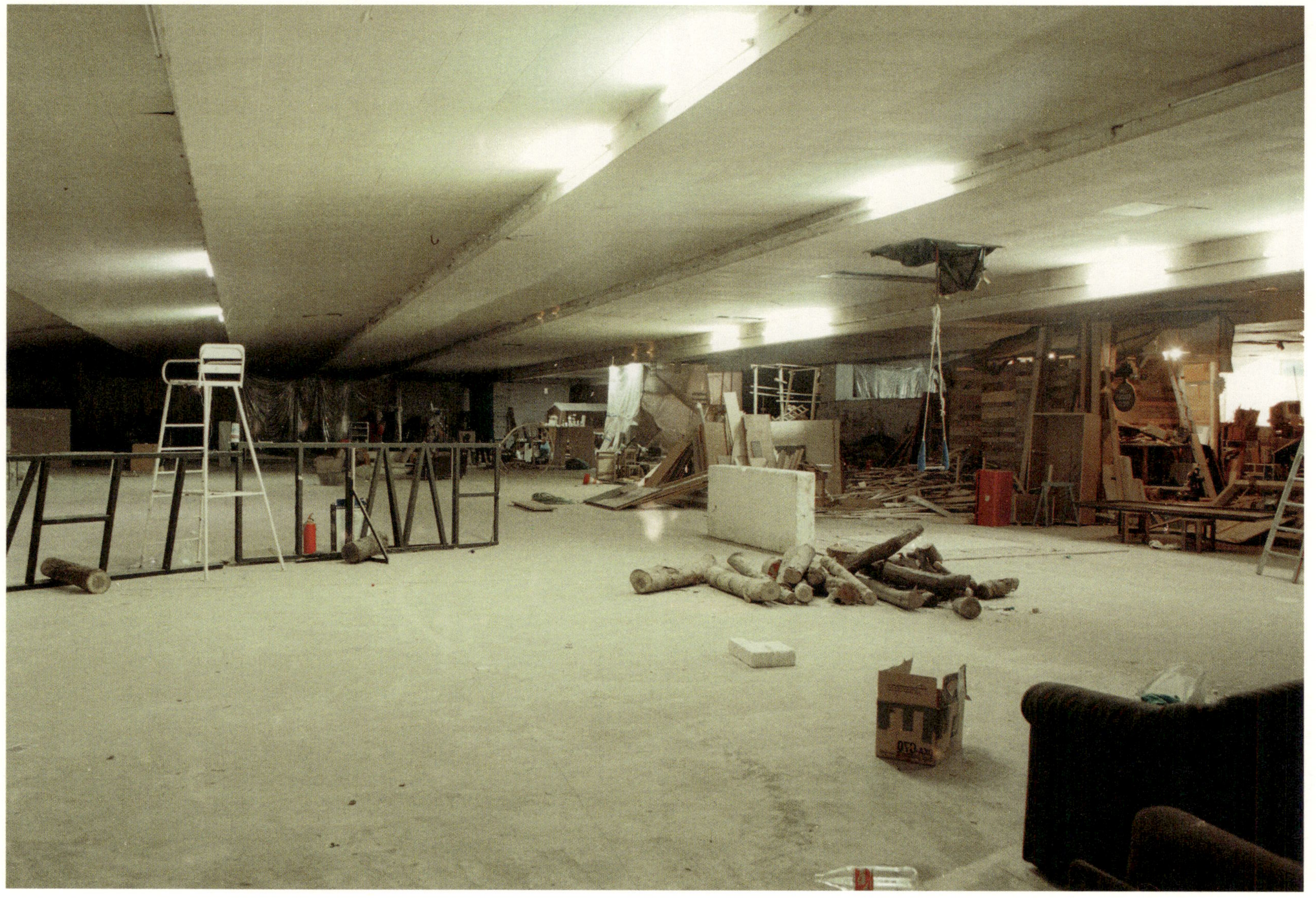

Let me start by saying: I haven't actually got the faintest idea who Thorsten Passfeld really is. Even though we've been friends for several years now. However what we have in common – among other things – is this very fact. He doesn't know either and sometimes we sit there and ponder. Throw our hands in the air and let them drop again. We do that when the silence does not suffice to express the extent of our perplexity. "It's actually pretty good like that. Everything", I say. I talk, often a

Always good, always not! [1]

little strangely. "Maybe without the brown jacket", I say. "Or the jeans a bit smaller".
But Thorsten shakes his head. "No", he says or shouts. Sometimes one doesn't really know with him. "It will have to do".
I often think that his immense creative urge is the expression of a search for something. For a cosmos, in which he can simply be who he is. Or for a different Thorsten. Then the world could stay the way it is.
He yearns for a completely perfect world that is like the one in children's storybooks. A world in which life has given people red cheeks. Everything smiles. Not only the people. The animals too. The flowers. The vegetarian food. Everything says "hey mate" and slaps the other asexually on the back. His earlier works seem as if they wanted to capture exactly this. Colourful, comic-like LSD cosmoses, which are only disturbed because of a few scribbled-look-ing words in the margins. Rallying calls for depressives.
Eventually he simply stopped painting altogether.
"Look, Sven", he said when I asked him why, and instead of answering, he fired at an earlier work with one of the airguns that had recently become his companions.
I suppose that he simply considered these pictures too small. They didn't offer him enough protection. Meta level, knickknack, but also completely real. Between you and me and the gatepost:

Megalomania is also a pair of shoes that Thorsten enjoys performing a few dance steps in.
It began with a harmless wooden typewriter. Then there was the lawn mower. A tractor. A rocket-launcher. Later whole houses. Towns. One got the feeling that he wasn't really concerned with what he built, just as long as it was big. Constructed using pieces of old wood that he more or less found outdoors in the city he was hiding from. This was a big part of the process. At night he drove exhausted through Hamburg and loaded his car with scraps of wood, however small. He could often be seen from a distance, his pale face glowing in the dark Passat.
Often the huge pile of wood in *Skam*, his former studio above what used to be club Mojo, was almost more impressive than the artworks Thorsten made with it. The pile seemed to grow day by day, regardless of how much of it Thorsten used for his construc-tions. As if it were a living organism that began to grow over Thorsten, to pupate and protect him.
Initially it was just a few planks. Later it was like a cocoon of wood that enclosed Thorsten, and I spent days sitting in front of it waiting for the wooden butterfly. However eventually it was again only Thorsten who crawled out of it. Dirty. Bearded. Pale.
A constant hammering and saw-ing sound could be heard from in-side. Sometimes light shone out. Meanwhile the pile was so big that the day no longer even man-aged to creep in.
To be honest, I have my suspicions that Thorsten often just sat there and randomly hit at any old plank of wood. Simply enjoyed being alone. Not having to do anything. He also yearns very much for this: doing nothing. Unspoken, like so much. I believe he is also driven by the feeling that life owes him something.
So you see: think, presume, as-sume – I'm not lying, I really have no idea.
Thorsten never simply sits around doing nothing. He is always roam-ing around. Picking things up and then putting them down again somewhere else. Breaking them in order to make them into some-thing new. Sometimes he simply breaks them. He always seems to be on the move. Even when we are sitting somewhere and I think we are having an animated conversation. Behind his back his searching hands flutter about, ap-pear here, then there again. They are searching for something that they can grasp, break or simply swirl around. They are like two

fat birds. They only move when I'm not looking.

This restlessness!

Thorsten always makes the impression that he is in a hurry. Even when we are only lying in the bar together getting drunk In Thorsten's case it is like a kind of sport and the first beer he downs triggers his desire to draw a boundary between himself and his life.

We once spent so long in the bar *Mutter* that a real barrier of beer bottles protected us from the other guests. They were standing everywhere.

At least he set them up around both of us. Perhaps the most touching gesture that he had ever shown me.

Later he walked around the bar all puffed up with pride, yelled, pointed at things. Shouted: "I'm going to make that out of wood! I'm going to make that out of wood!"

Eventually he began to point to the guests. "I'm going to make you out of wood! And you! And you! Better. Much better."

More recently in particular I have suspected that he could have long ago made a copy of himself in wood. When I visit him in his new studio, I send him out to get beer. In the Hafencity district it takes much longer than in St. Pauli. While he is away I search his studio.

Somewhere I must be able to find him, a Thorsten made completely of wood. A perfect image of himself. *Always good, always yours!* A smiling Thorsten in a white sequin suit. Standing a little straighter than the real one. A little taller. His hands delicate and always poised to wave. Wearing shoes with little heels. And arms so long that they could hug many things. Hair combed to a neat parting. A little moustache as a symbol of respectability. A small lid that one can lift off his head in order to look inside. It is all neat and tidy in there. Different rooms. Doors, with signs bearing words such as *guilt* or *atonement*. But also the word *past*. Behind it there is a room with shelving systems. Two rows of shelves and above them the word *Dinslaken*. On the shelves are small pictures made of wood showing Thorsten fooling around with his friends. With his brother Holger at a table while the latter explains the functions of a frog to him. Or building an electric fence out of wood with his father.

He must be here somewhere, this Thorsten. He must be lying somewhere ready to come out when the two of them are alone. He will stand next to Thorsten in his goddam beautiful shoes and always tower above him. Like a stepfather he will put his hands, exhausted from waving, on his shoulders and say: "See Thorsten, what you are doing is completely wrong. And, my friend, it is not only wrong but it is also really really bad. It has to be better. Not just something, but a lot of things. Otherwise it's no use at all. You know? Otherwise *you* are no use! Art is basically like Catholicism. A tough business, one that you have to really believe in if it's going to be any fun. Art can be a punishment, but also a penance. It is in your hands, my friend."

And with these words he destroys what Thorsten has made so that Thorsten can make it again. Over and over again. Always new.

Sven Amtsberg

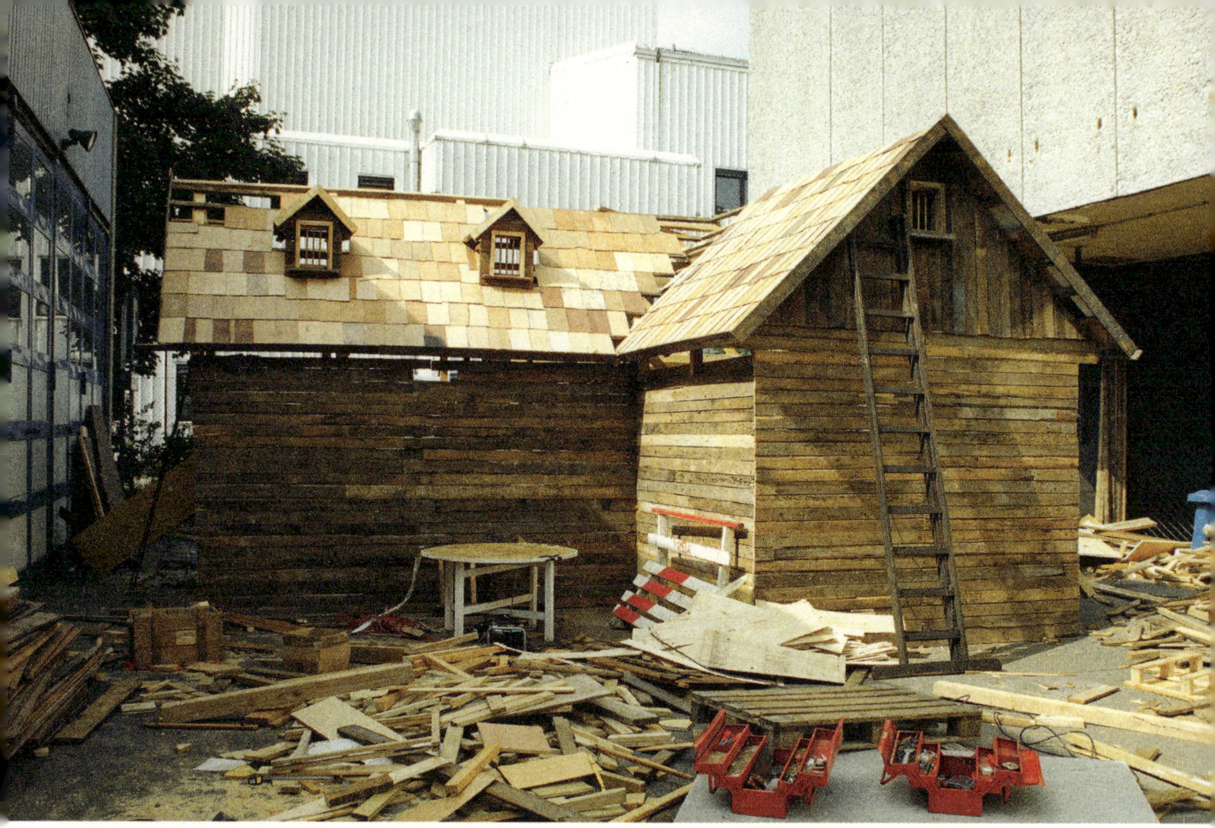

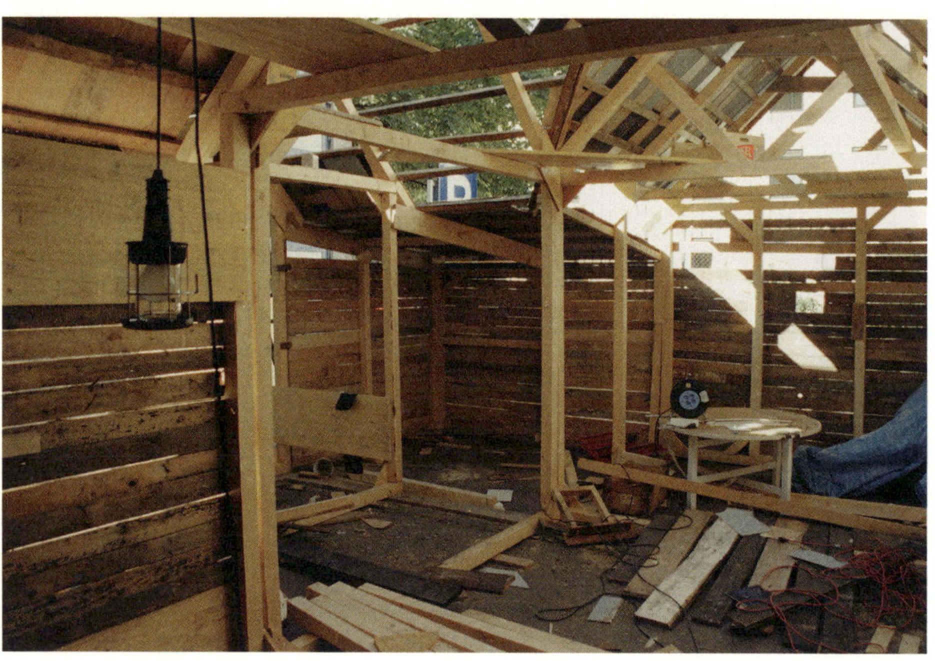

   Haus aus Holz, 2002

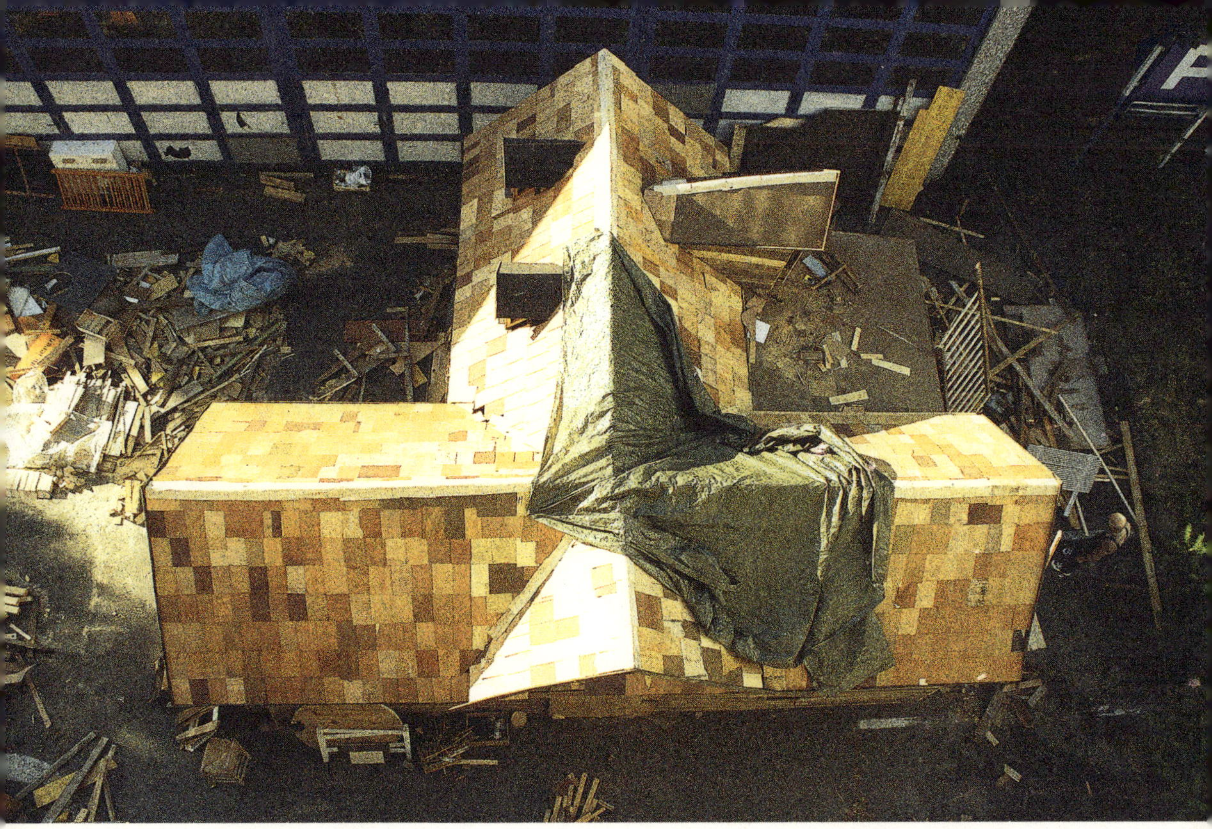

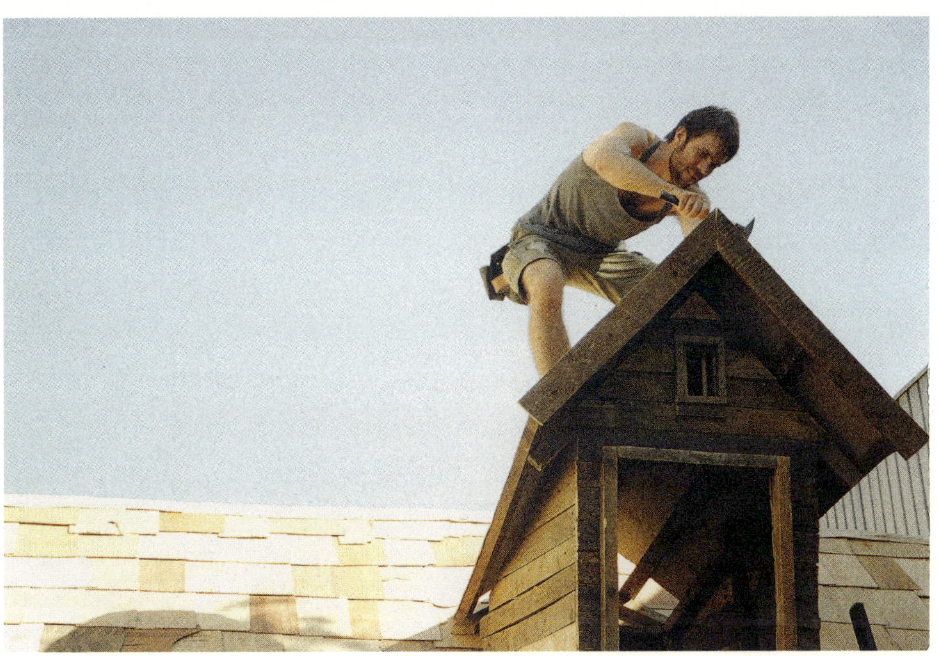

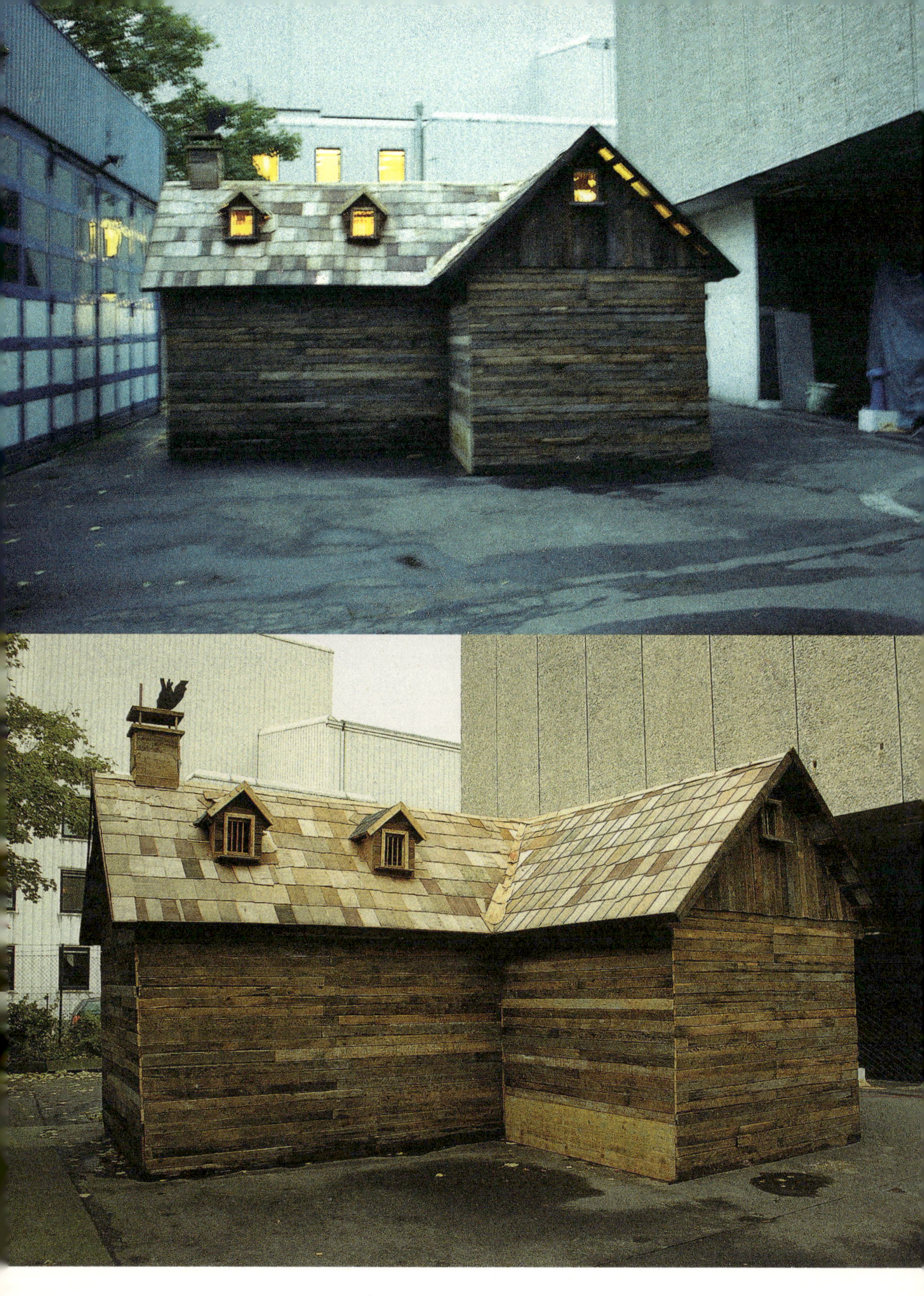

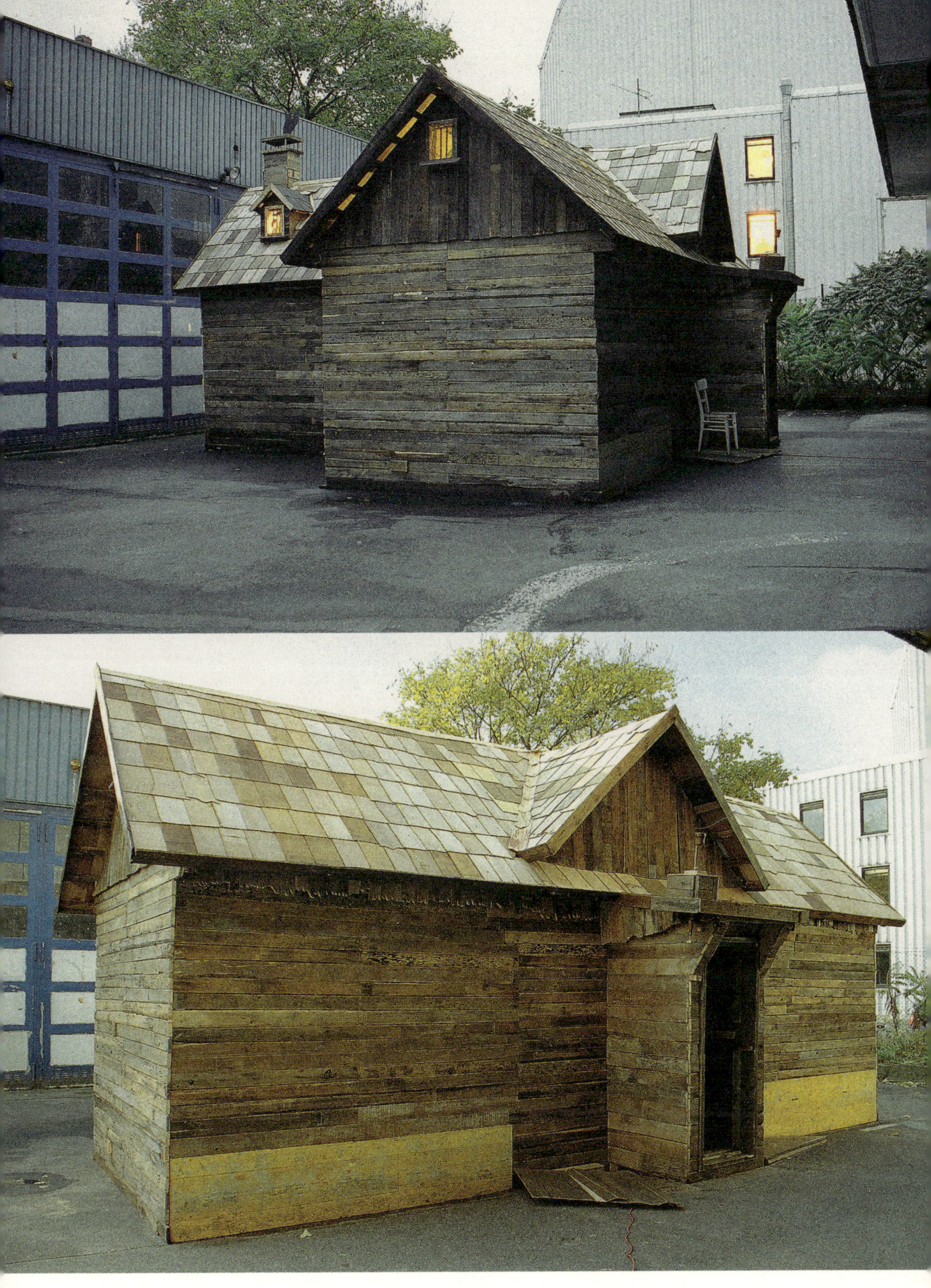

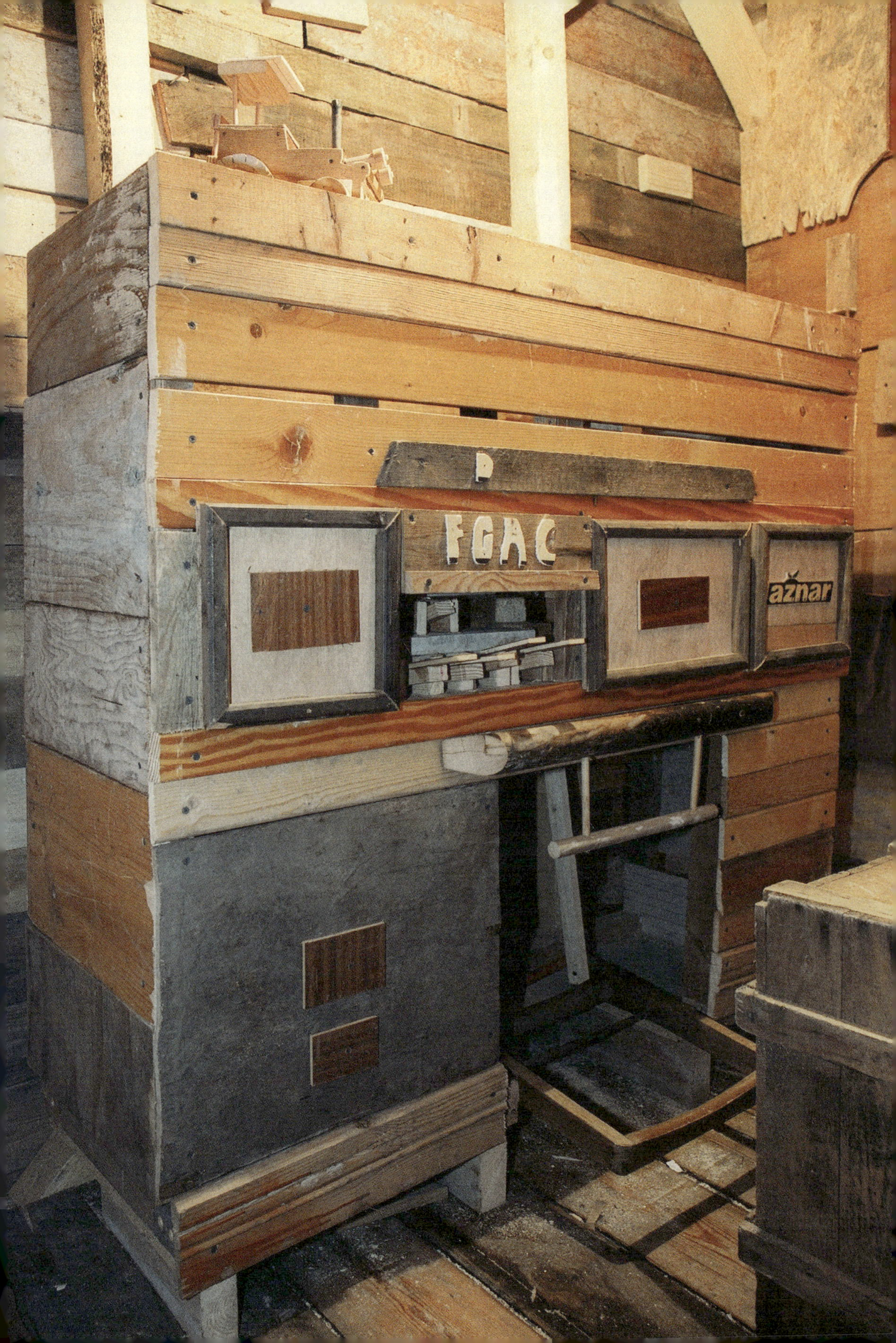

P
FGAC
aznar

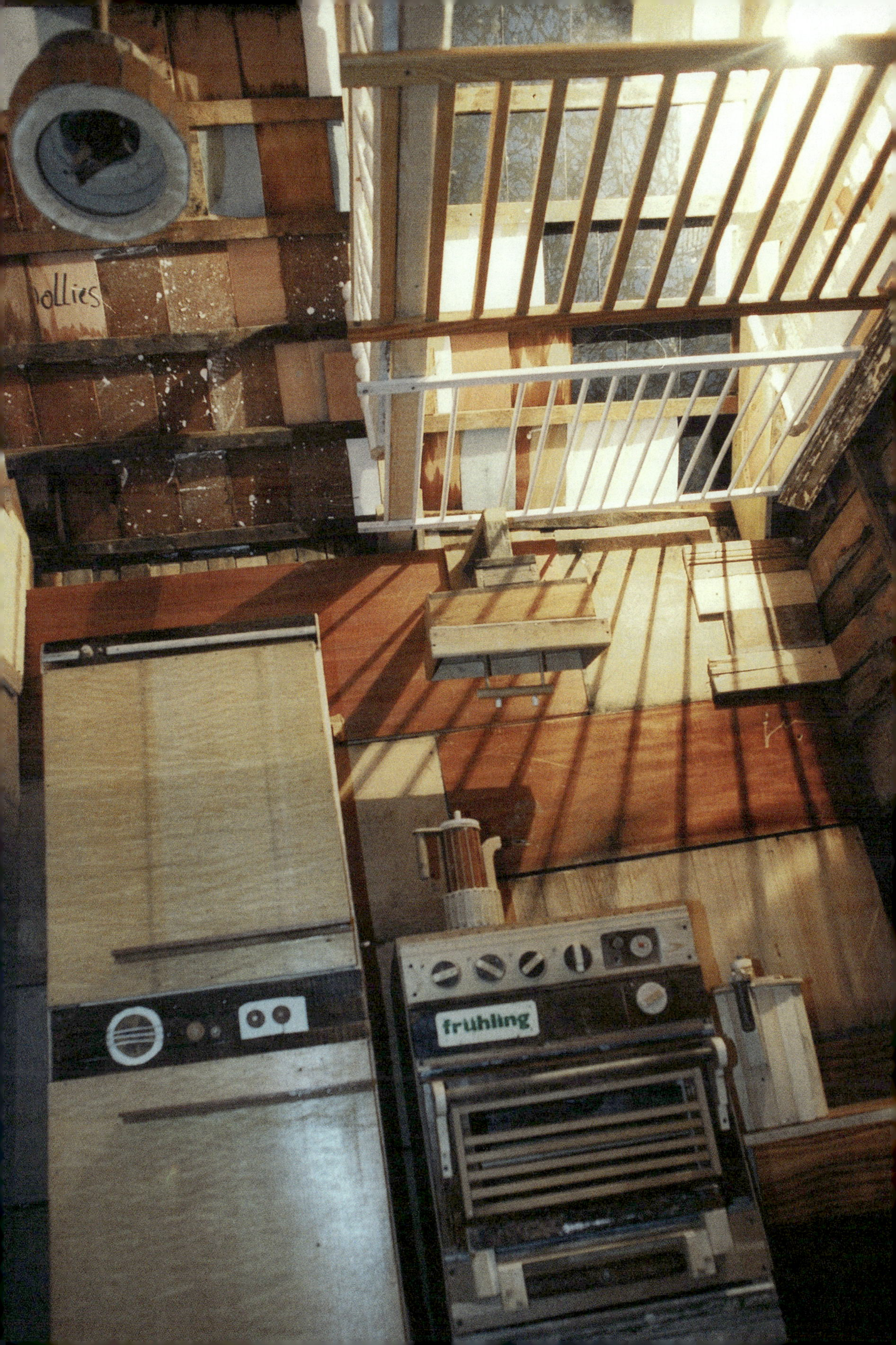
ollies
frühling

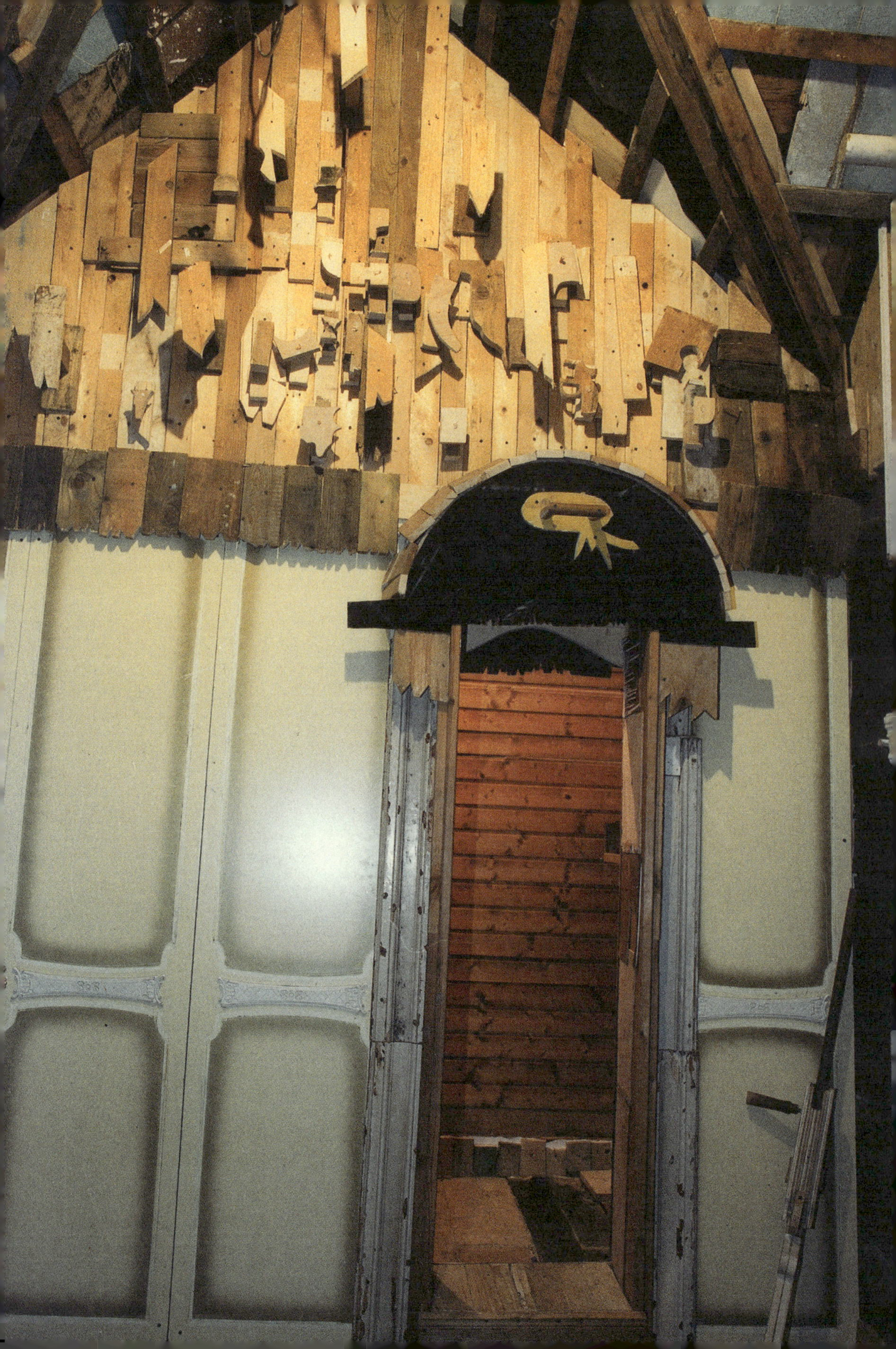

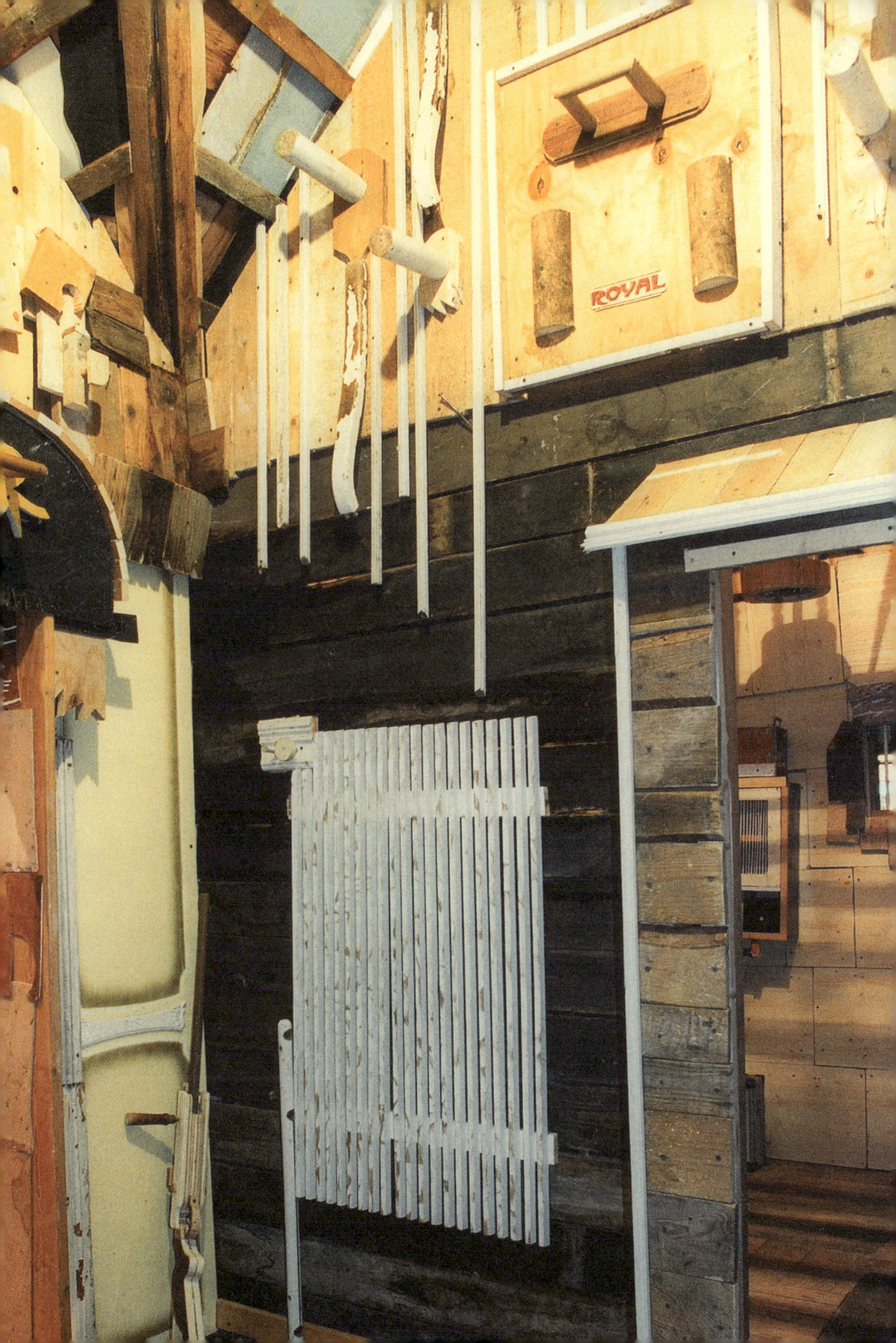
ROYAL

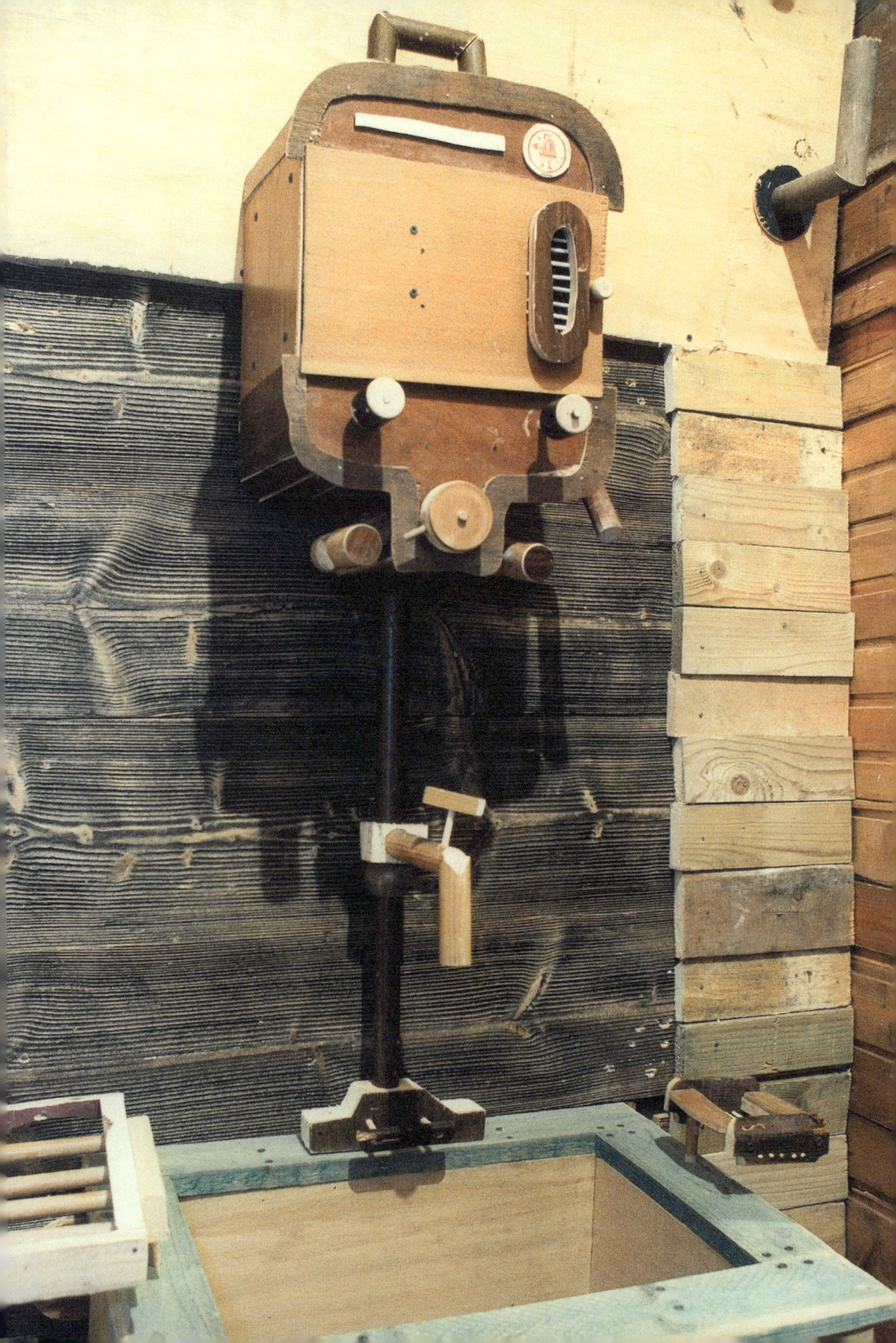

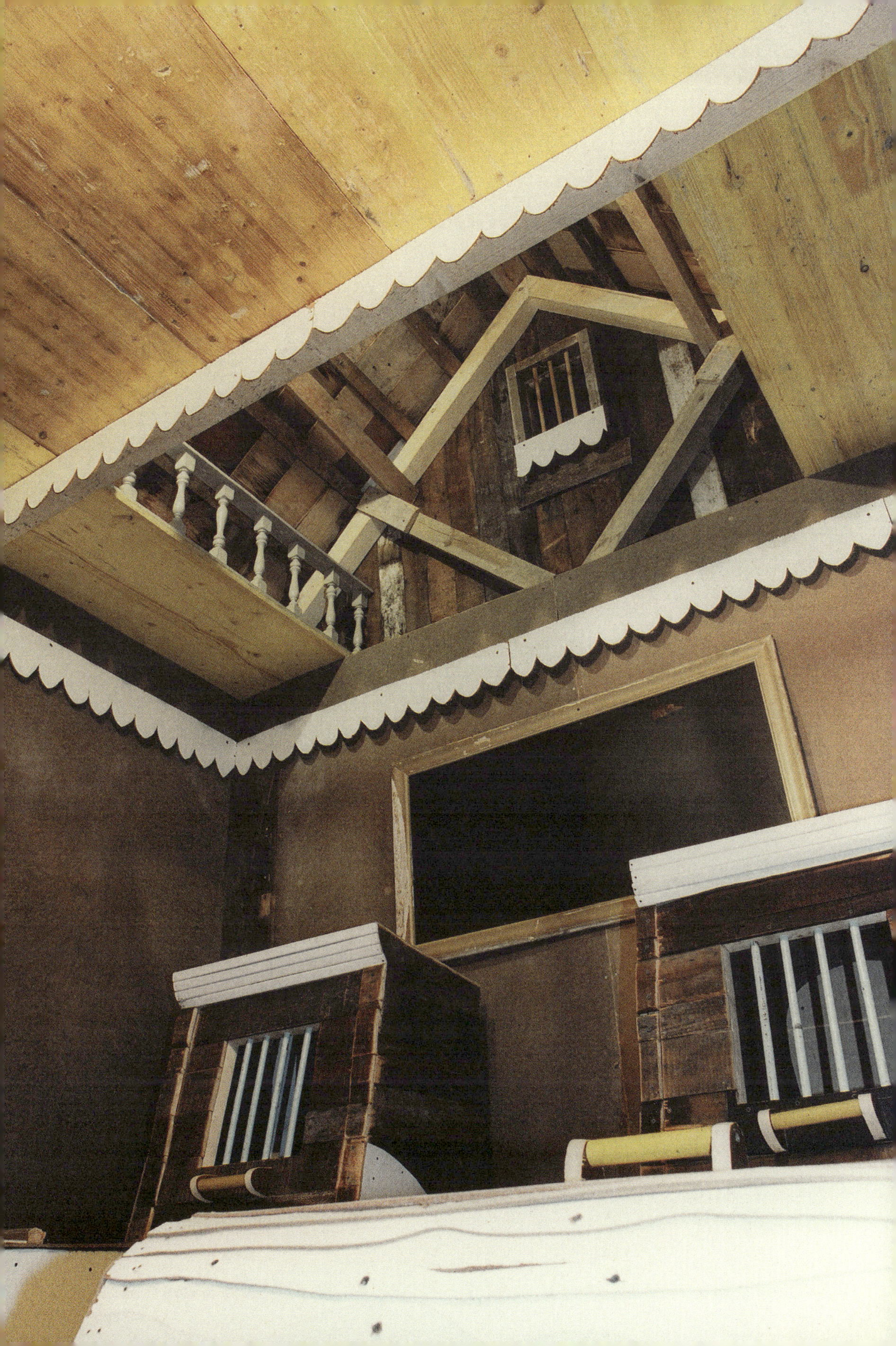

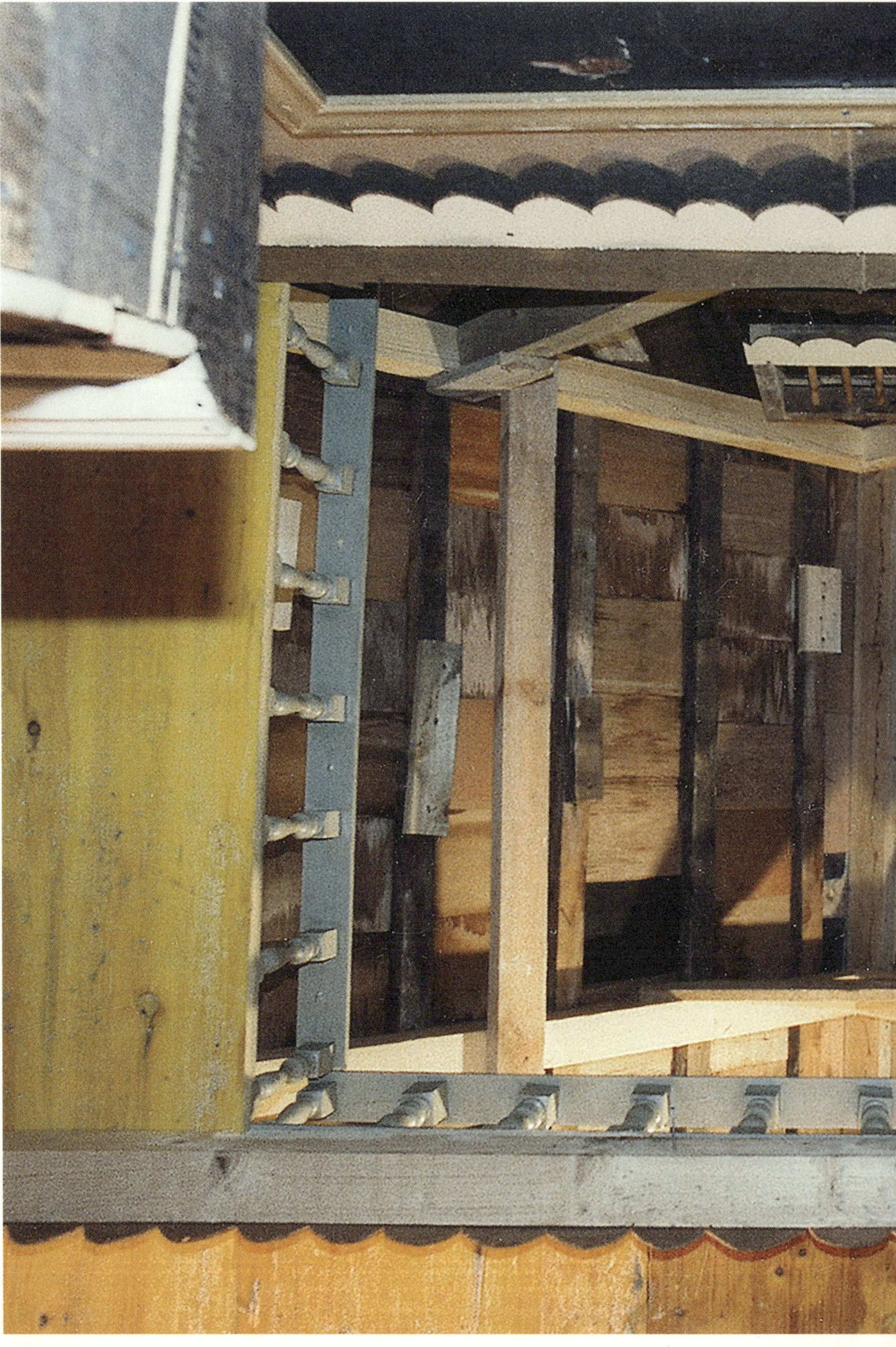

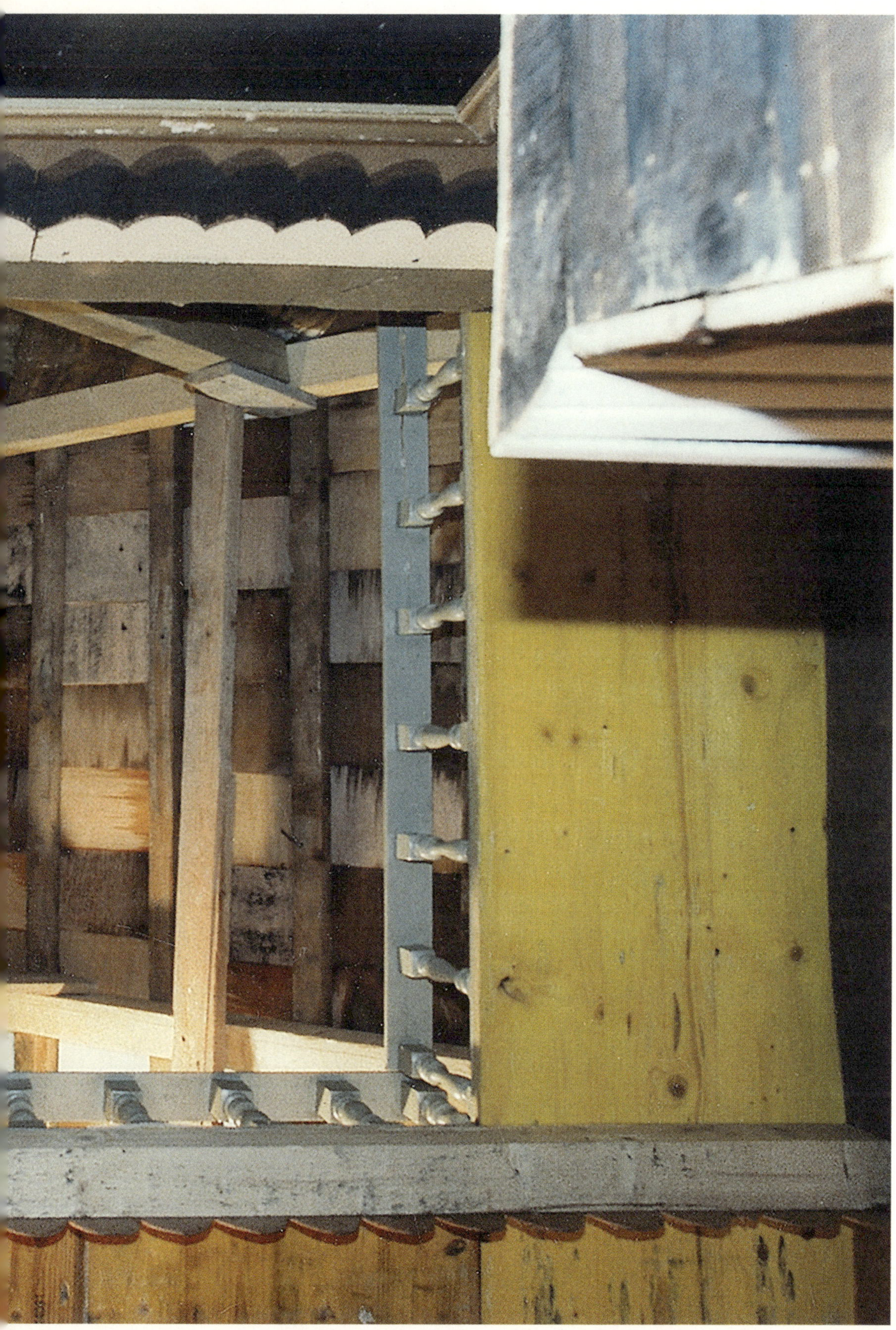

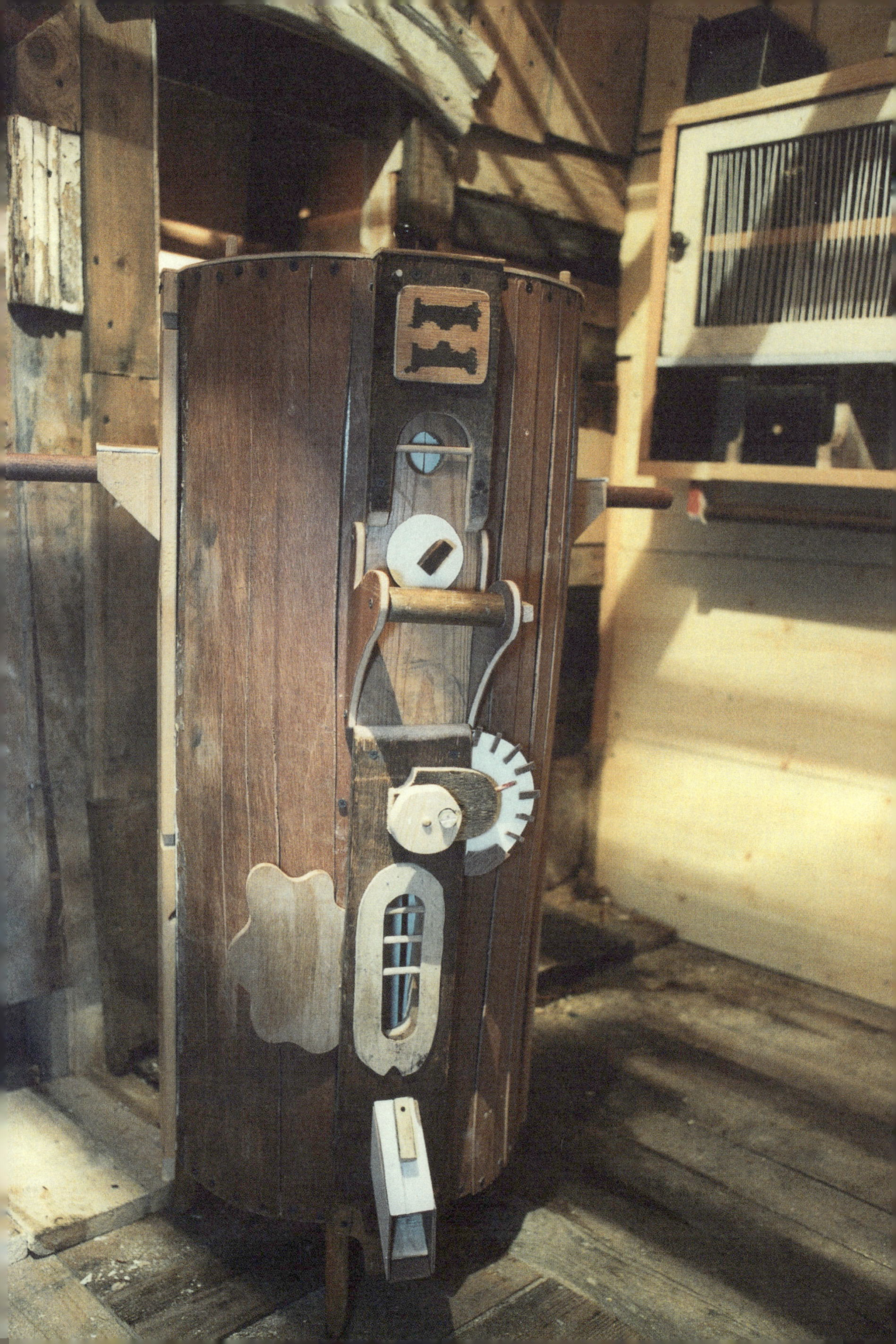

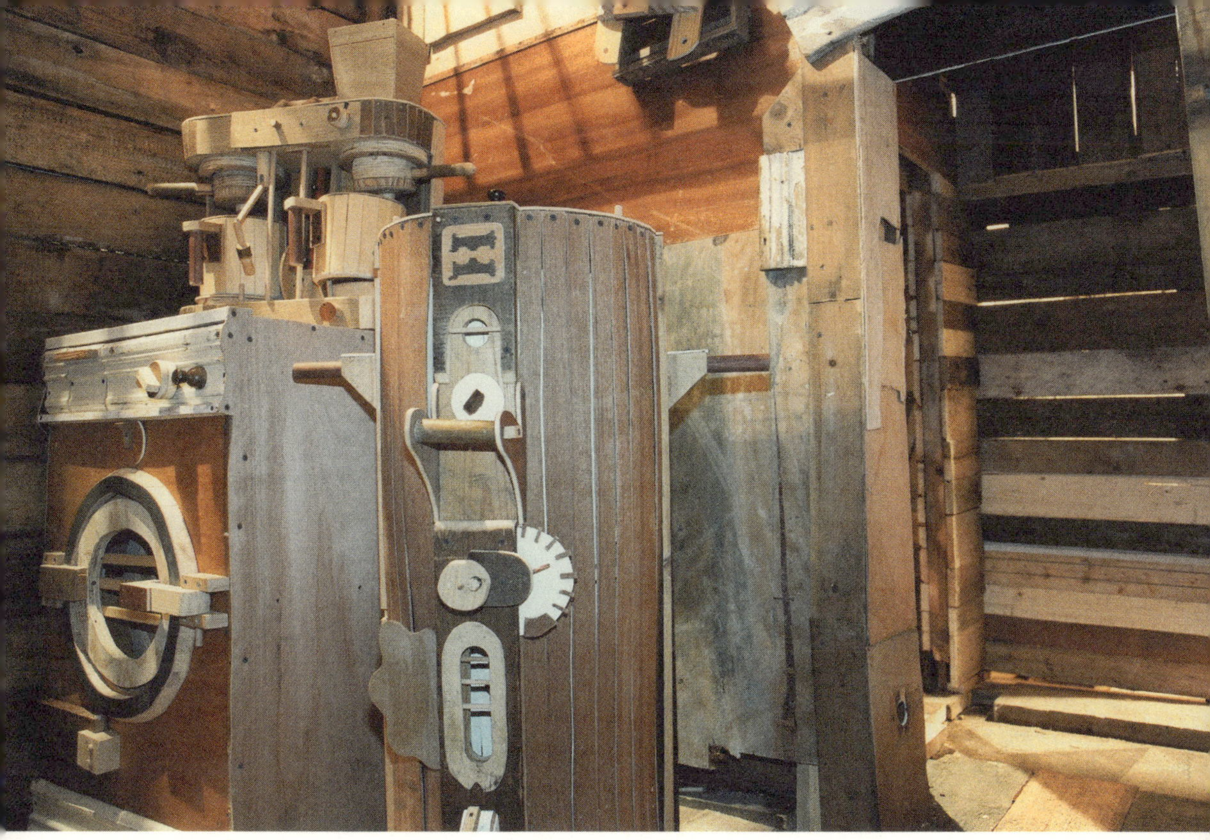

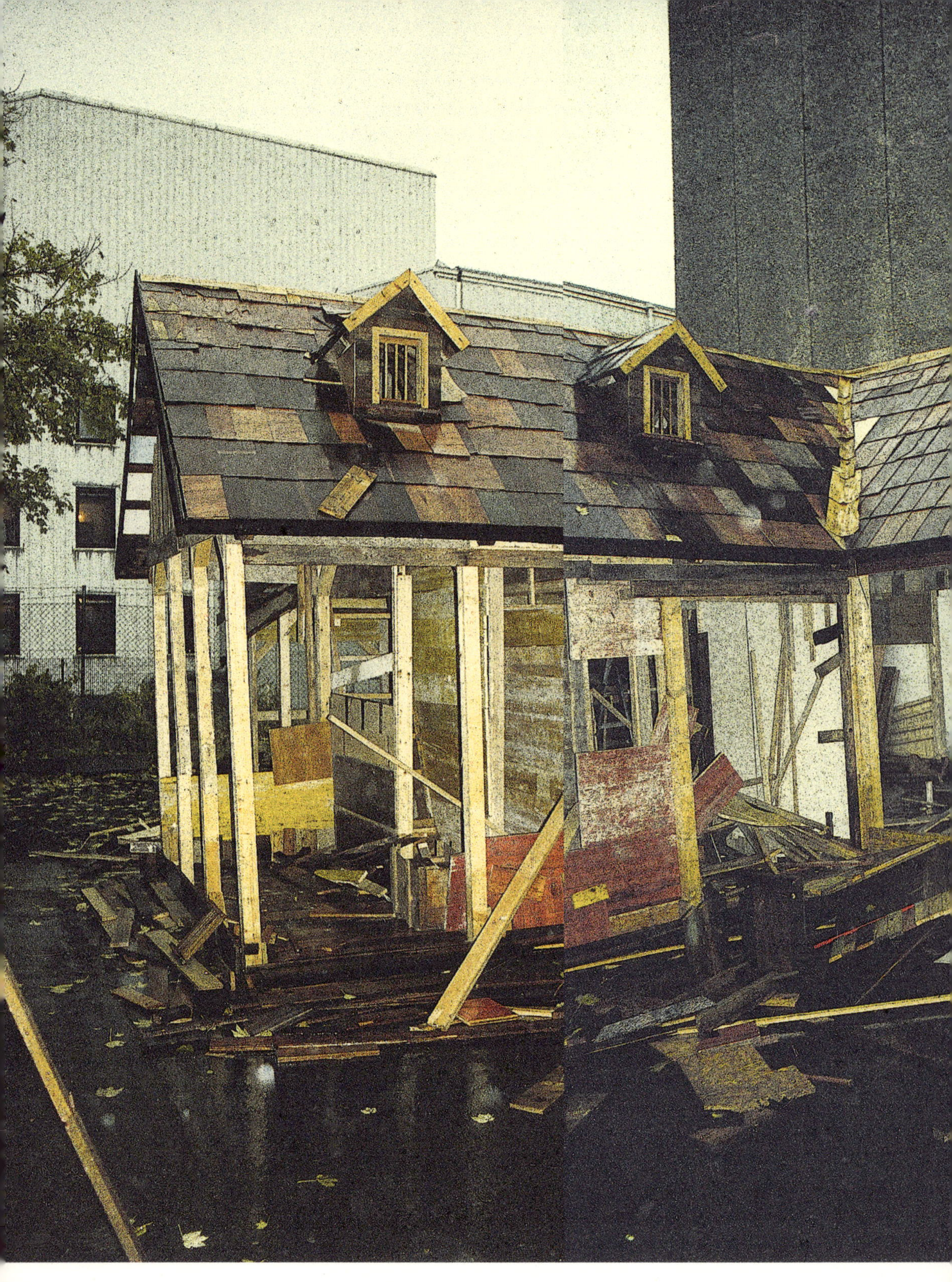

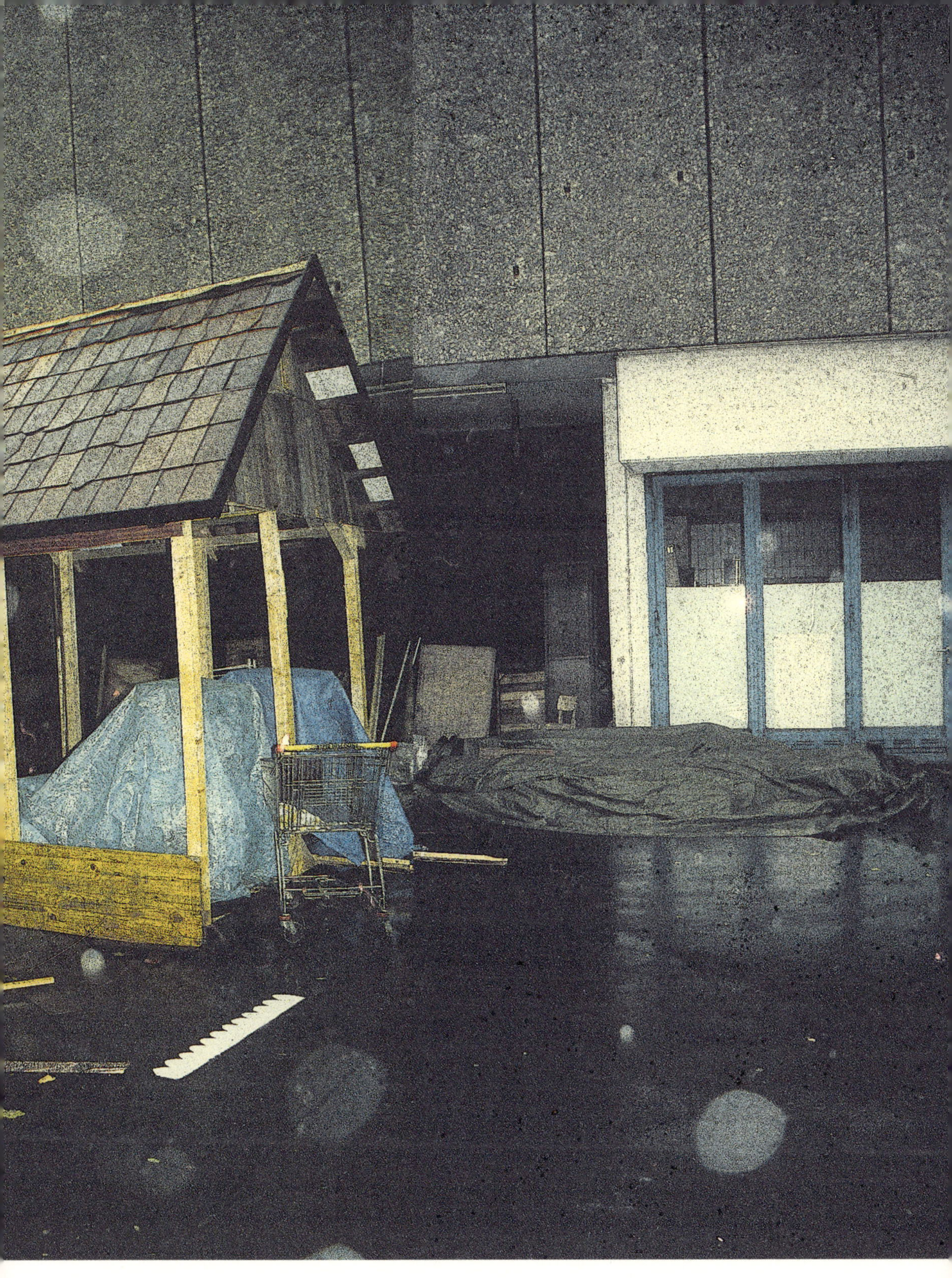

Hinter dem Schauspielhaus Ecke Ellmenreich- und Baumeisterstraße fällt eine offene Fläche in ansonsten dichtester Bebauung auf, umgrenzt von Gebäuden und Straßen. Räudiger Rasen, zwei Kastanien, Müll. Etwas »Zusätzliches«, »Überflüssiges«. Ich hatte von einem Hamburger Künstler gehört, der mit Farbe, mit Holz, mit Musik, Film und Texten arbeitete. Nach einem Besuch im »Atelier« von Thorsten Passfeld war klar, dass er der Richtige war für die Gestaltung dieser Fläche. Er saß

Vergänglichkeit in Holz

Thorsten Passfelds

»Hoftheater Vierlinden«

hinter dem Deutschen Schauspielhaus

in Hamburg (2004)

im ehemaligen Mojo-Gebäude am Anfang der Reeperbahn als typischer Künstler-Zwischennutzer in eisiger Kälte einer wahrscheinlich asbestverseuchten ehemaligen Bowlingbahn und erzählte mir, dass er auf das künstlerische Arbeiten mit Holz eigentlich gekommen sei, weil in der Kälte die Ölfarben immer eingefroren waren. Man beachte: Da beschwerte sich nicht jemand über miserable Arbeitsbedingungen, sondern wollte nur klarmachen, dass er keine Lust gehabt hatte, so lange nichts machen zu können! (Nebenbei: 2009 musste das Gebäude von den Künstlern geräumt werden und wurde abgerissen für die »Tanzenden Türme« von Te-

herani und Konsorten, ein Hochhauskomplex, der dort bis 2012 entstehen soll. Nutzung: Büros, Hotel, Mojo. Die Arbeitssituation für Bildende Künstler in Hamburg ist nach wie vor ausgesprochen schwierig).

Nachdem Thorsten Passfeld das Holz in die Hand genommen hatte, ließ es ihn nicht mehr los und es entstanden sein erstes Gebäude *Haus aus Holz* hinter der Reeperbahn (2002), das er wie alle späteren Häuser nach Projektende wieder abriss, und viele wunderbare Holz-Objekte. Seine Arbeiten aus Altholz haben etwas Raues, Schlicht-Einfaches, sind hölzern stabil und verströmen eine Atmosphäre archaischer Heimatlichkeit. Zugleich sind sie von irritierender Fragilität, im Detail akribisch genau und verweigern sich im »falschen Material« ganz selbstbewusst Funktionalität und Nützlichkeit.

Recycling von Material, ein Arbeitsprozess im öffentlichen Raum an einem vergänglichen Produkt – Passfeld und das Theater passen gut zusammen. So entstand der gemeinsame Plan zu einem kleinen Theater aus Holz, das zur Spielzeiteröffnung 2004/05 auf dem Grün hinterm Schauspiel-

haus entstehen sollte. Thorsten Passfeld baute den Sommer über in wochenlanger Kleinarbeit. Wie bei allen anderen Holzarbeiten verwendete er Altholz, das er in nächtlichen Streifzügen in Sankt Pauli aufspürte und bei Abrissunternehmen, auf Baustellen und aus Containern sammelte. Immer wenn man hinter dem Schauspielhaus vorbeiging, war er am Bauen, ganz allein, in akribischer Kleinarbeit, viele, viele Stunden lang.

Im September stand es fertig da: Das *Hoftheater Vierlinden.* Erbaut unter zwei Kastanien, mit Foyer, Zuschauerraum, Bühne – und sogar eine Bar gab es und viele kleine Kunstwerke an den Wänden. Rund 130 Quadratmeter groß, mit tausend kleinen und größeren Accessoires ausgestattet für die Zuschauer, die mit kindlicher Entdeckerfreude überall herumgingen und Holzobjekte entzückt kommentierten, die mit der Funktionalität ihrer Vorbilder spielten, wie der lebensgroße Zigarettenautomat, das Wandtelefon ganz aus Holz oder die vielen Vogelkästen mit vergittertem Einflugloch.

Eine Woche lang war das *Hoftheater Vierlinden* Ort für ein exquisites kleines Musik- und Theaterprogramm mit Theaterprojekten der Regieassistenten und der Kapelle des Schauspielhauses mit den ewig unvergessenen Lieven Brunckhorst, Martin Engelbach und Dirk Ritz. Von »draußen« hatten wir die Schischischos Sven Amtsberg, Michael Weins und Alex Posch geholt, Rocko Schamoni und Heinz Strunk mit ihren Lesungen und Jacques Palminger &

Reverend Dabeler mit einer Body
Painting Performance. Es gab einen Kindernachmittag, und die
»Lange Nacht der Theater« war zu
Gast in unserem kleinen Theater.
Den Abschiedsabend gestaltete
Passfeld selbst mit Lesung, Musik
und Film.
Am nächsten Tag fing er mit dem
Abriss an, zum größten Bedauern
von Zuschauern und Theatermit-
arbeitern - programmgemäß. Er
selbst sagte dazu, er baue seine
Häuser »aus Höflichkeit« wieder
ab, die seien eben für eine kurze
Zeit der große Aufriss, erhielten
sehr viel Aufmerksamkeit, was ja
auch sehr schön sei, aber dann
sei es auch mal genug und die
müssten dann wieder weg.
Es ist unbedingt wieder Zeit für
ein neues Projekt im öffentlichen
Raum nach all dem, was in Hamburg 2009 so passiert ist…

Tom Stromberg

*Tom Stromberg, Leiter des Thea-
terfestivals »Impulse« (gemeinsam
mit Matthias von Hartz) und Thea-
terproduzent, war von 2000 bis
2005 Intendant des Deutschen
Schauspielhauses in Hamburg.
Auf seine Einladung hin realisier-
te Thorsten Passfeld 2004 das
Hoftheater Vierlinden in St. Georg
hinter dem Deutschen Schauspielhaus.*

Behind the Schauspielhaus at the corner of Ellmenreich- and Baumeisterstraße an open space surrounded by buildings and streets strikes the eye in what is otherwise an area of heavy building density. A mangy lawn, two chestnut trees, rubbish. Something "additional", "superfluous". I had heard about a Hamburg artist who worked with wood, music, film and text. After visiting Thorsten Passfeld in his "studio" it was clear that he was the right person to commission with the design of this area. He sat in the former Mojo building at the entrance to the Reeperbahn, with a typical artist's temporary utilization contract, in the icy cold of a former bowling alley that was probably contaminated with asbestos, and told me that he had started to work with wood because his oil paints always froze in the cold. One should note however: This was not someone complaining about appalling working conditions, he just wanted to make it clear that he didn't want to spend such a long time doing nothing! (By the way: In 2009 the artists had to vacate the building and it was demolished to make way for the "dancing towers" designed by Tehrani and consorts, a high-rise building complex that is to be completed by 2012. Utilization: offices, hotel, Mojo. The working conditions for fine artists in Hamburg is still extremely difficult).

Once Thorsten Passfeld had picked up his first piece of wood, he could no longer let it go and his first building *Haus aus Holz* (wooden house) was created behind the Reeperbahn (2002), a house that he demolished at the end of the project, just like all the others, in order to turn the pieces into wonderful objects in wood. His works made out of scrap wood have something rough about them, something straight and simple. They are clunky and stable and radiate an atmosphere of archaic homeliness. At the same time they are irritatingly fragile, their details are meticulously precise, self-confidently defying functionality and usefulness by means of the "wrong material."

The recycling of material and work in progress in public space using a perishable product – Passfeld and the theatre fit well together. This formed the basis for a collaborative plan for a small theatre made of wood that was to be constructed on the lawn behind the Schauspielhaus for the opening of the new season 2004/05. Throughout the summer, Thorsten Passfeld built the theatre, right down to the smallest detail, week after week. As with all his other works in wood, he used scrap wood that he tracked down on his nightly wanderings through Sankt Pauli or that he collected from demolition companies, building sites or containers. On passing the back of the Schauspielhaus, one could see him building away, completely alone, in painstaking detail, piece by piece, hour after hour.

In September it was ready: The *Hoftheater Vierlinden*. Built beneath two chestnut trees, with a foyer, auditorium and stage – and it even had a bar with lots of small works of art on the walls. About 130 square metres, equipped with thousands of small and large accessories for the spectators who went around everywhere with childish enthusiasm and commented with delight on the wooden objects that played on the functionality of those they were based on. For example the life-sized cigarette vending machine, the wall phone made completely of wood or the large number of bird boxes with grilles over the entrances.

For a week the *Hoftheater Vierlinden* was the location for a small, exquisite music and theatre programme with theatre projects run by the Assistant Director and the Schauspielhaus band with the ever-unforgettable Lieven Brunckhorst, Martin Engelbach and Dirk Ritz. From "outside" we

Perishability in wood

Thorsten Passfeld's

"Hoftheater Vierlinden" behind

the theatre Deutsches Schauspielhaus

in Hamburg (2004)

brought in the schischischos Sven Amtsberg, Michael Weins and Alex Posch, Rocko Schamoni and Heinz Strunk with their readings, and Jacques Palminger & Reverend Dabeler with a body painting performance. There was a children's afternoon, and we even hosted the event "Lange Nacht der Theater" (long night of the theatre) in our small theatre. Passfeld created the programme himself for the farewell evening, with readings, music and film. The next day he began with the demolition as planned, much to the regret of the audience and theatre employees. He himself said that he dismantled his houses "out of politeness", they were only intended for a short time, to pull a big crowd, they drew a lot of attention which was of course really nice, but then it was enough and they had to be done away with again.

It is most definitely time for a new public art project after everything that happened in Hamburg in 2009…

Tom Stromberg

Tom Stromberg, Director of the theatre festival "Impulse" (together with Matthias von Hartz) and theatrical producer was Artistic Director of the Deutsche Schauspielhaus in Hamburg from 2000 to 2005. In response to his invitation, in 2004 Thorsten Passfeld realized the Hoftheater Vierlinden *in St. Georg behind the Deutsche Schauspielhaus.*

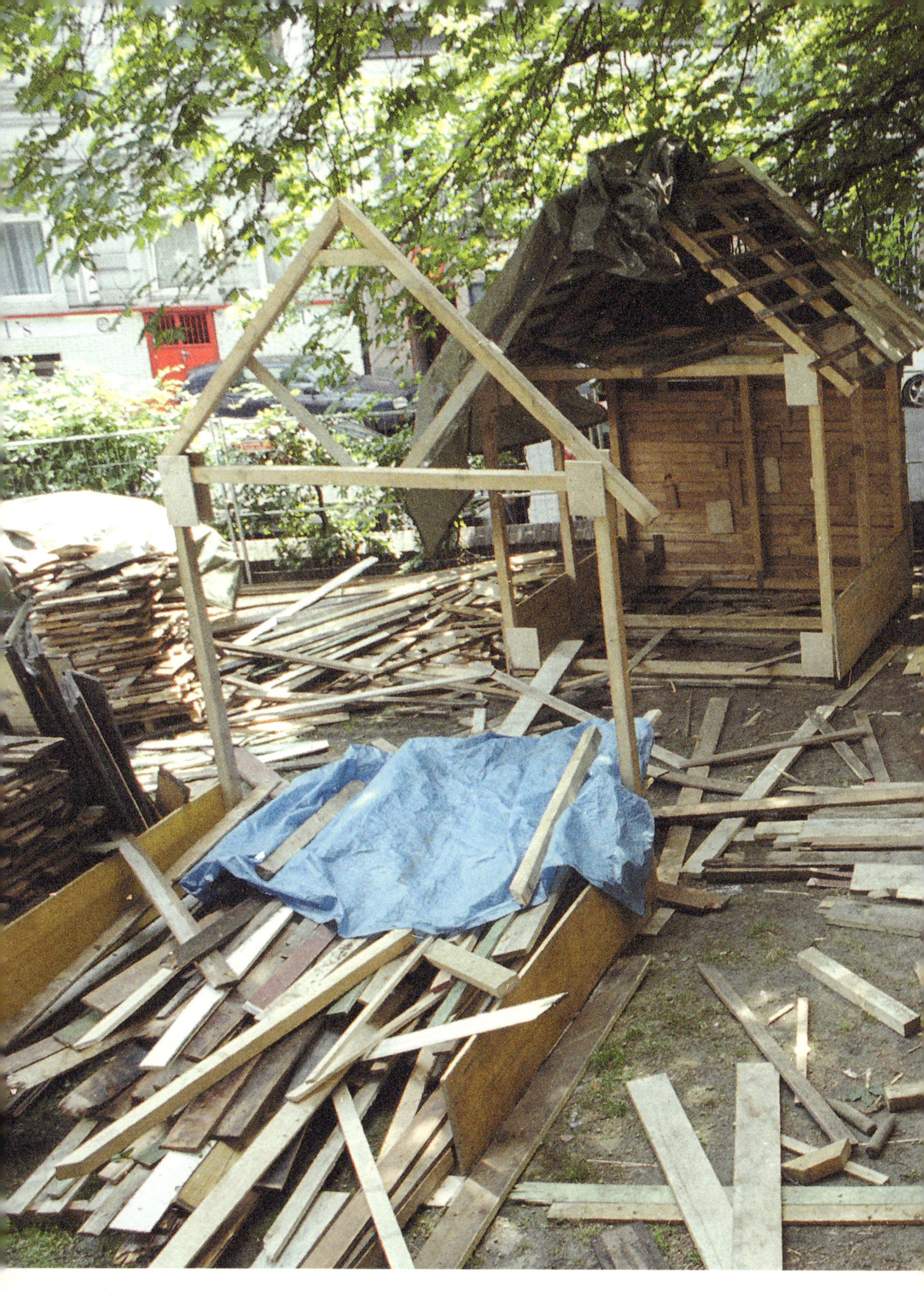

 Hoftheater Vierlinden, 2004

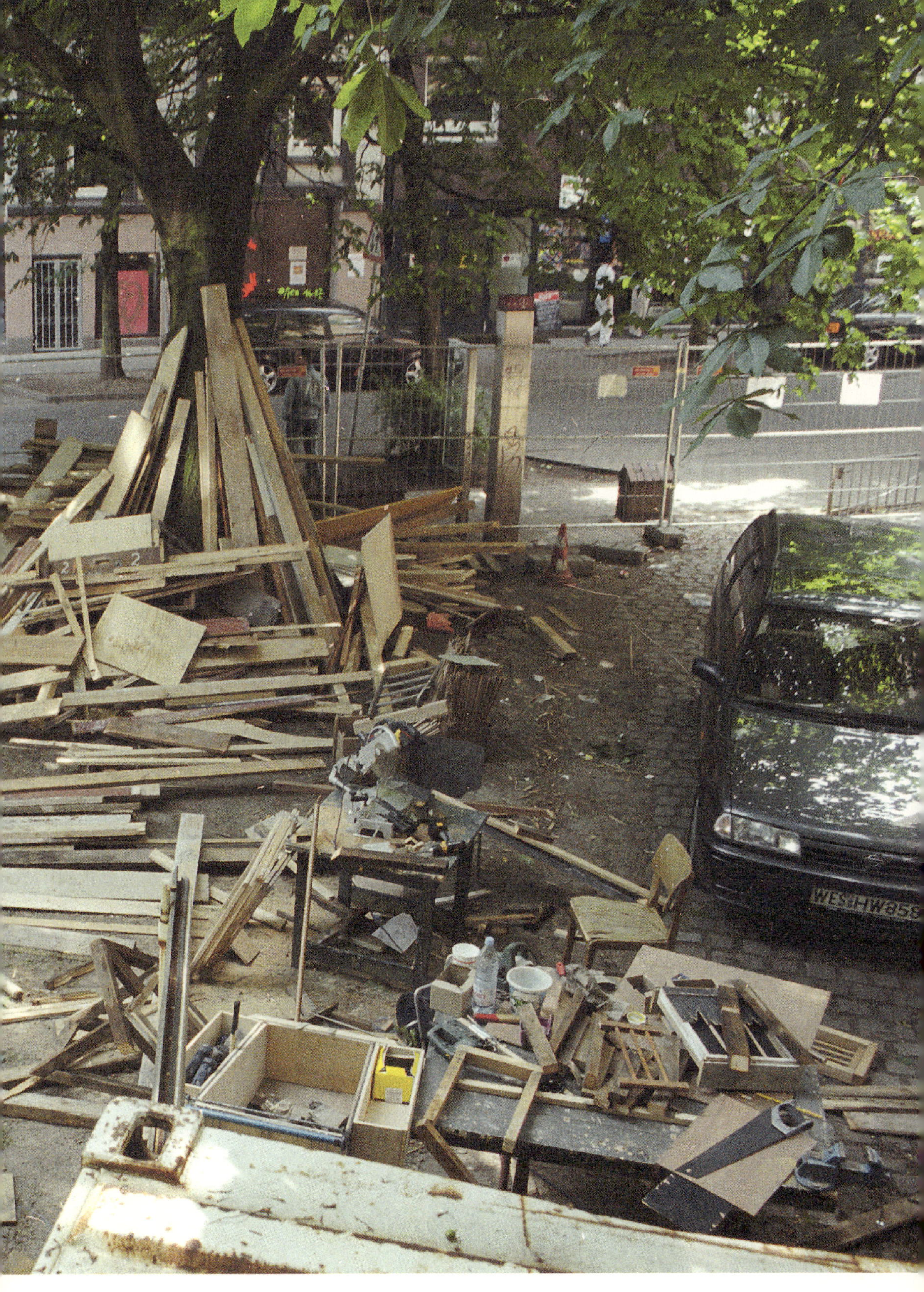

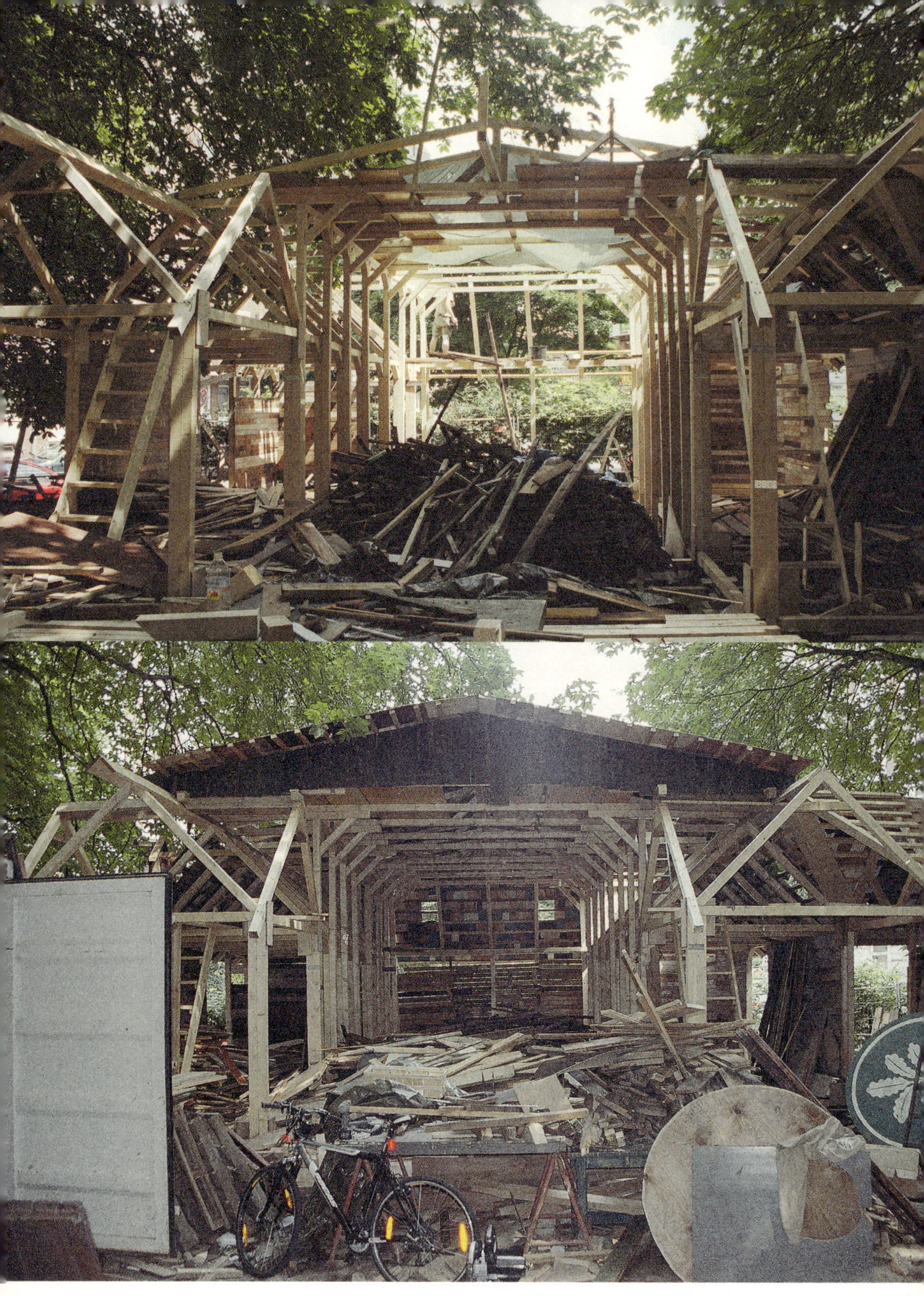

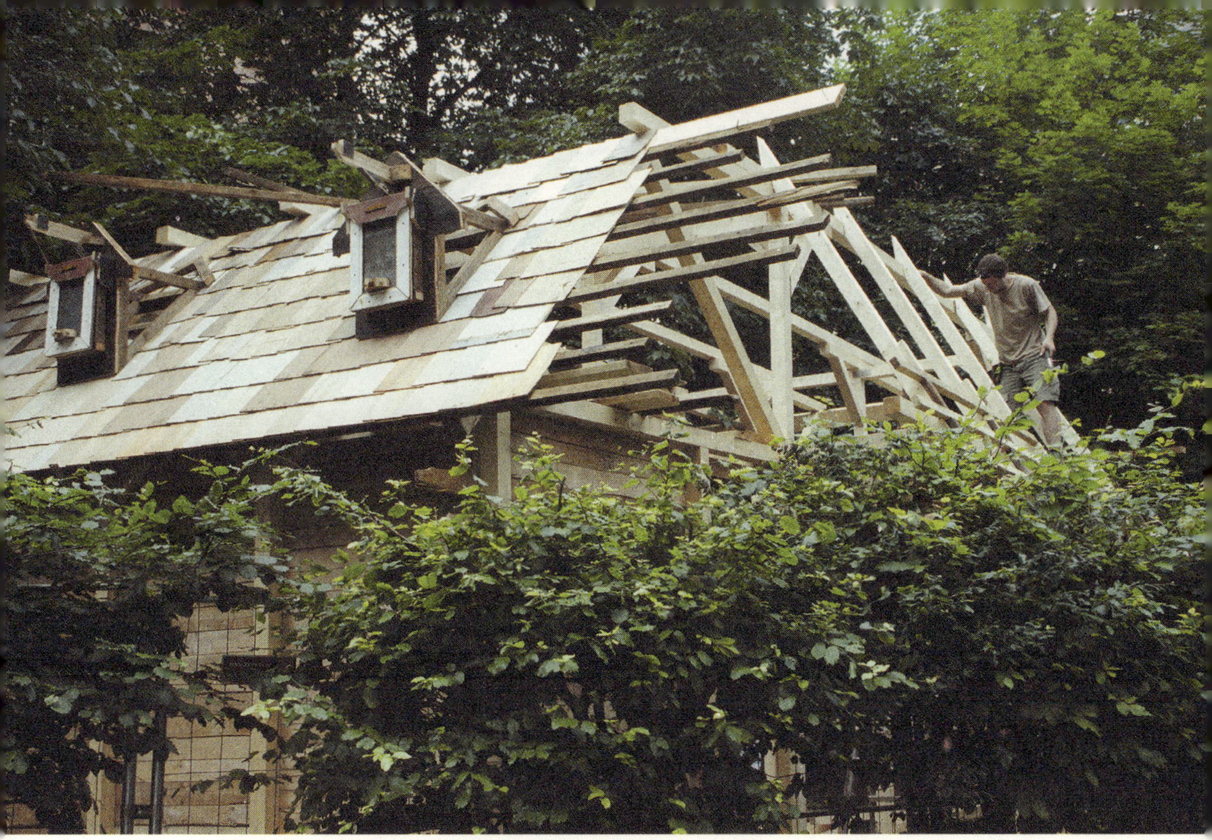

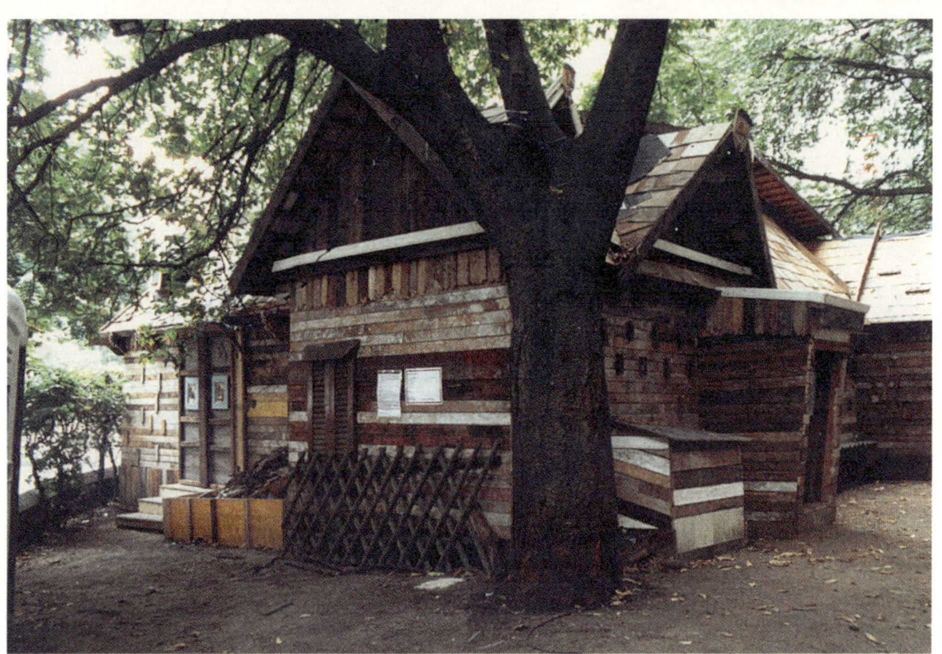

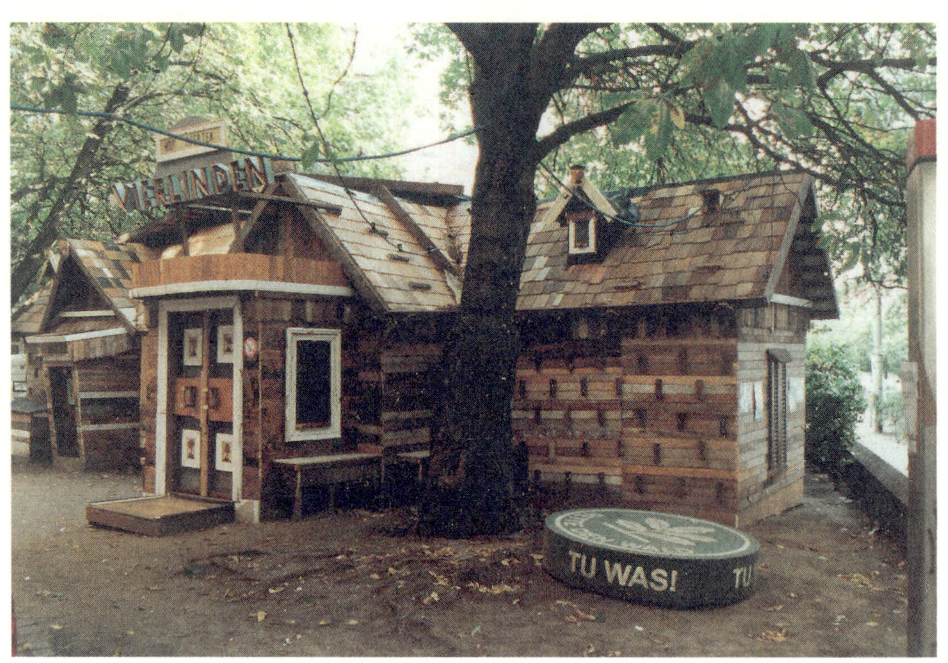

VIERLINDEN
TU WAS!   TU

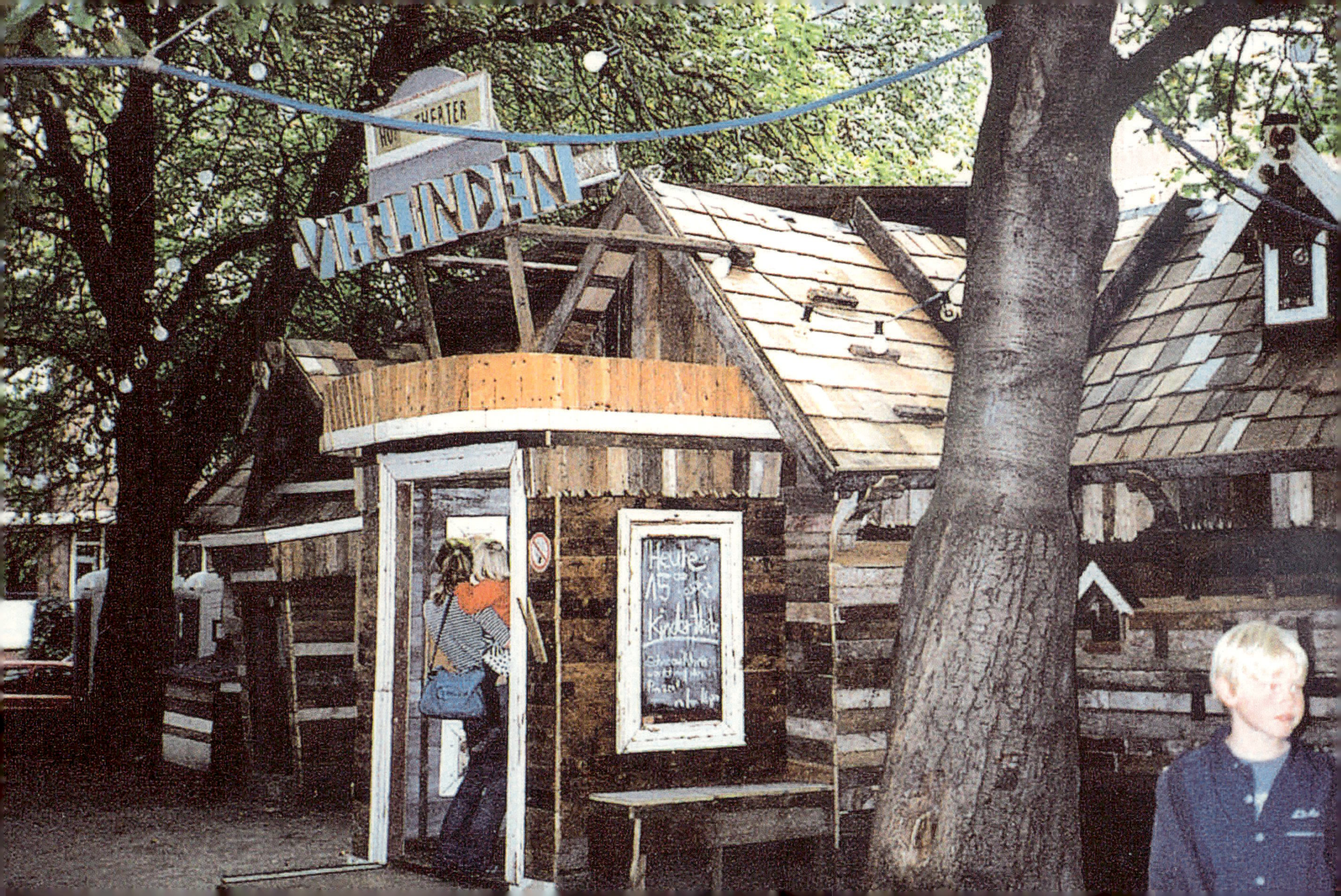
HOF THEATER
VIERLINDEN
Heute
15
Kinder

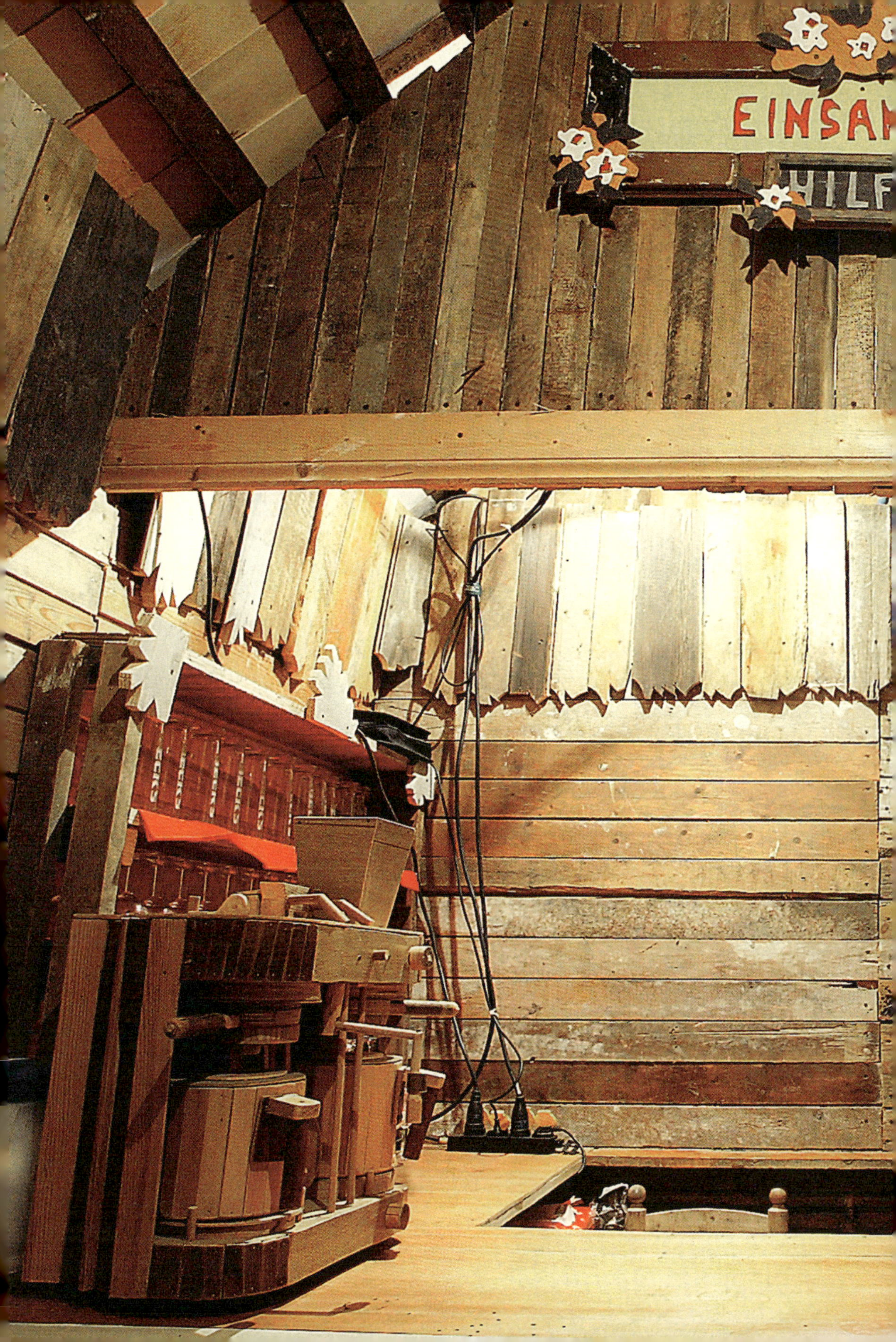

EINSAM
HILF

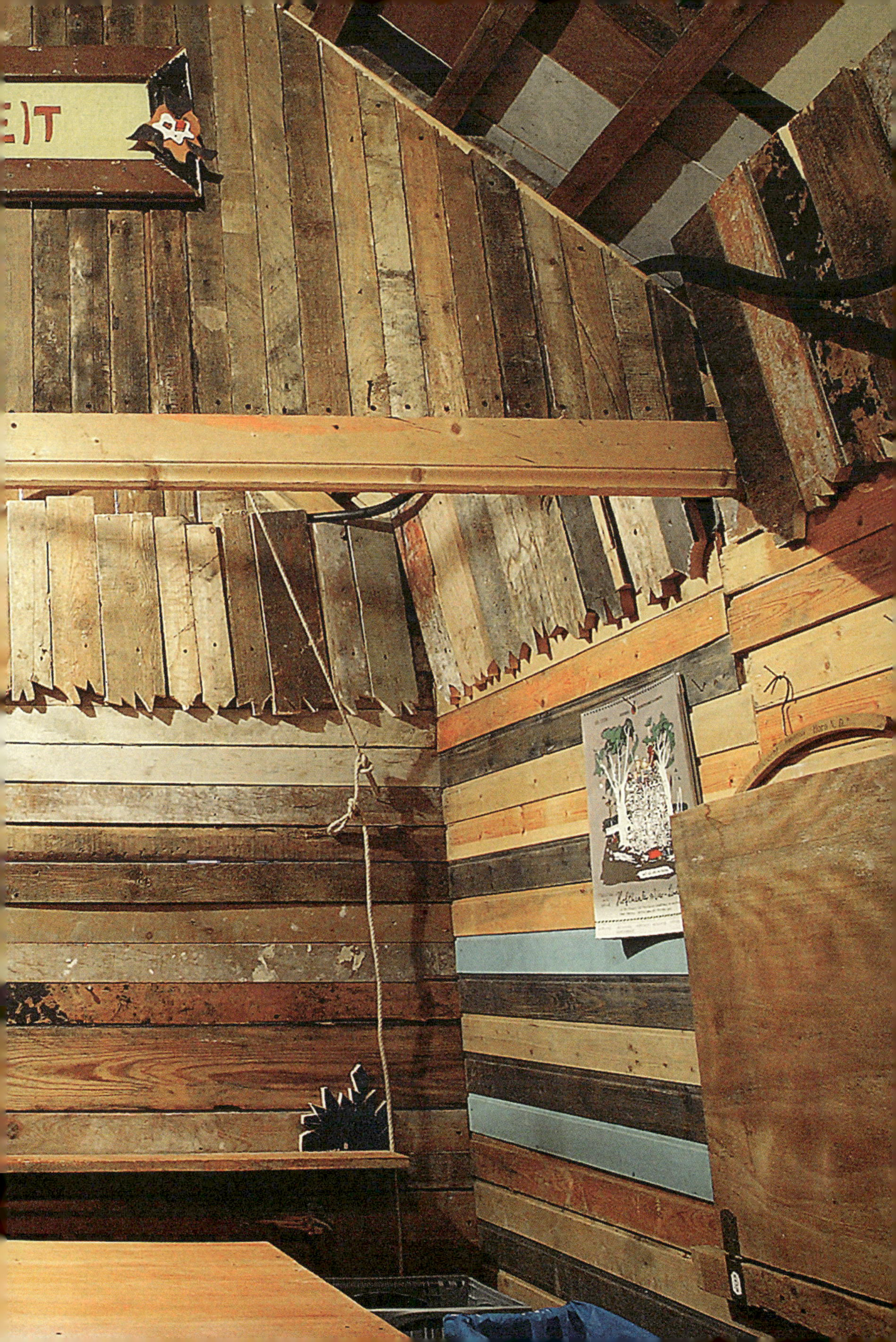
E)T

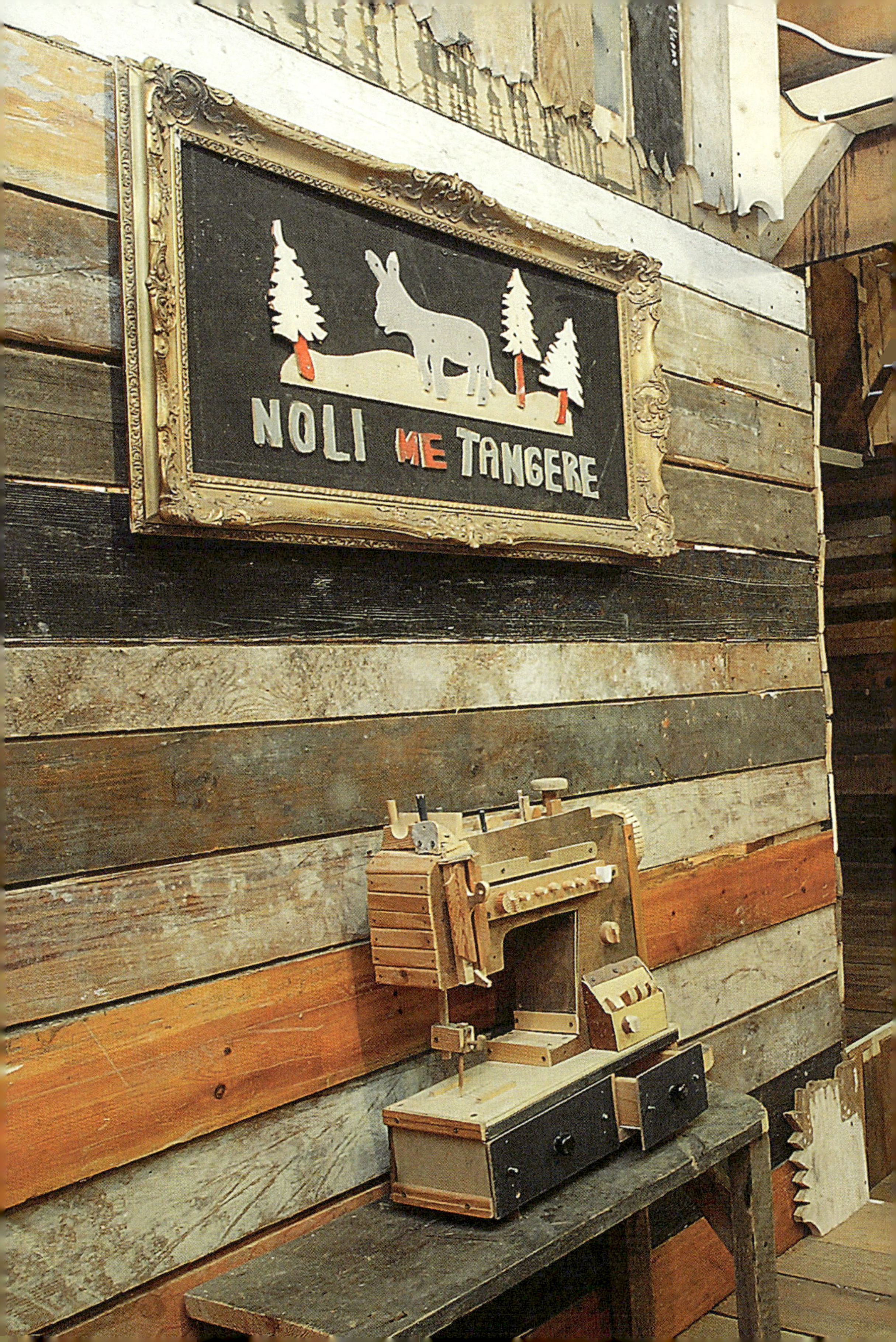

NOLI ME TANGERE

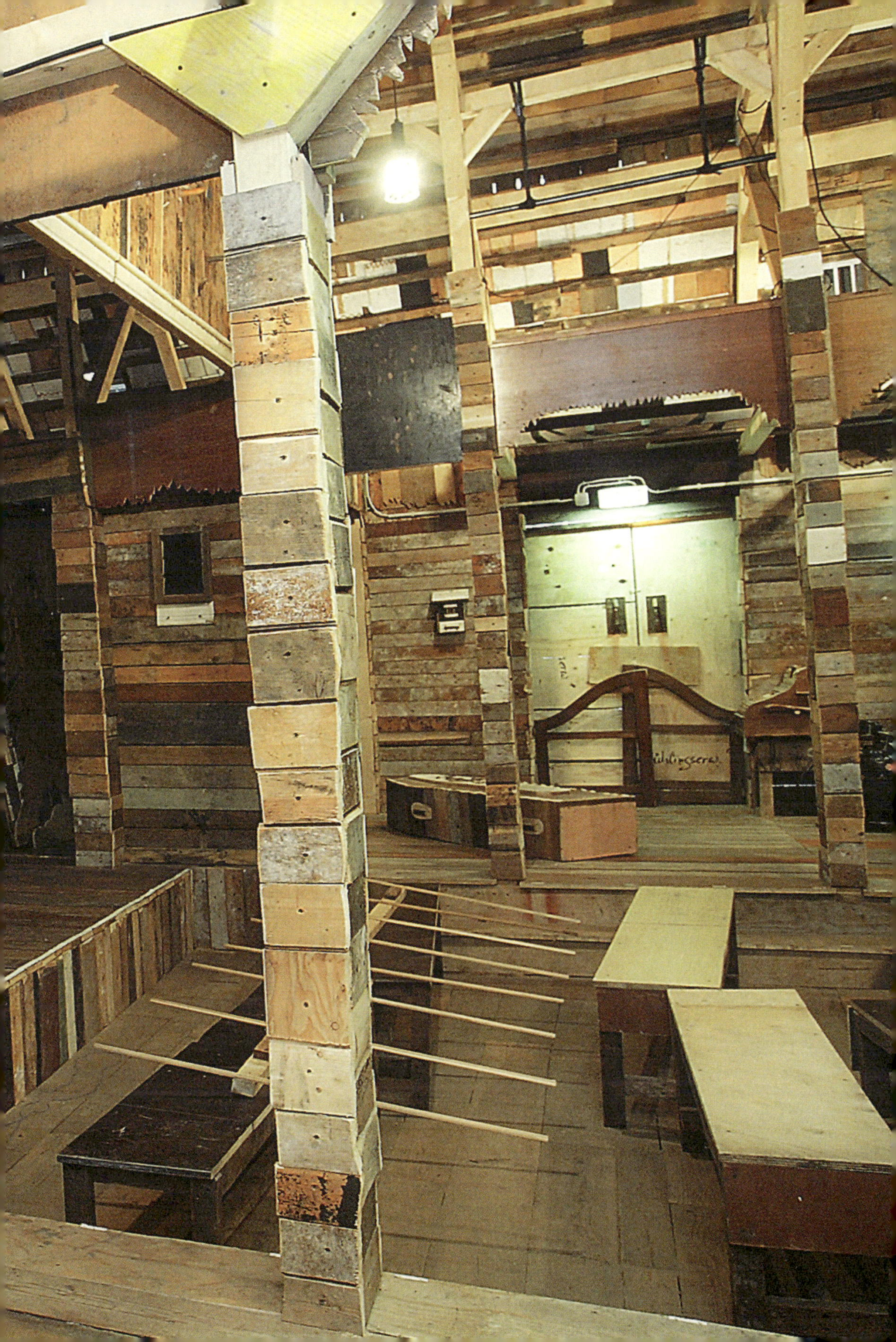

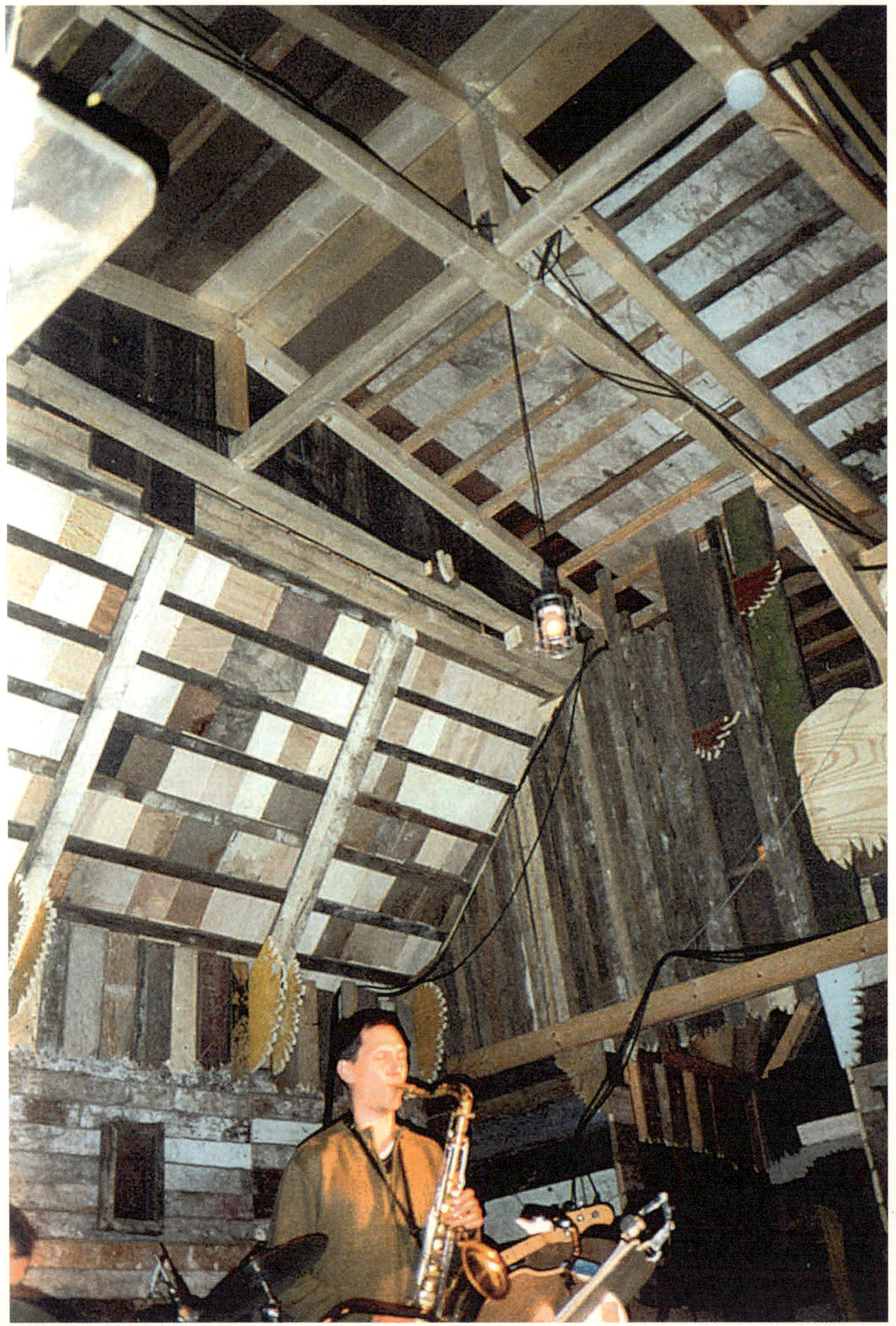

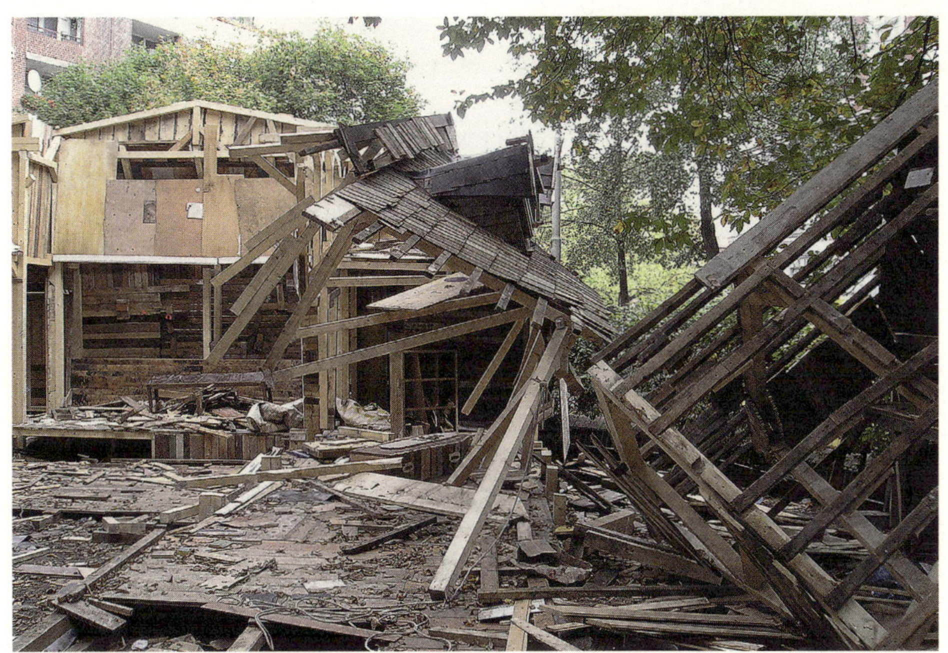

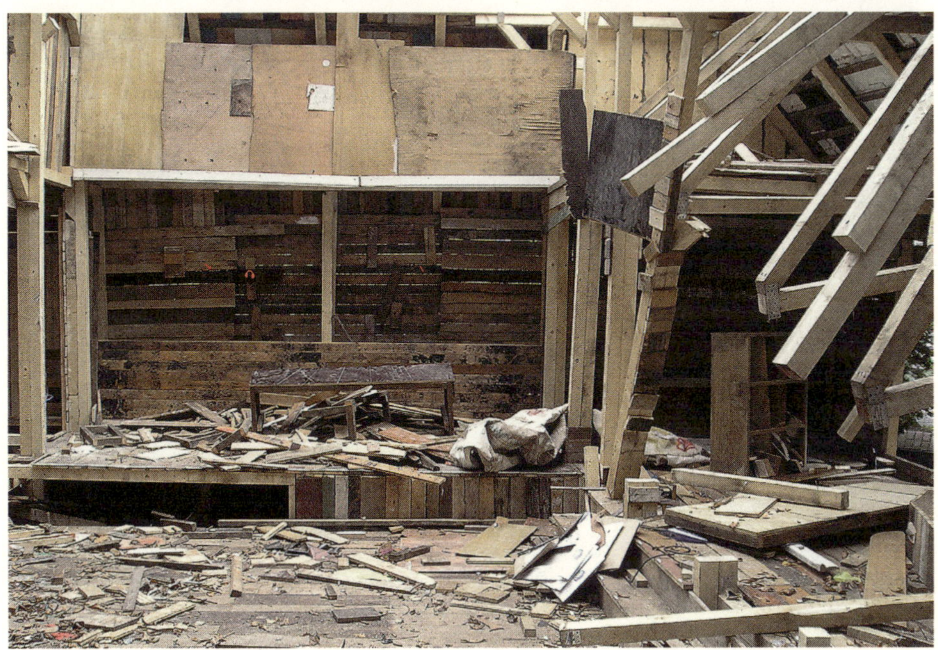

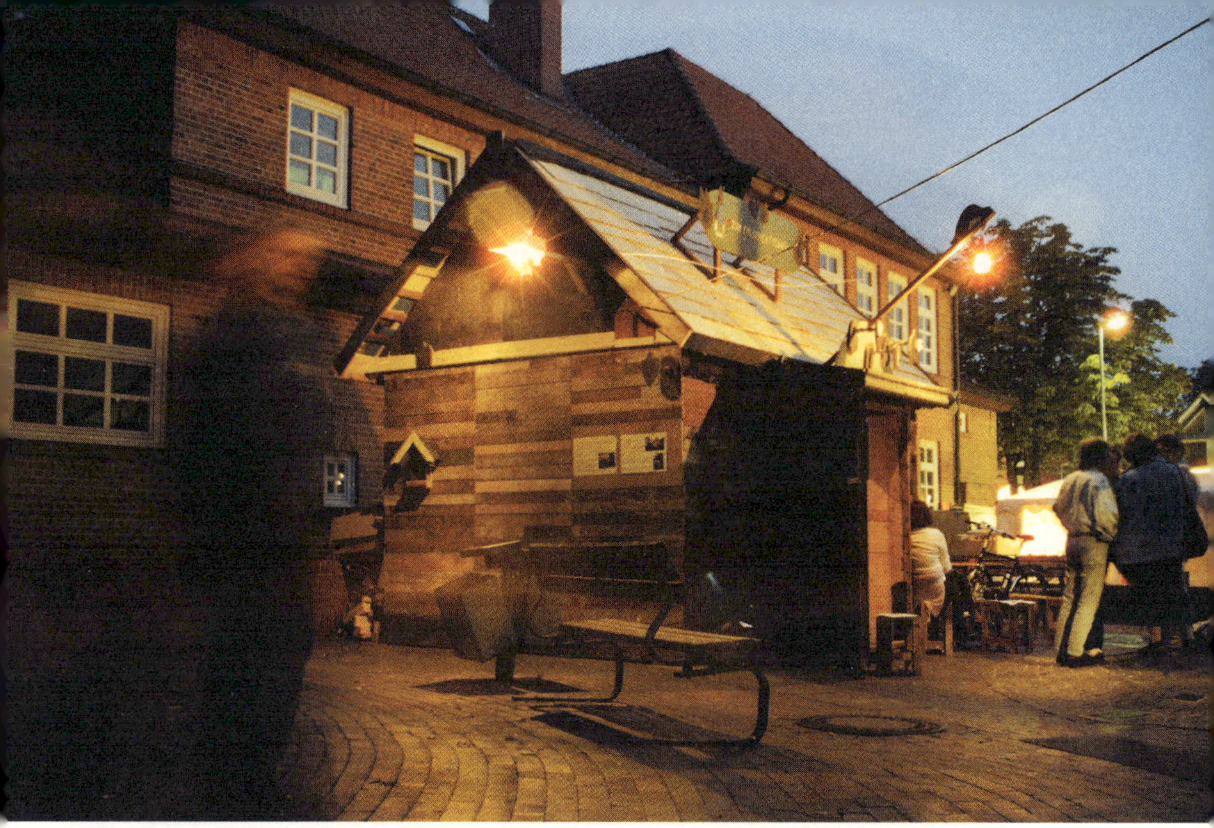

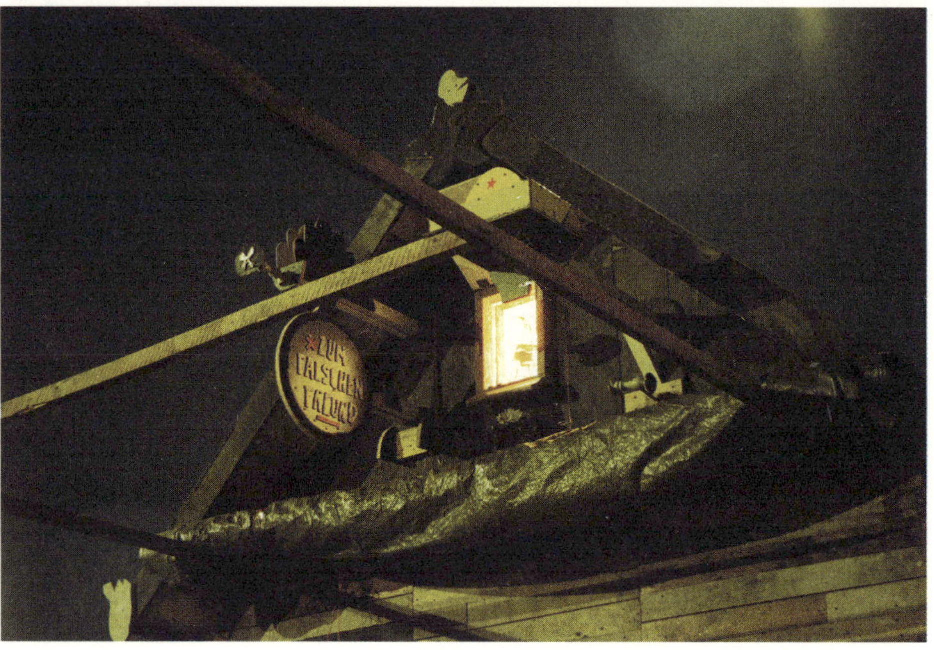

  Zum Falschen Freund, 2005

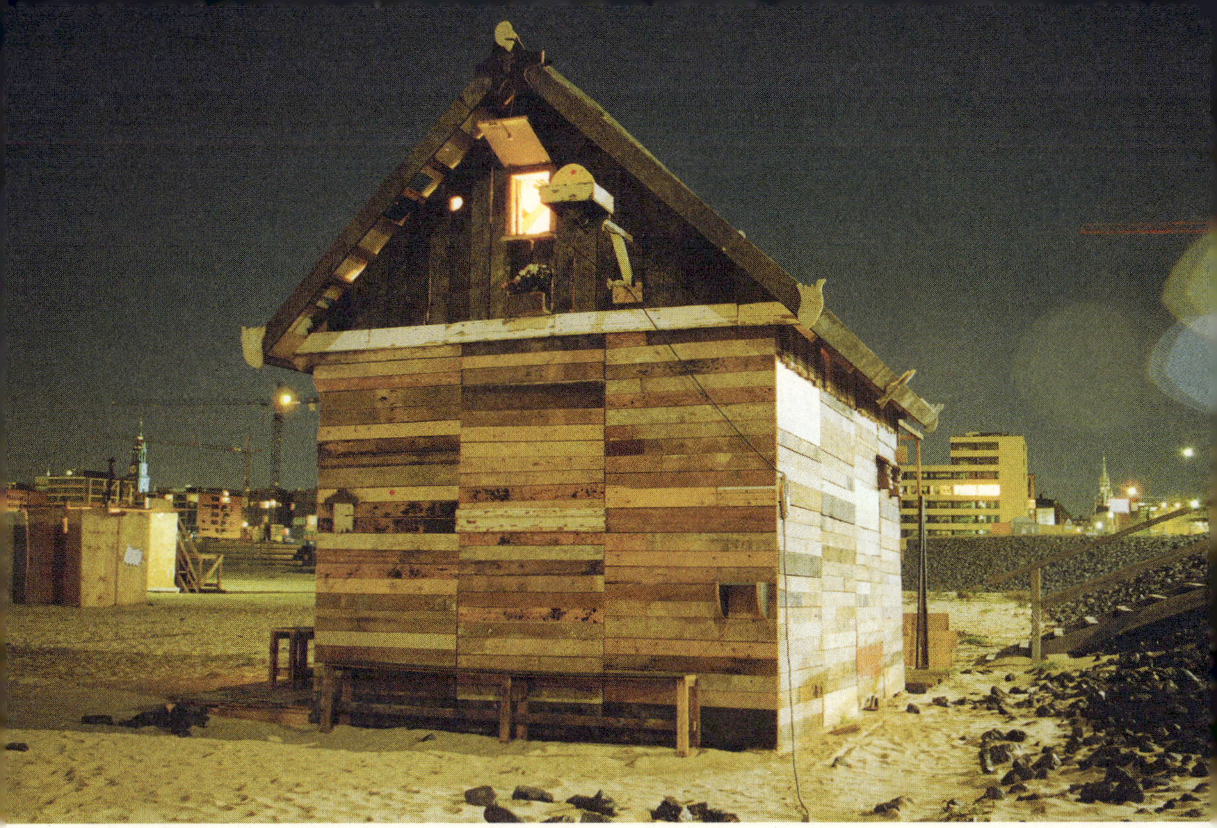

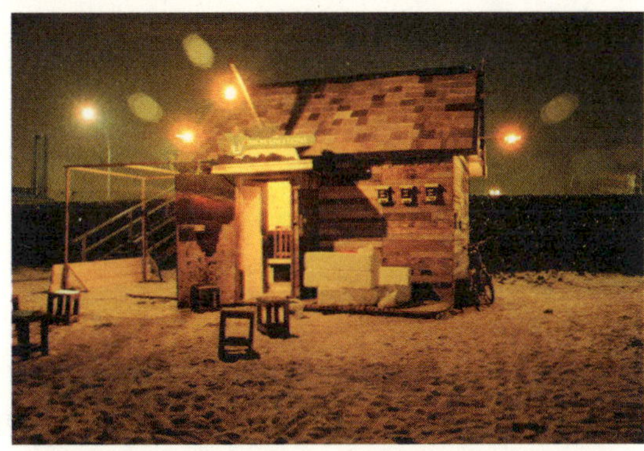
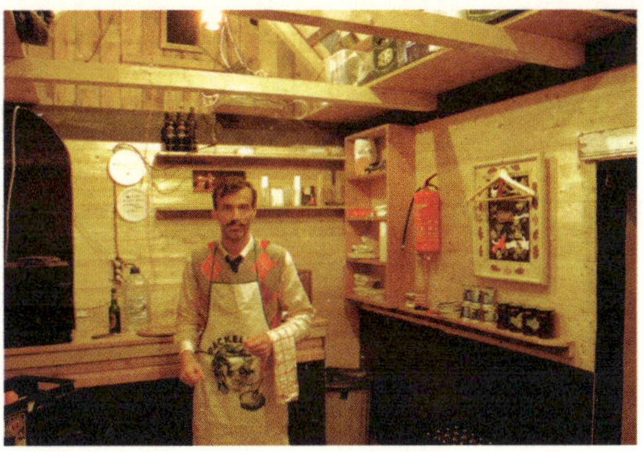
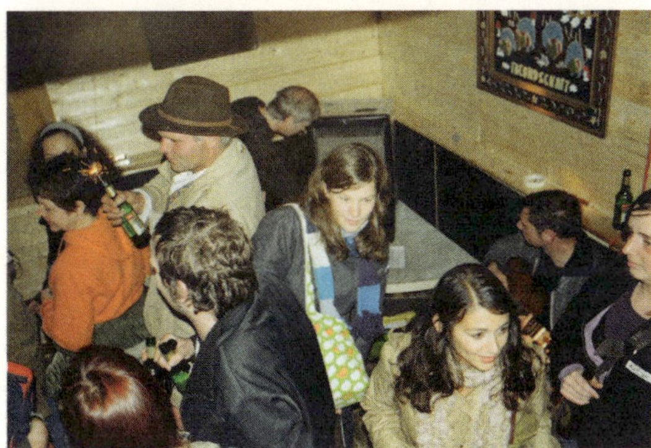

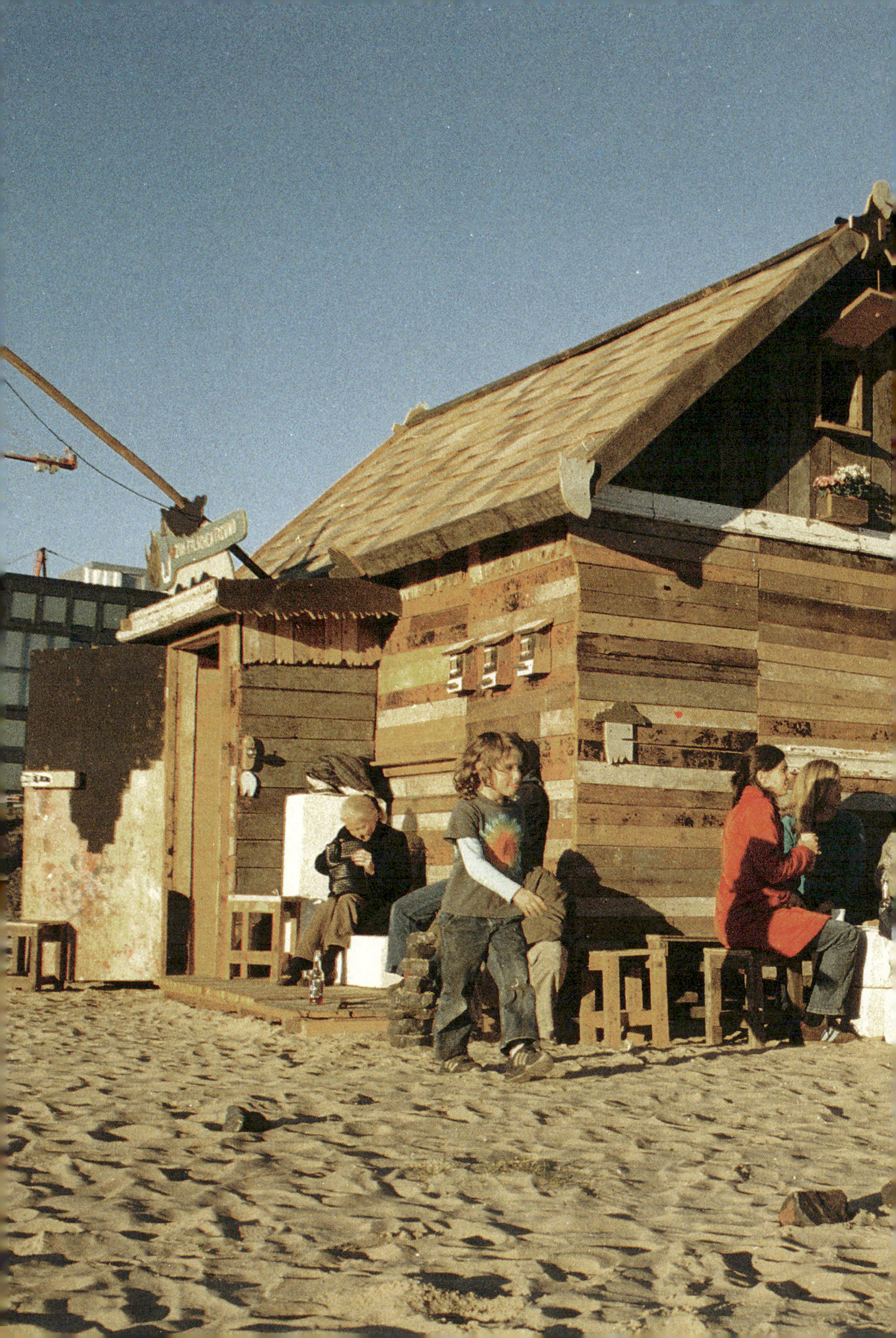

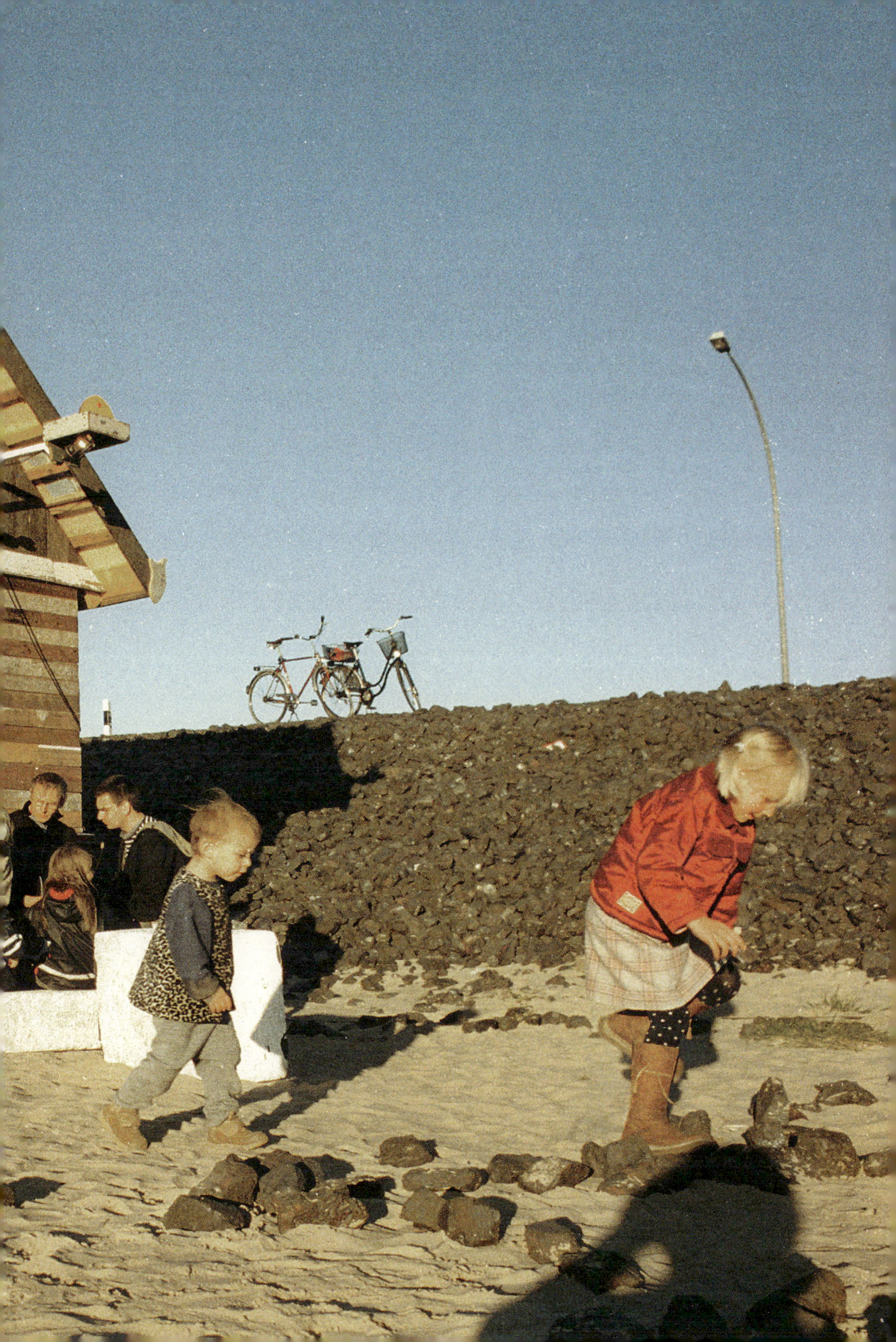

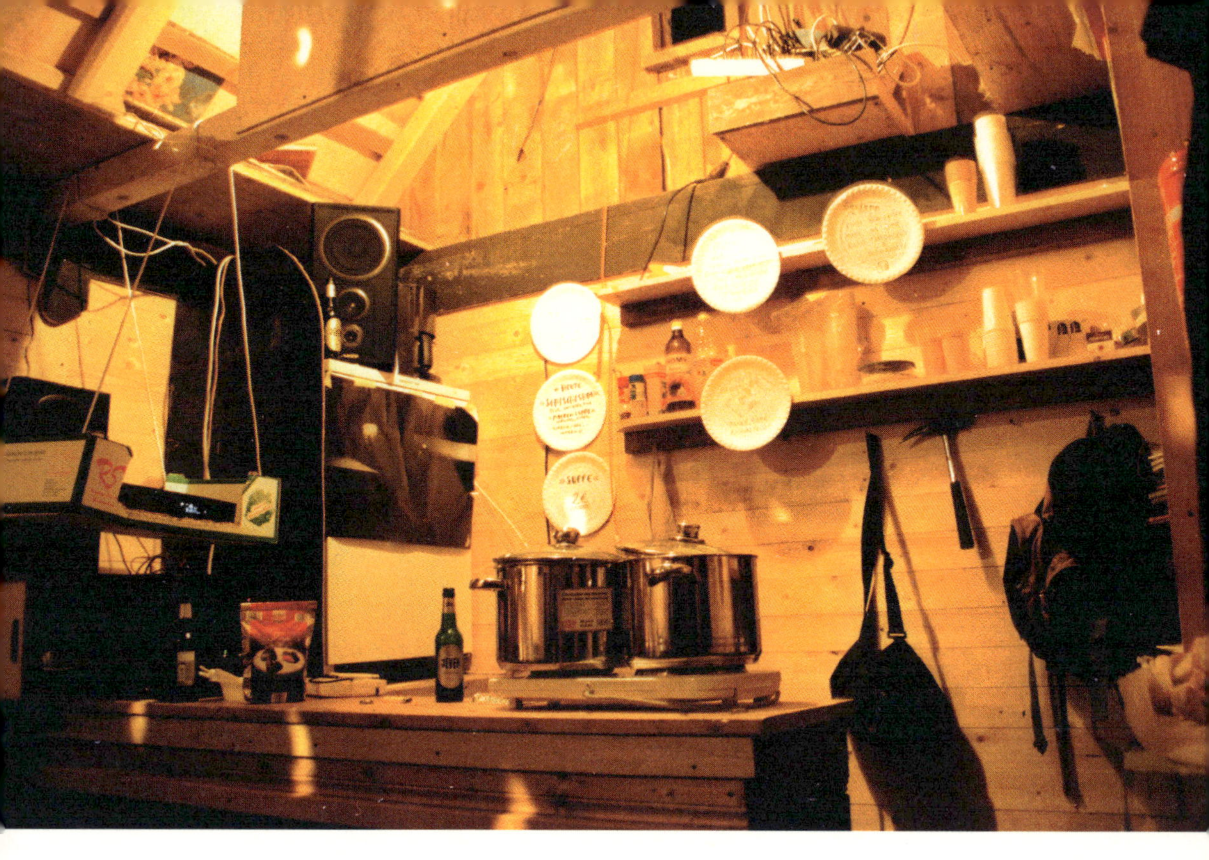

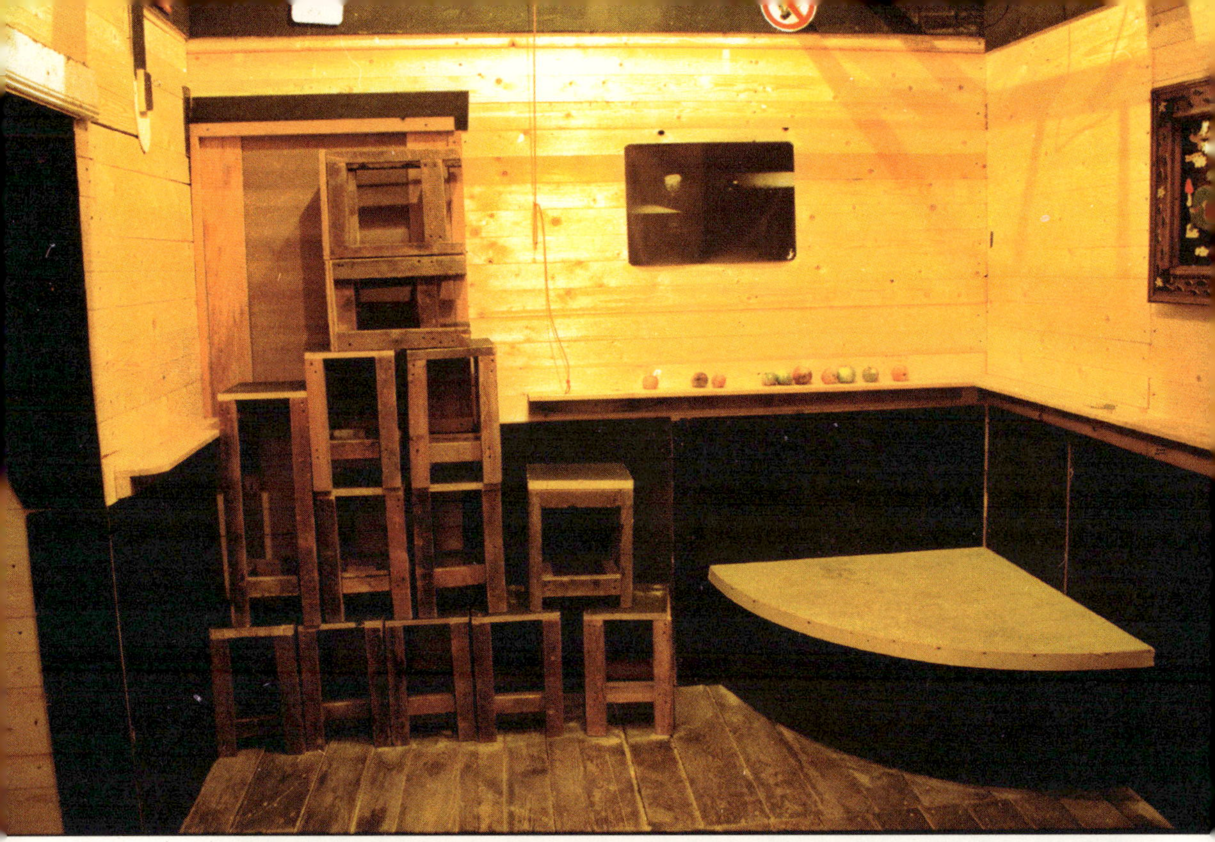

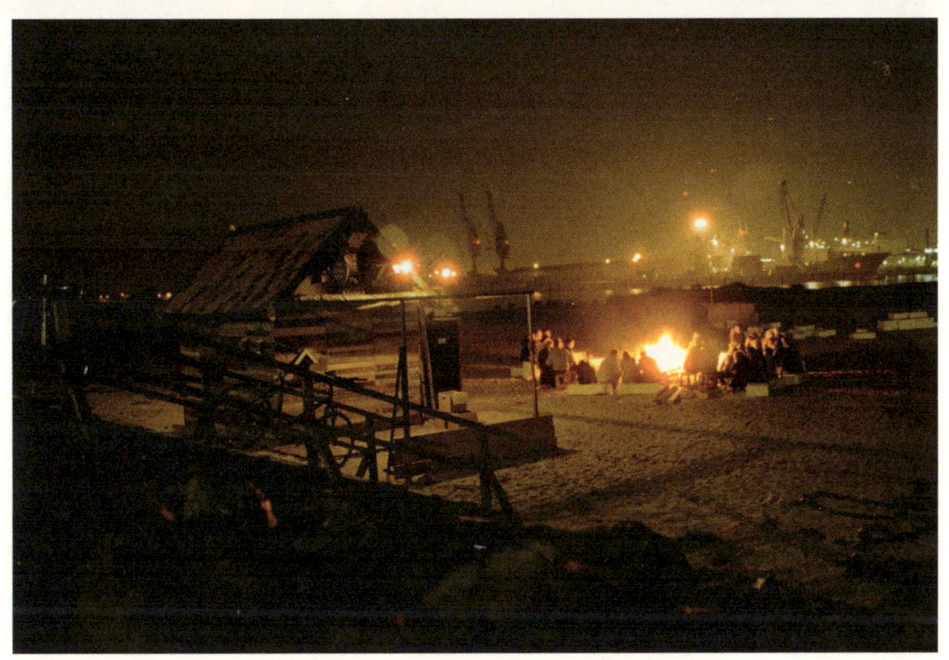

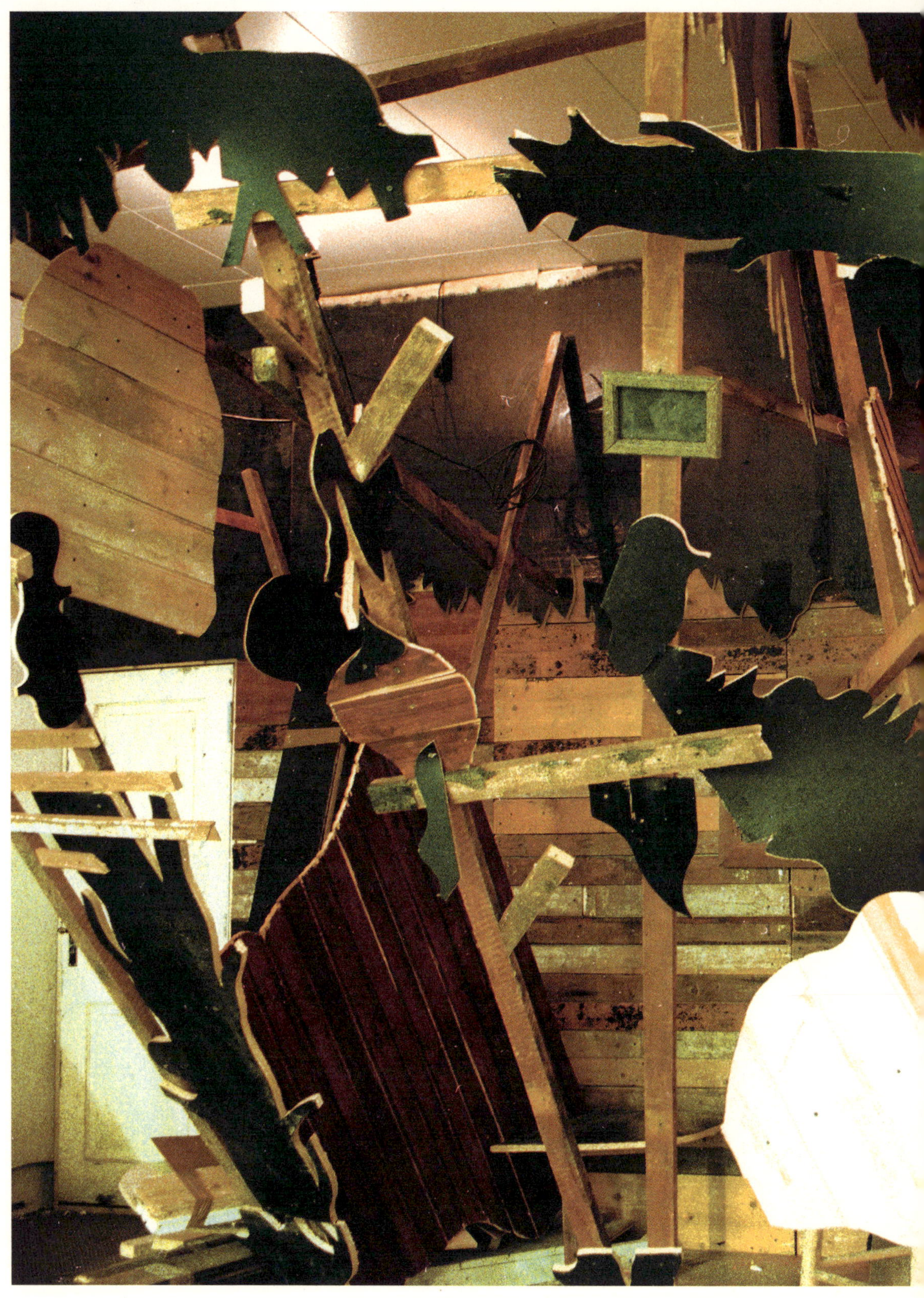

 Erholungsheim für schuldbewußte Großstädter, 2006

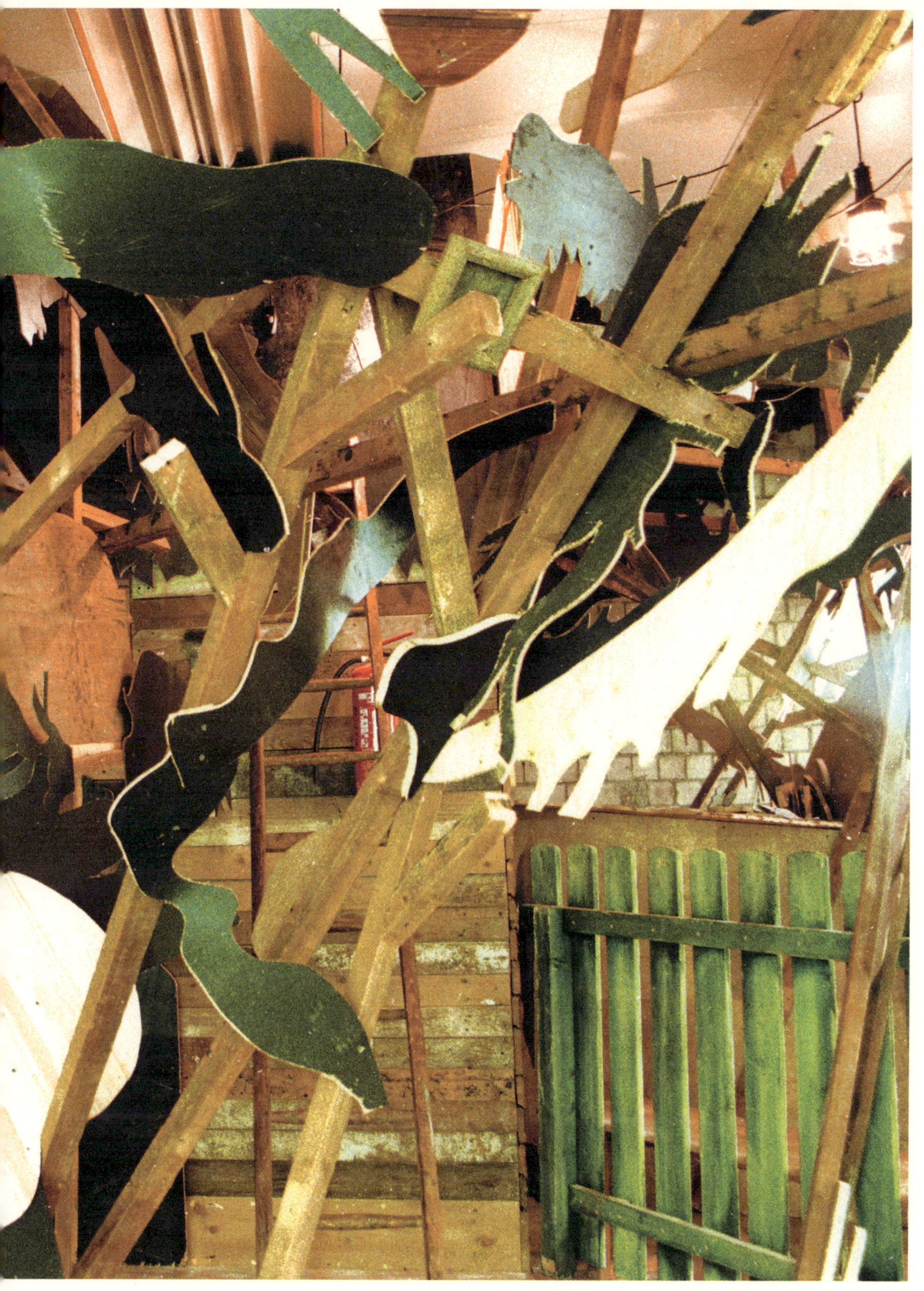

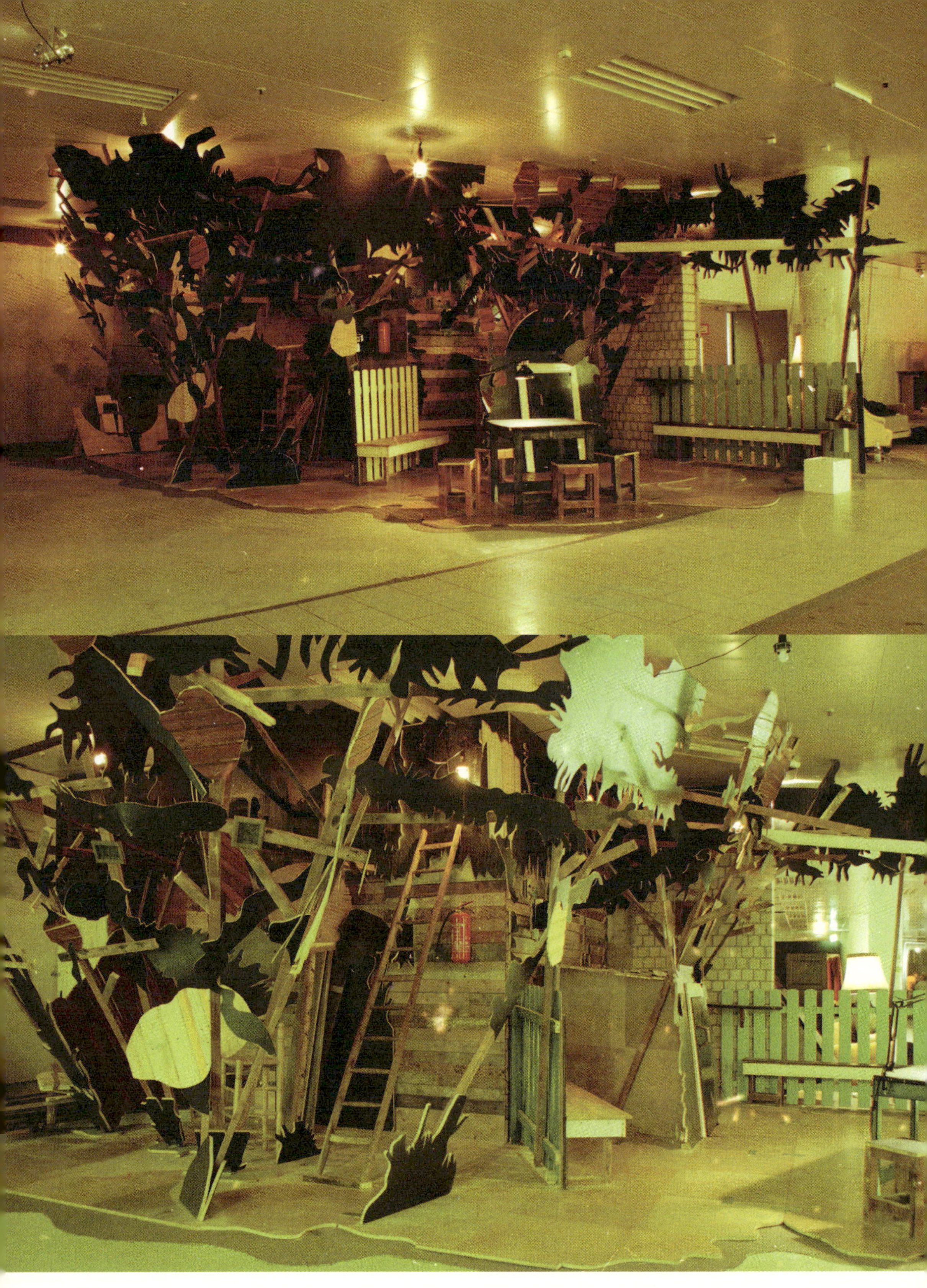

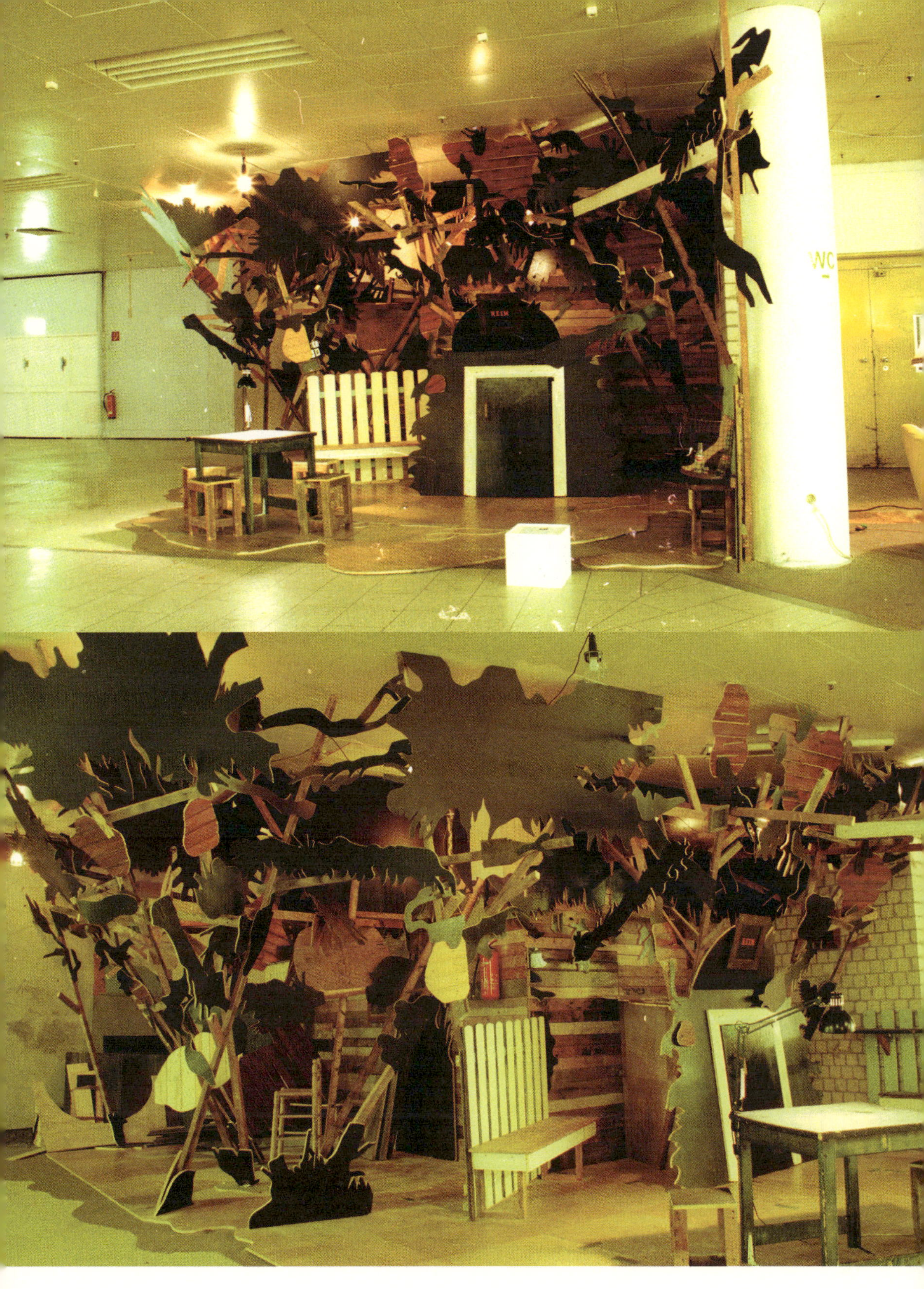

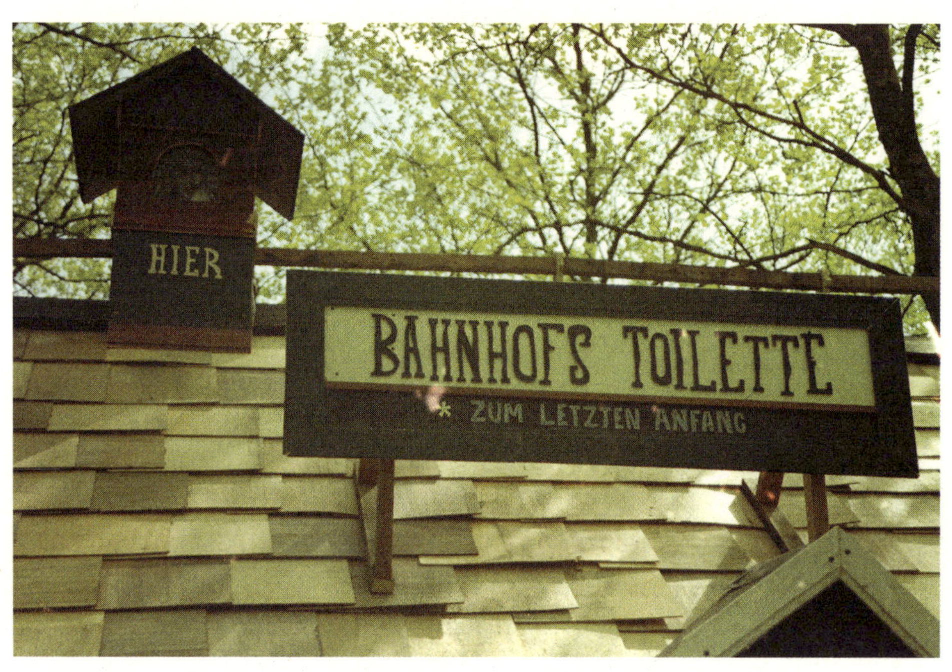

98   **Bahnhofstoilette zum letzten Anfang, 2006**

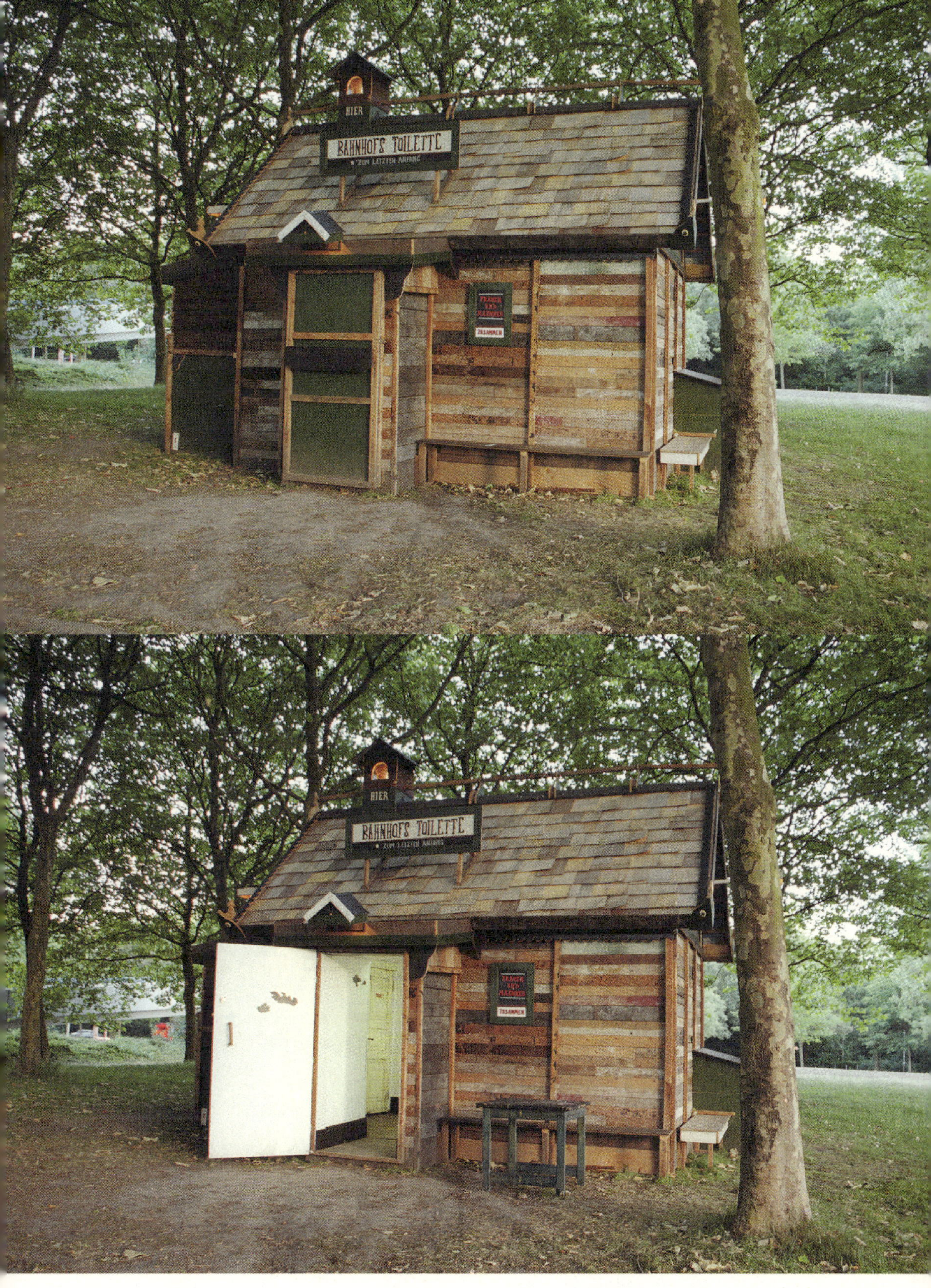
HIER
BAHNHOFS TOILETTE
ZUM LETZTEN ABGANG

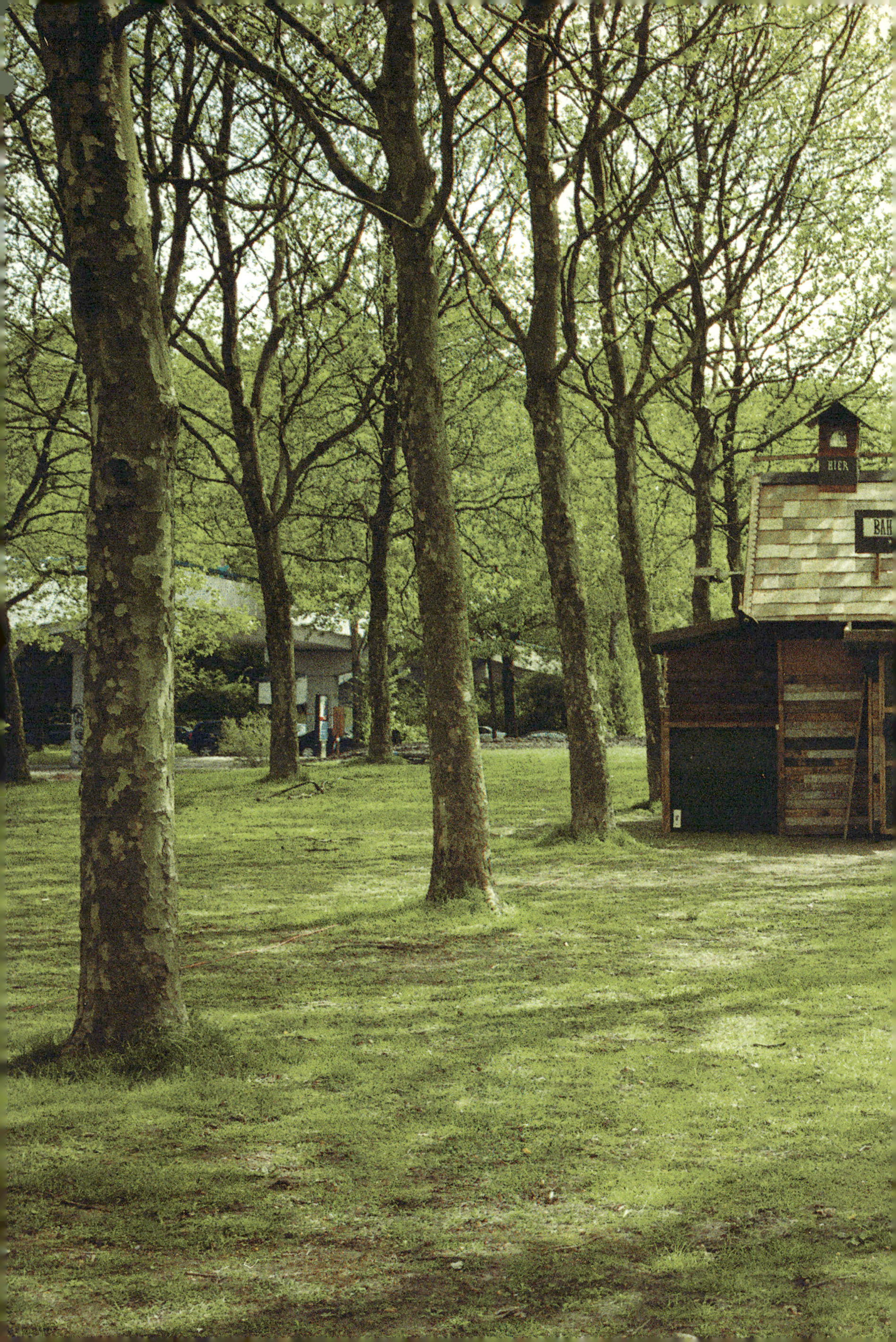

HIER
BAH

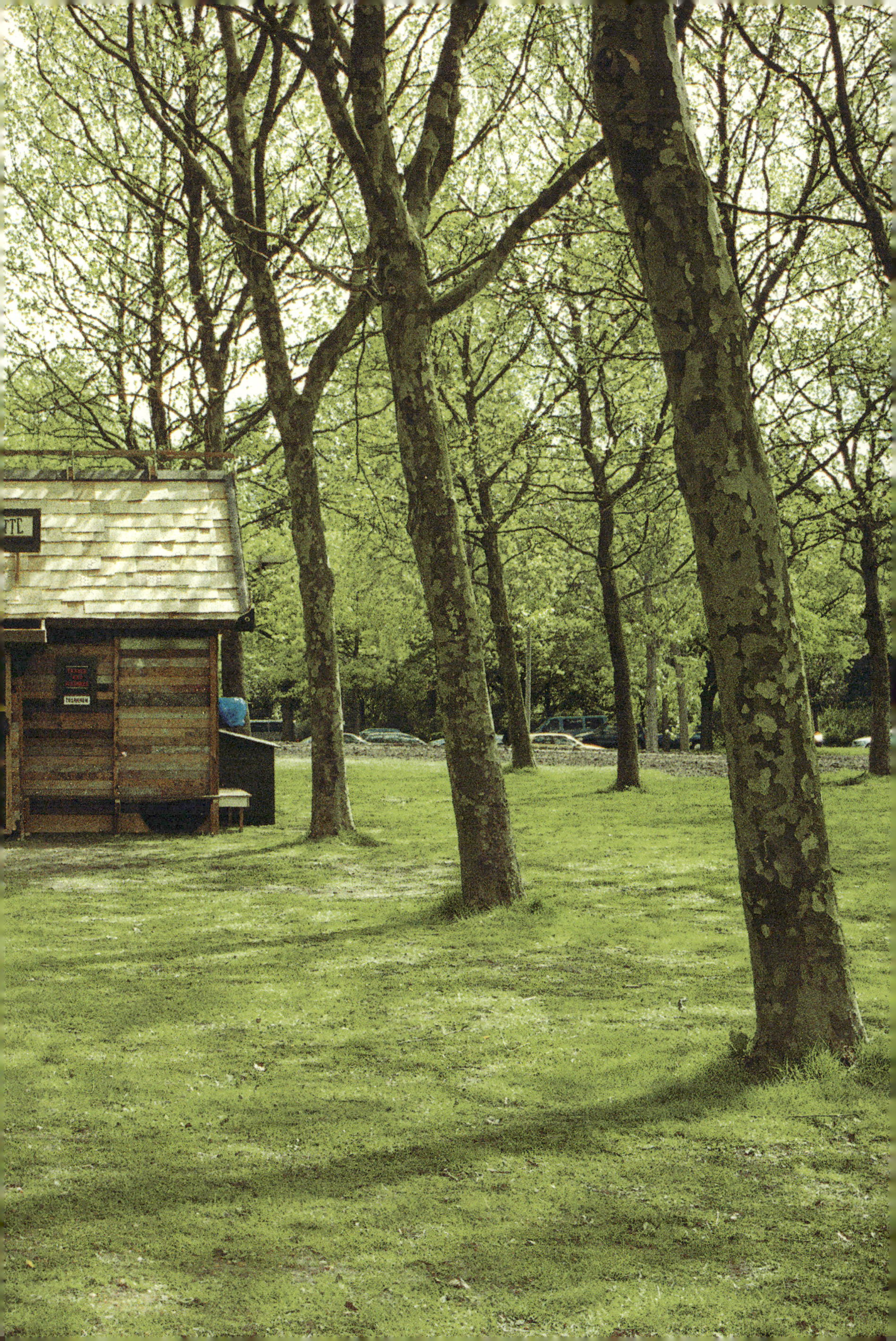

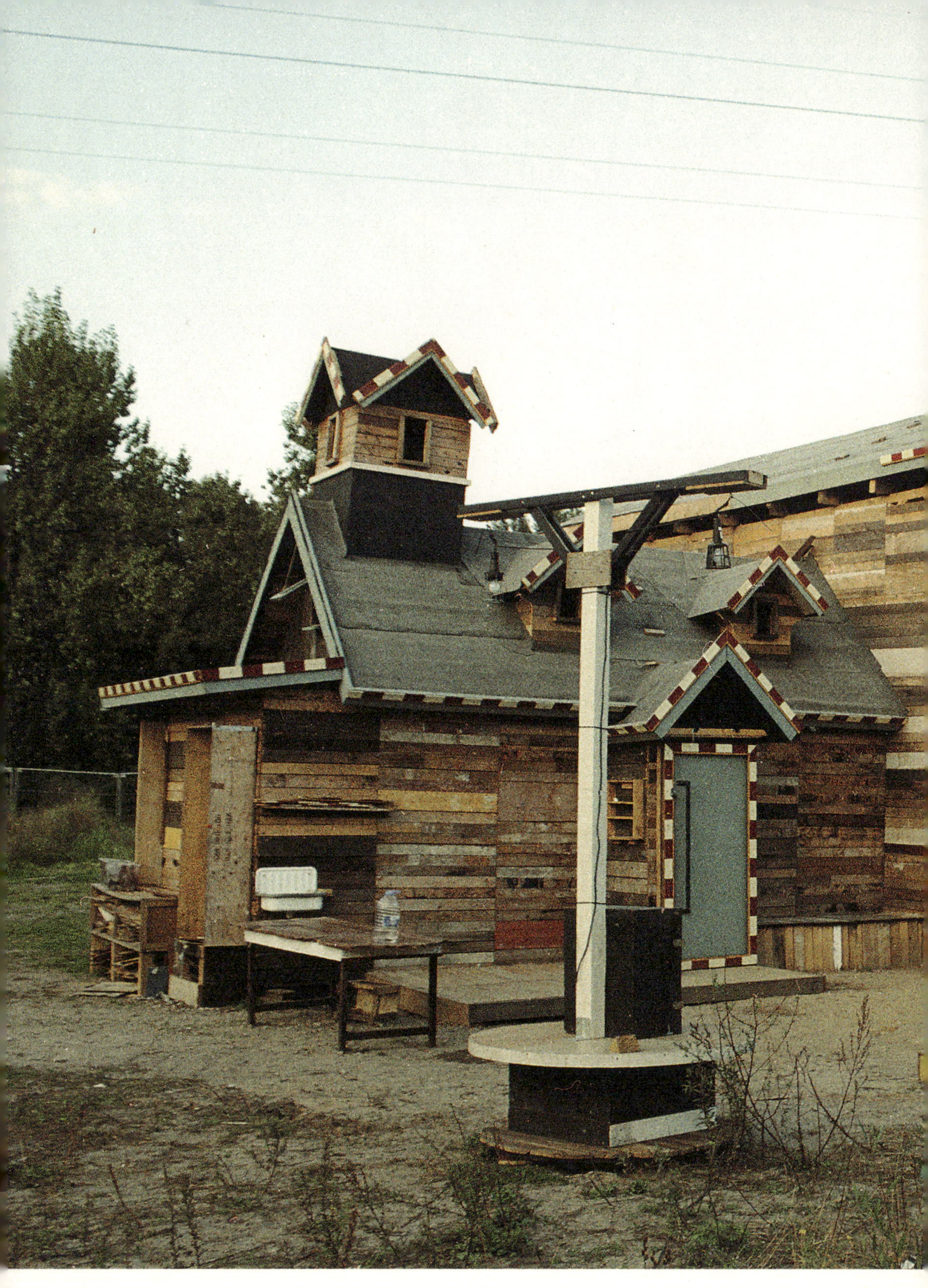

102 **Kirche des guten Willens, 2007**

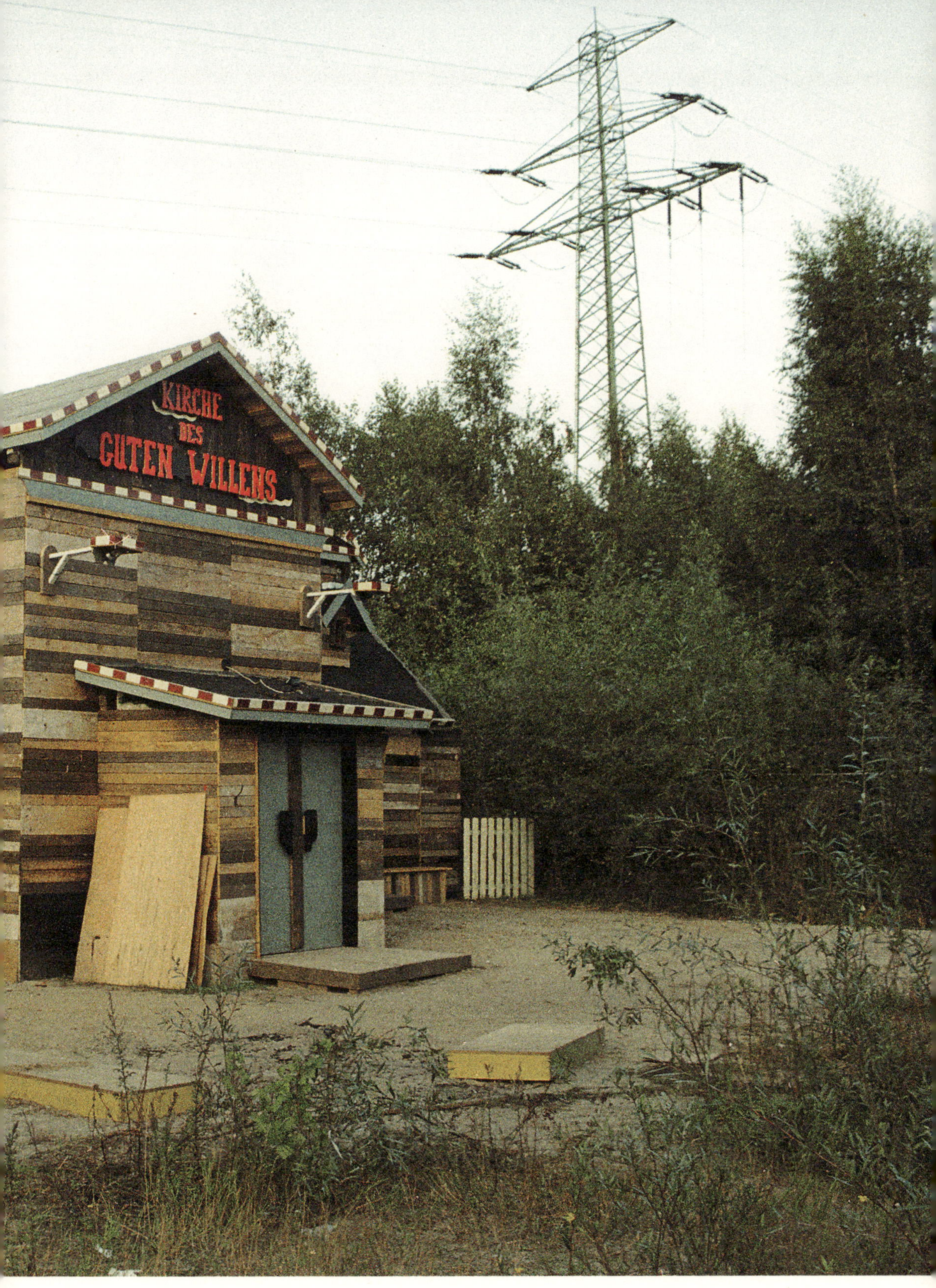

KIRCHE
DES
GUTEN WILLENS

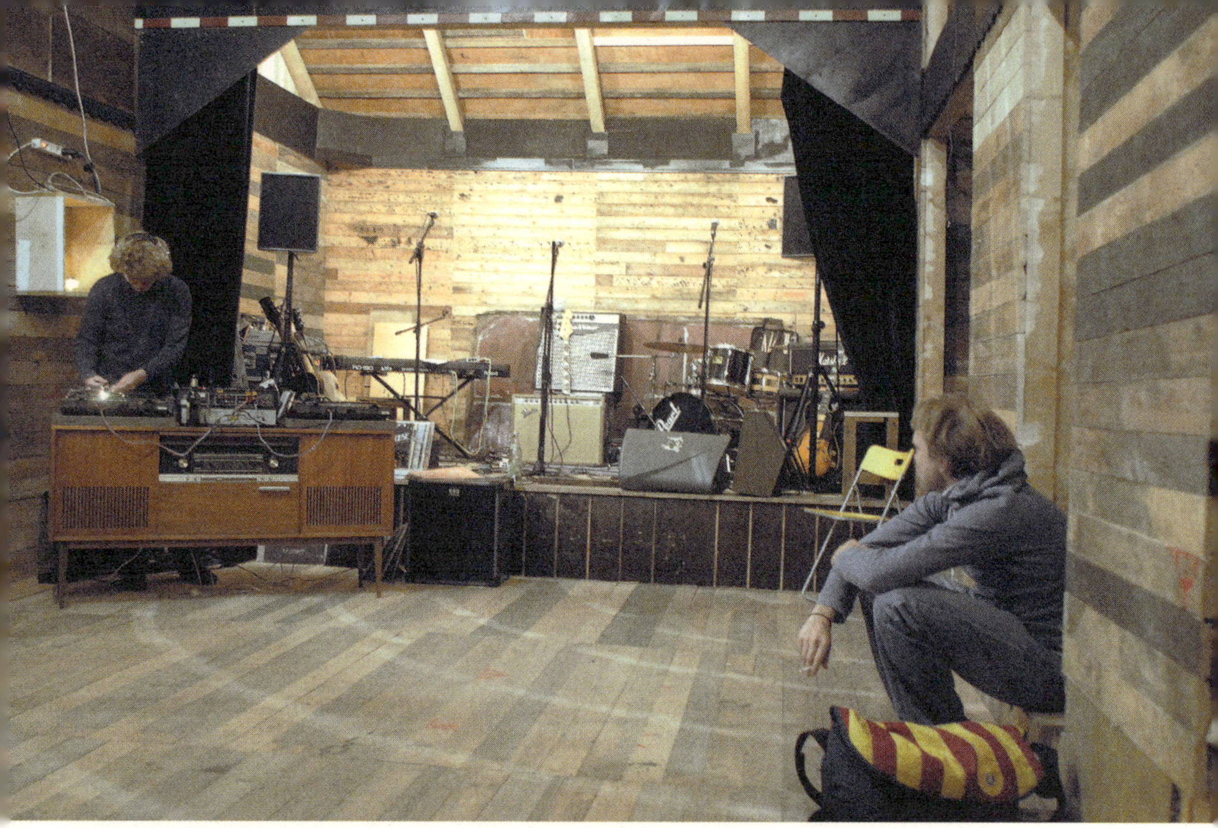

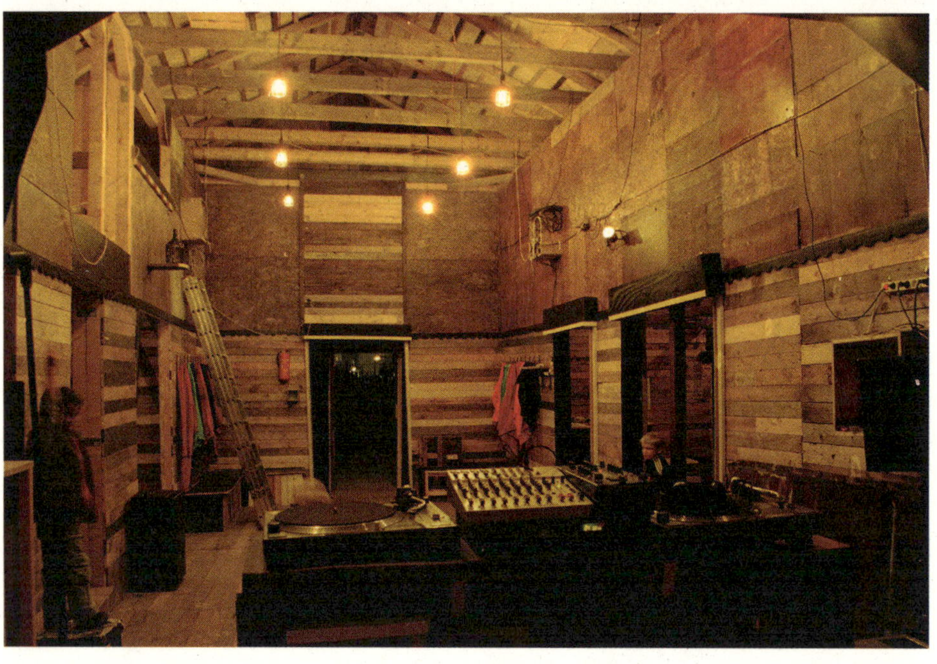

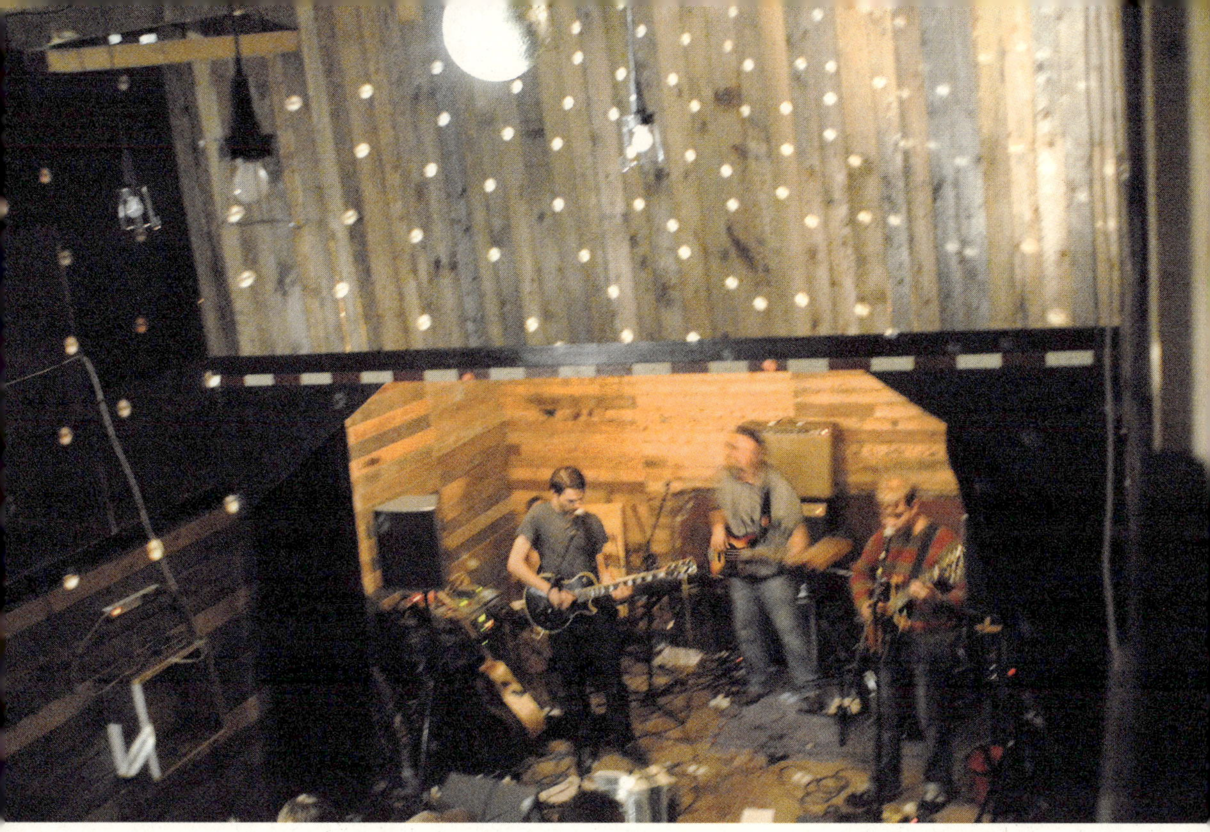

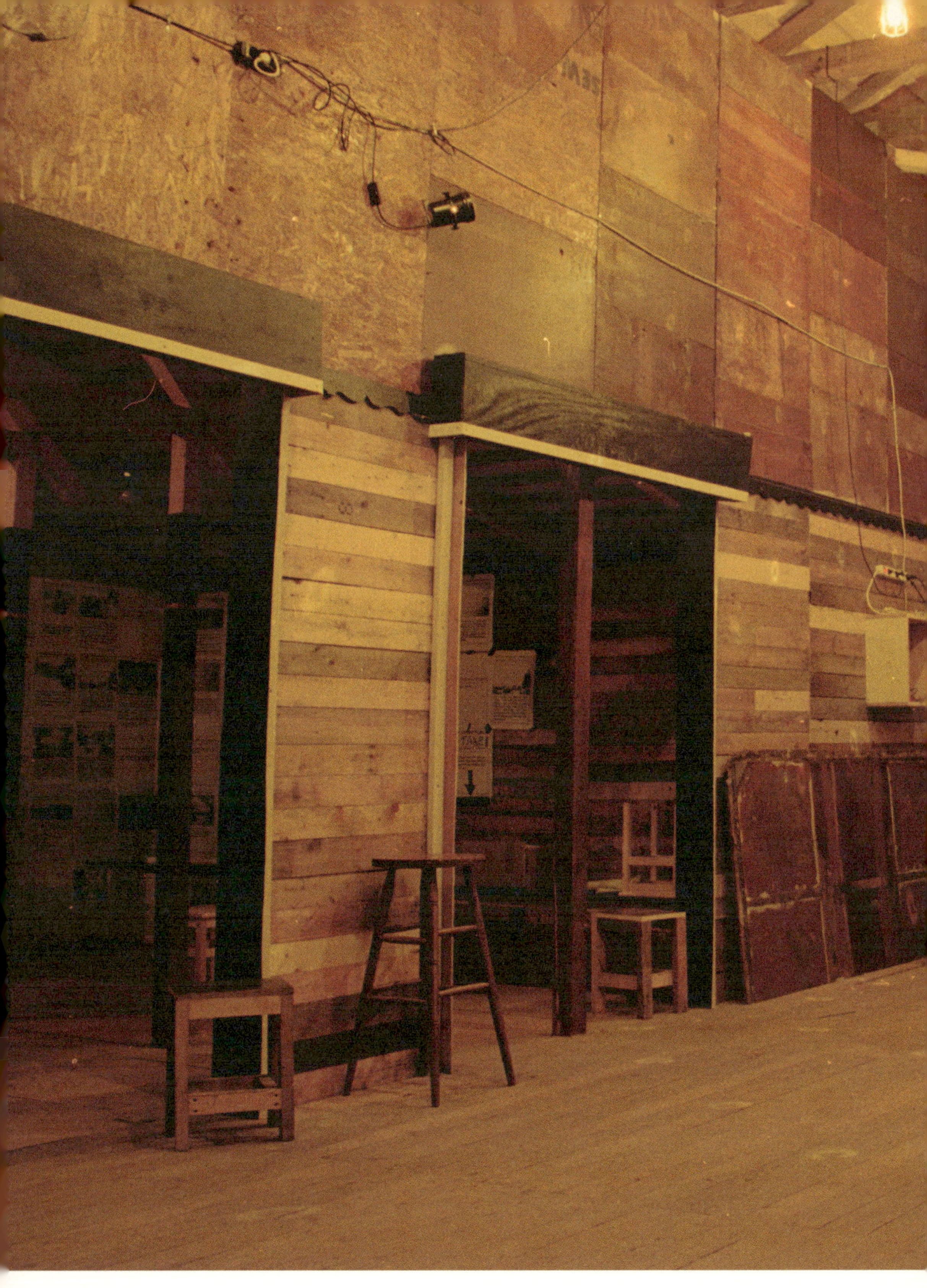

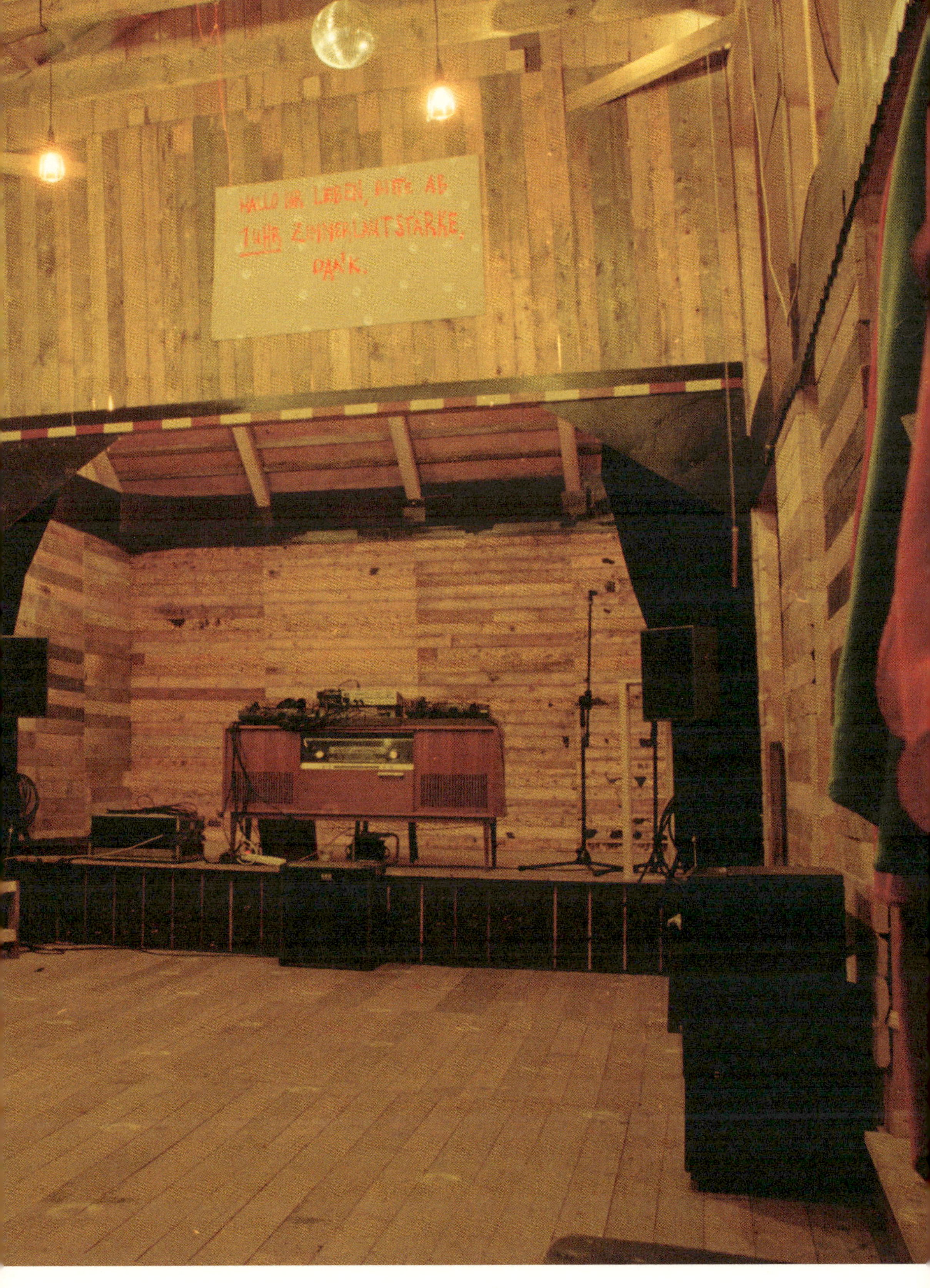
HALLO IHR LIEBEN, BITTE AB
1 UHR ZIMMERLAUTSTÄRKE.
DANK.

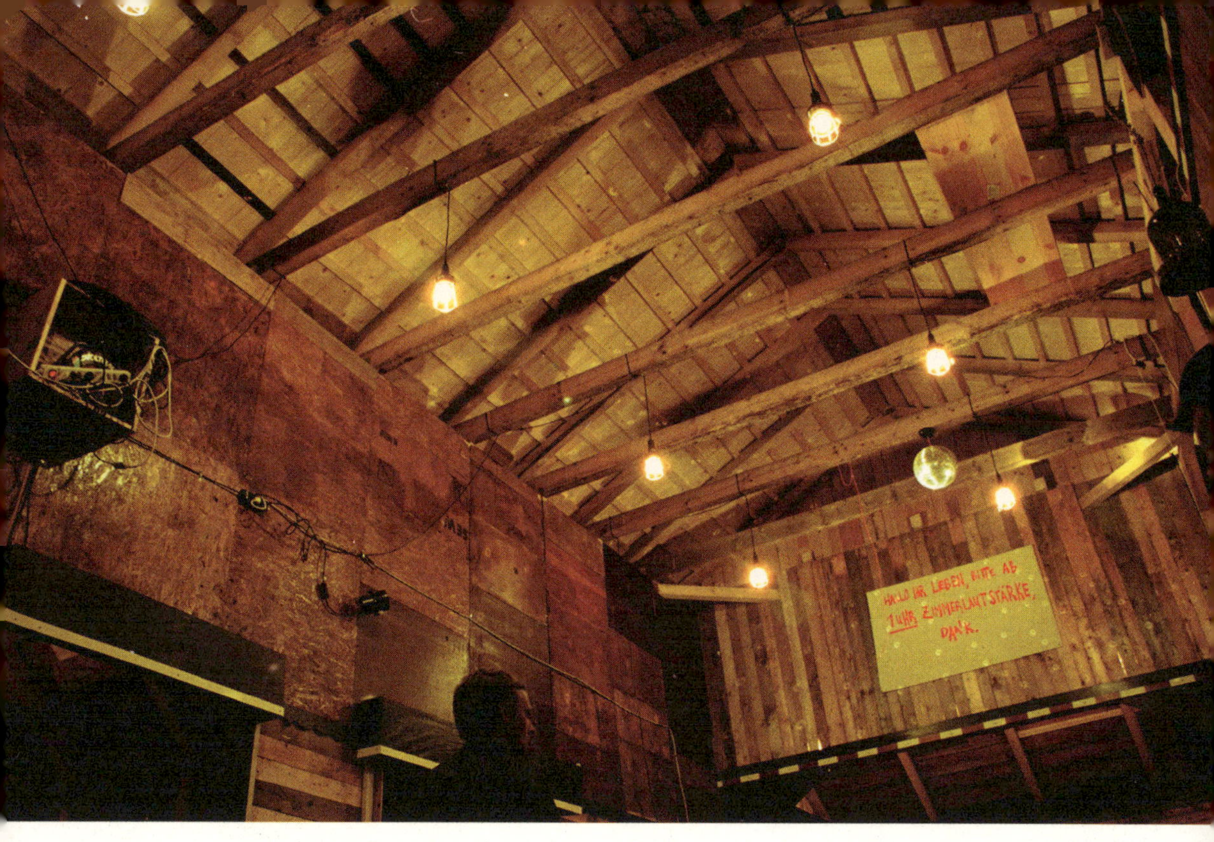

HALLO IHR LIEBEN, BITTE AB
1 UHR ZIMMERLAUTSTÄRKE.
DANK.

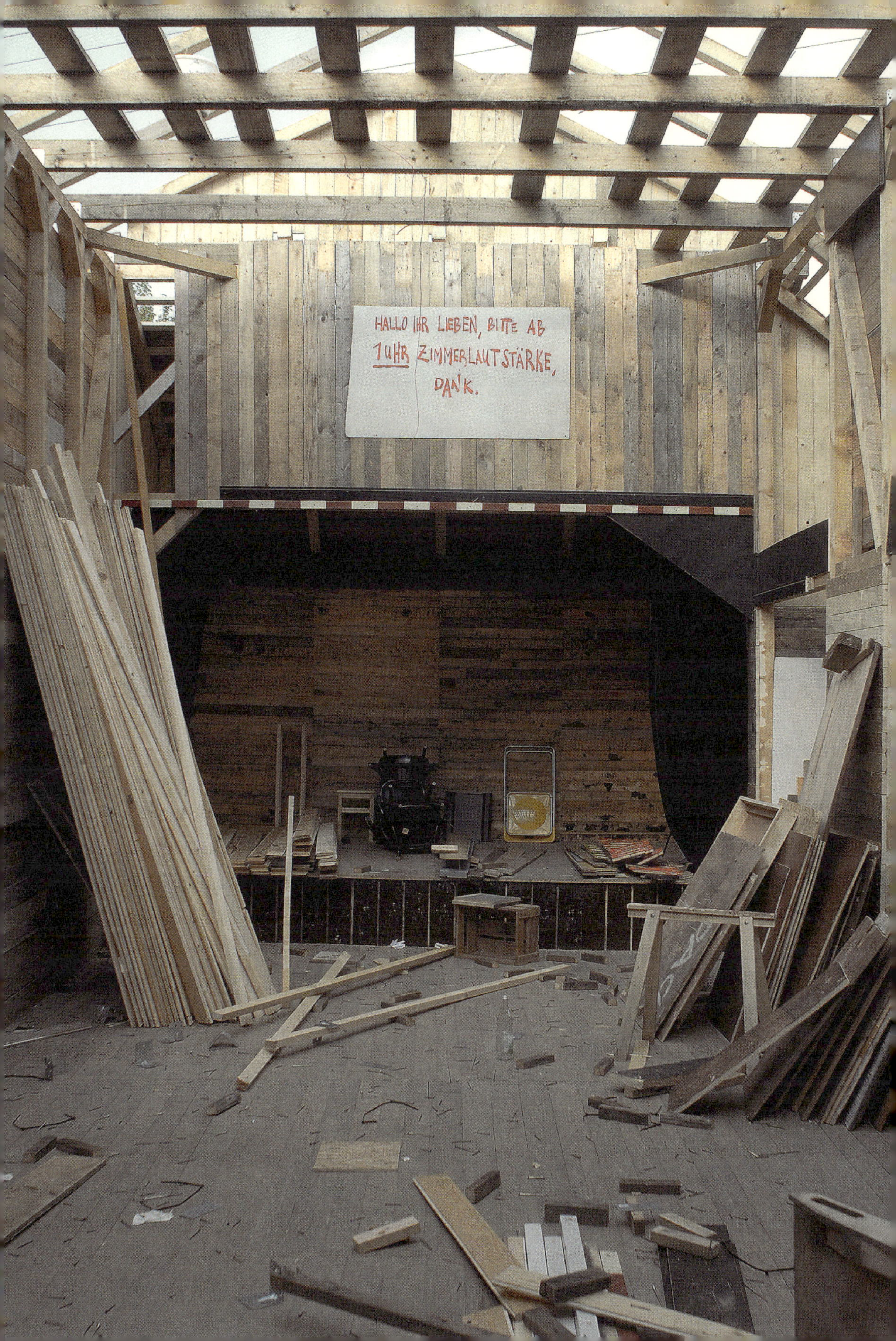

HALLO IHR LIEBEN, BITTE AB
1 UHR ZIMMERLAUTSTÄRKE,
DANK.

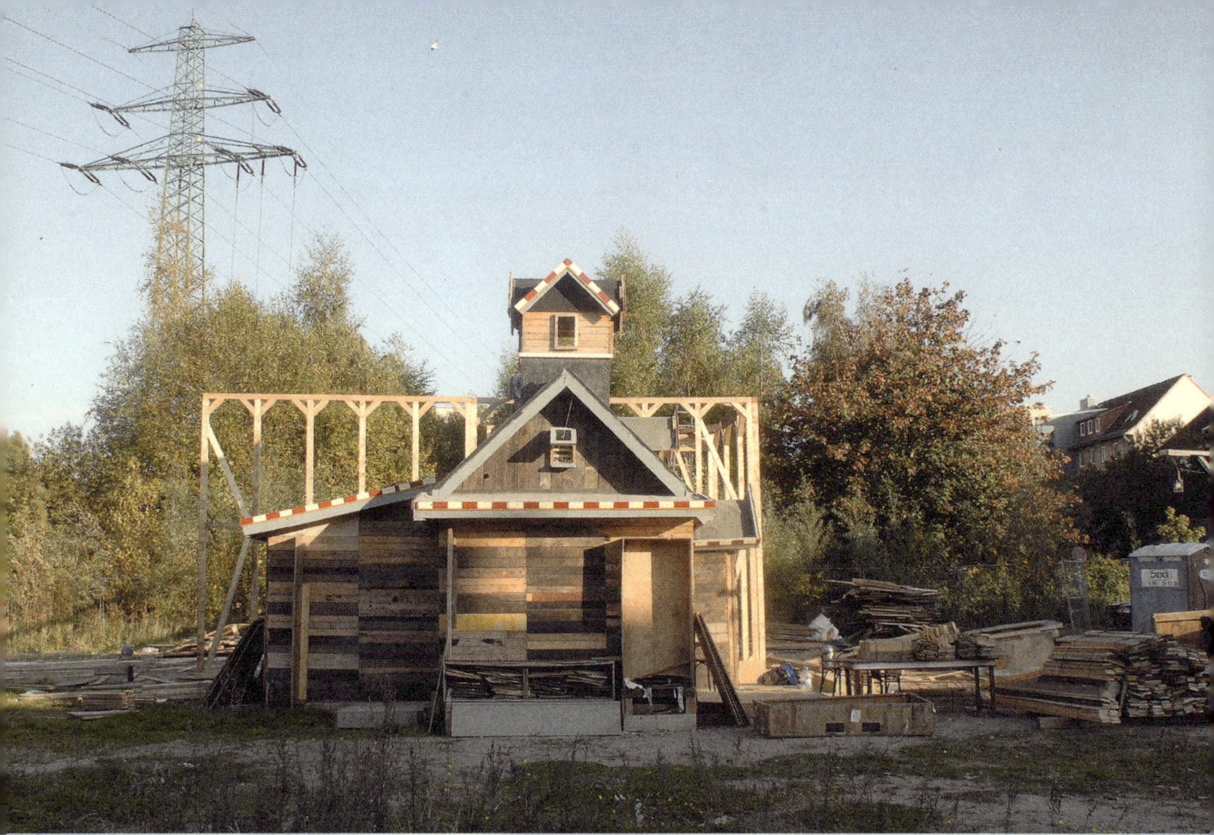

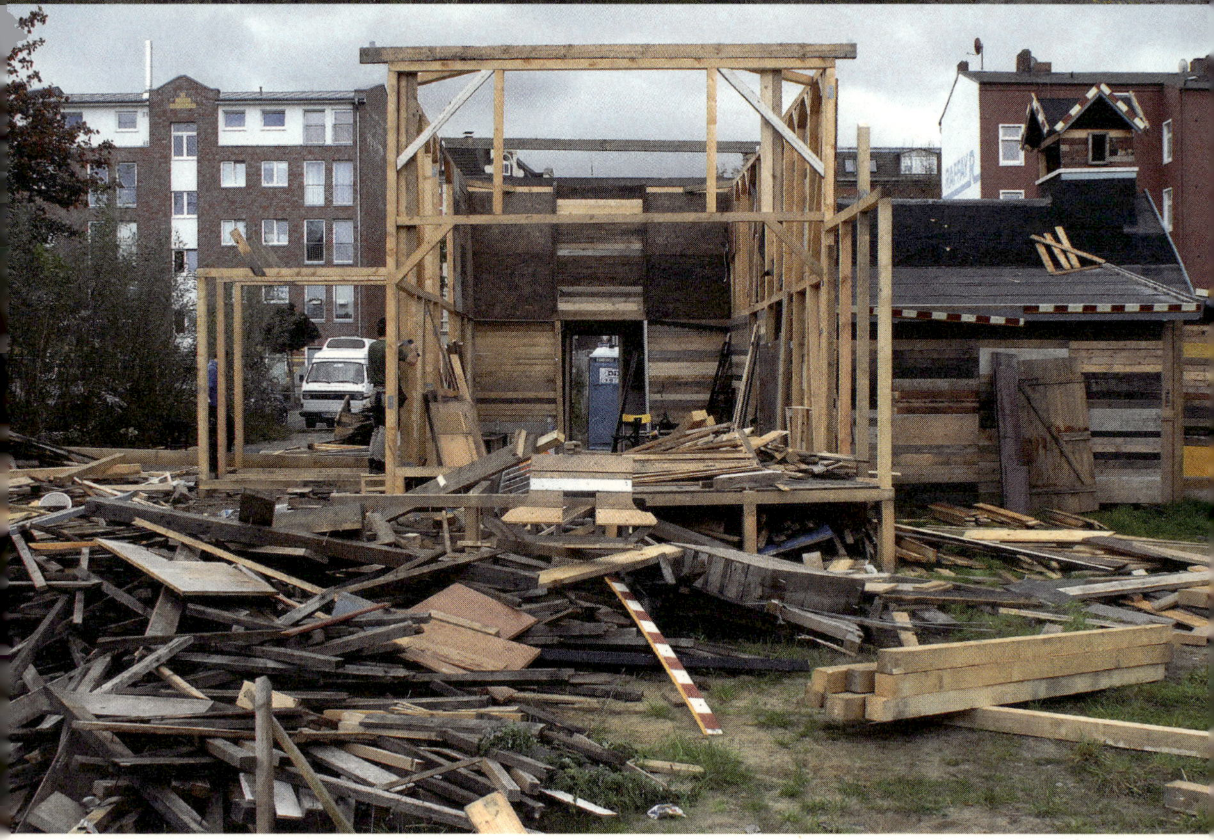

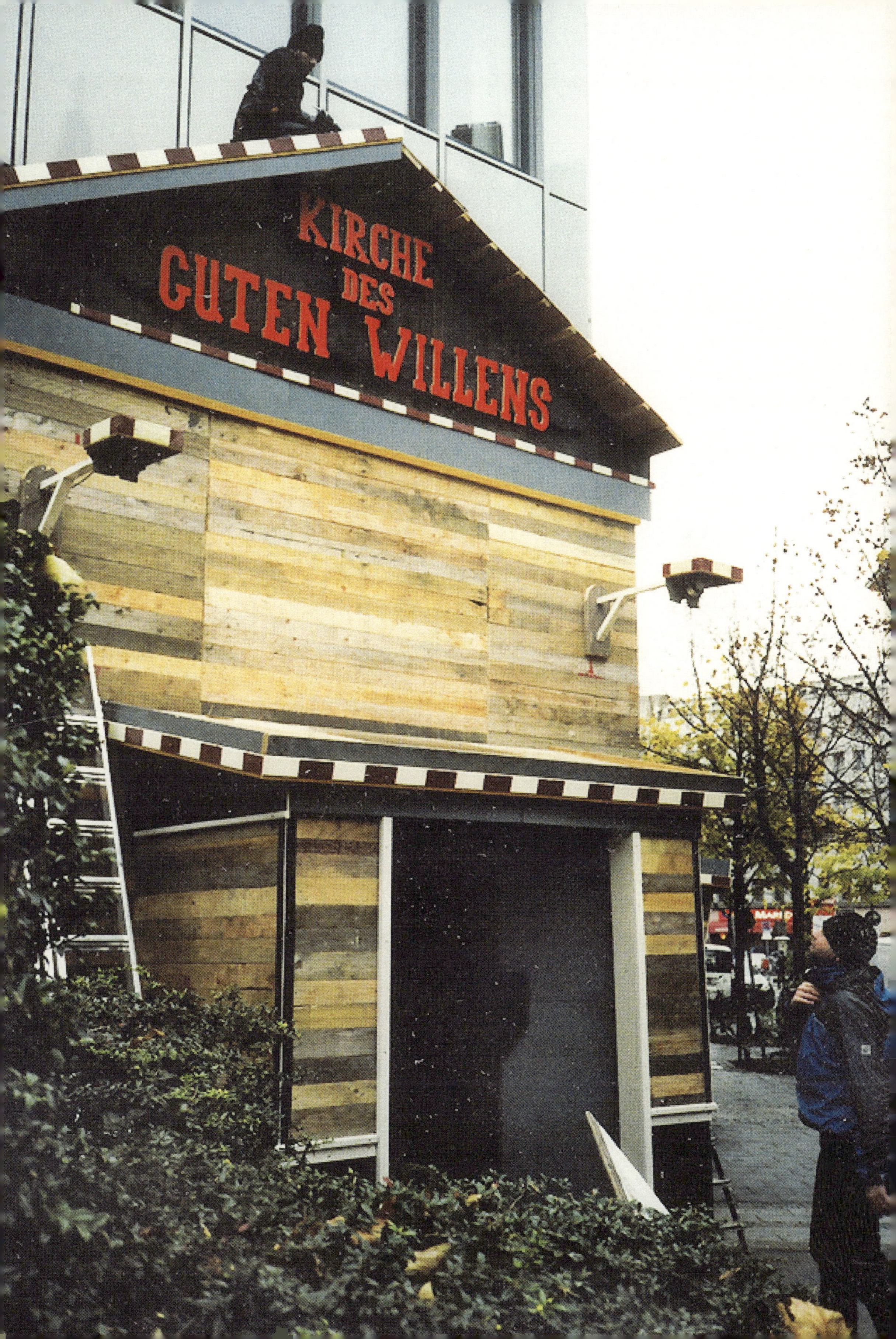

KIRCHE
DES
GUTEN WILLENS

Eine Welt im Keller / A World in the Basement *Jaques Palminger*

Ich sehe eine Frau im Badeanzug, die mit Taucherbrille und Schwamm die Scheiben eines riesigen Aquariums von innen putzt. Der Mann ist wohl gerade Fische kaufen. Ich sehe eine Tochterfrau, die am Bein eines alten Mannes einschläft. Der Mann greift in die Welt und stellt ein neues Haus auf. Er ist der gutmütige Herrscher einer eigenen Welt. Grob gearbeitet, aber lebendig. Ja, die kleinen Männchen leben. Eine wundervolle Ruhe liegt über dem Städtchen, ein Hauch von Märchenglück. Das Miniaturmodell im Keller, kleinteilige Zeitlupe, weltvergessen und endgültig. Noch ein Tisch, und die Welt da draußen verschwindet für immer. Es gibt so viel zu tun. Die Logistik der Kleinststadt fordert eine Bahn, die Gleise sind schon fertig. Hundert neue Männchen warten darauf, aus der Kiste geholt zu werden. Keine Frage, der Mann ist glücklich. Und die Frau?

Sie stützt, wischt und hält aus. Man gewöhnt sich, und vielleicht ist es sogar gemütlich. Maximale Glückserwartung warmer Keller. Das ist strukturelle Gewalt: Herbert Wehner krakeelt, seine Tochter schmiert ihm die Leberwurstbrote. Für mehr ist kein Platz. So gesehen ist das Bild in seiner melancholischen Verdichtung schwer wie Blei. Nur der Hund an ihrer Hüfte ist fein raus: Er schläft des schönsten Haustierschlaf und hält so das Bild gerade.

I can see a woman in a bathing suit cleaning the interior glass walls of a huge aquarium with diving goggles and a cloth. Her husband is off buying fish. I can see a daughter-in-law falling asleep against the leg of an old man. The man reaches into the world and constructs a new house. He is the good-natured ruler of his own world. A bit rough-and-ready but alive. Yes, the little men are alive. A wonderful calm settles over the small town, a whiff of fairytale happiness. The scaled down model in the cellar, small portions of slow-motion, oblivious to the outside world and ultimate. One more table and the world out there will disappear forever. There is a lot to do. The logistics of the small town require a train, the platforms are already finished. Hundreds of new little men are waiting to be taken out of the box. The man is happy, without a doubt. And the woman?

She braces herself, keeps on mopping and enduring. One can grow accustomed to it and perhaps it is even cosy. The maximum expectation of happiness is a warm cellar. That is structural violence: Herbert Wehner brawls, his daughter spreads liver sausage on his bread. There is no room for more. Viewed in this light the image is heavy as lead in its consolidated melancholy. Only the dog leaning against her hip is off the hook: it is sleeping the blissful sleep of a household pet and in this way keeps the picture straight.

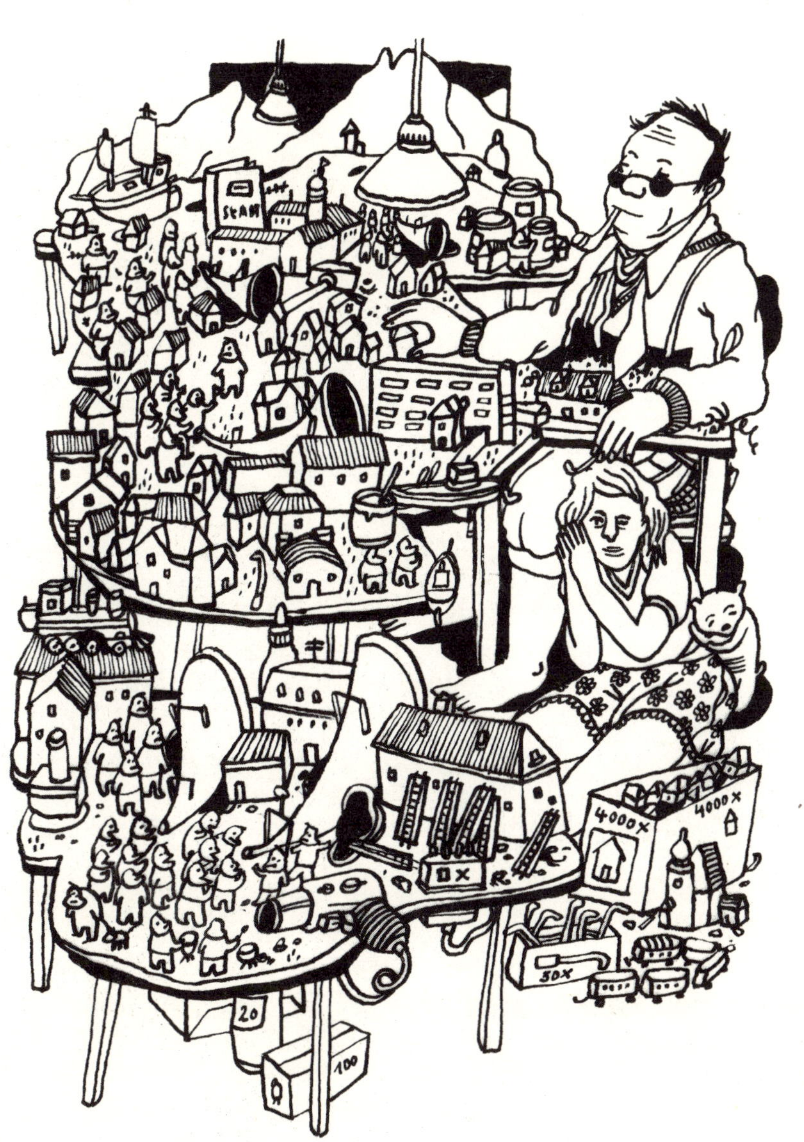

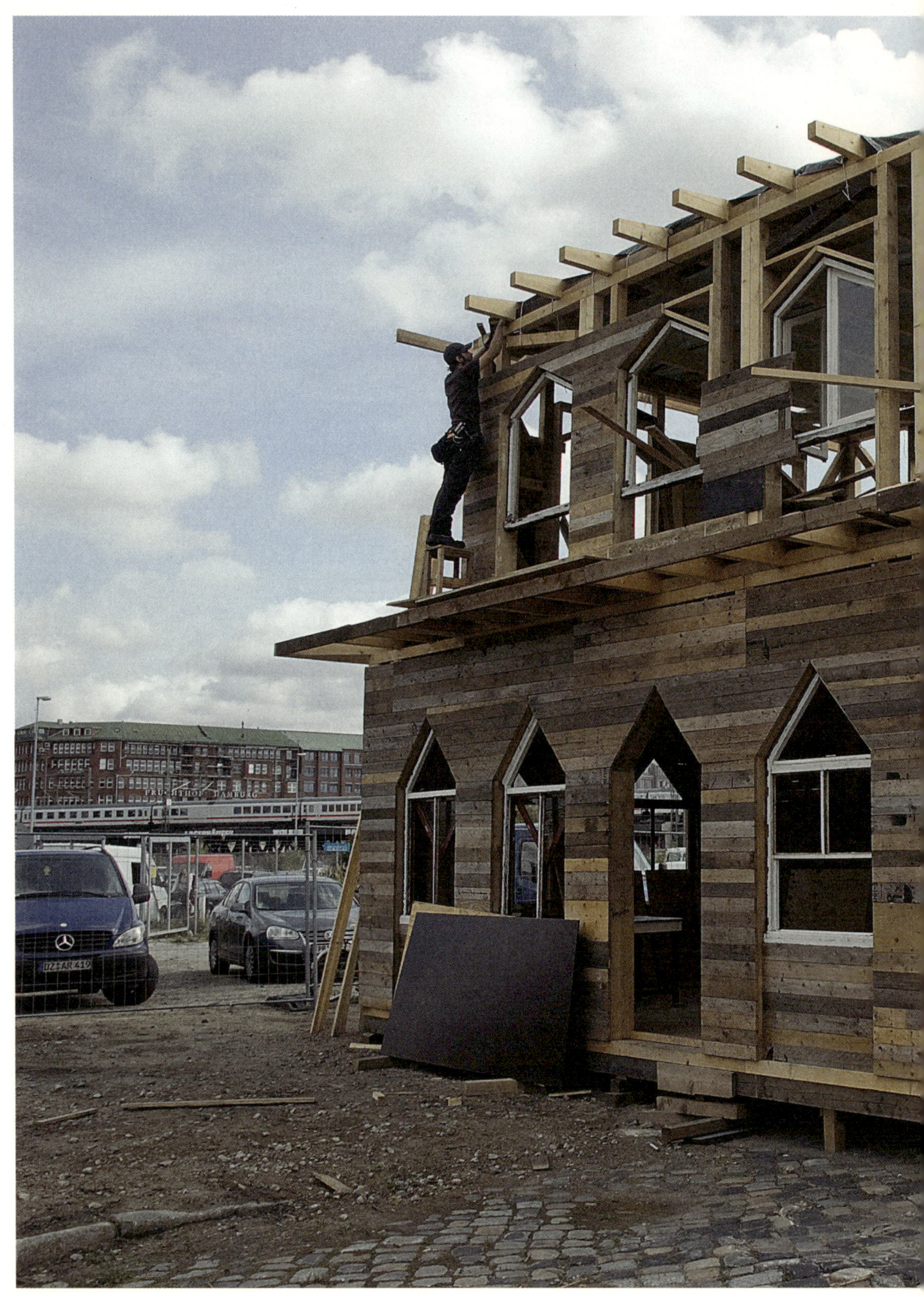

114   **Oberhafenkantine Replika, 2008**

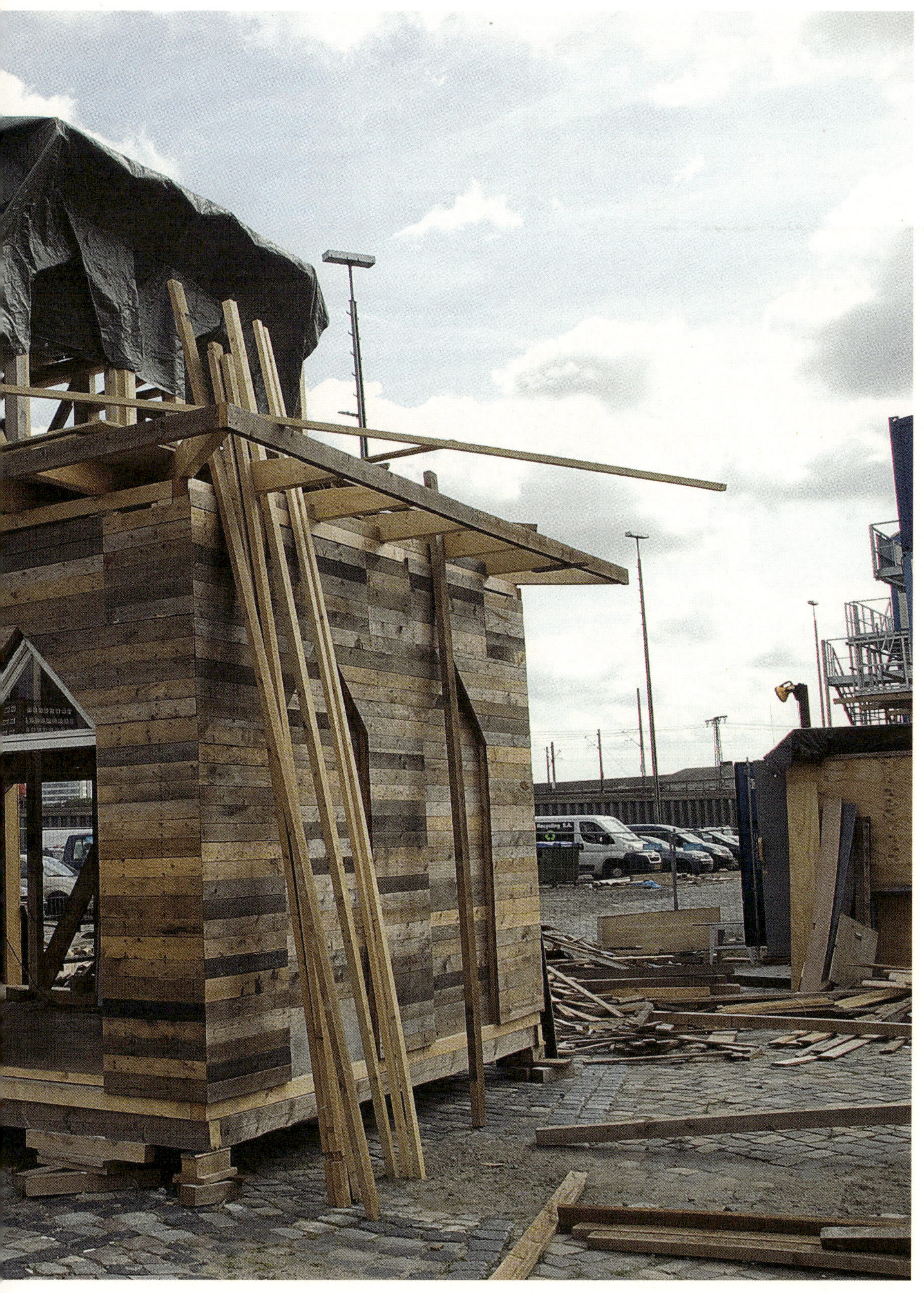

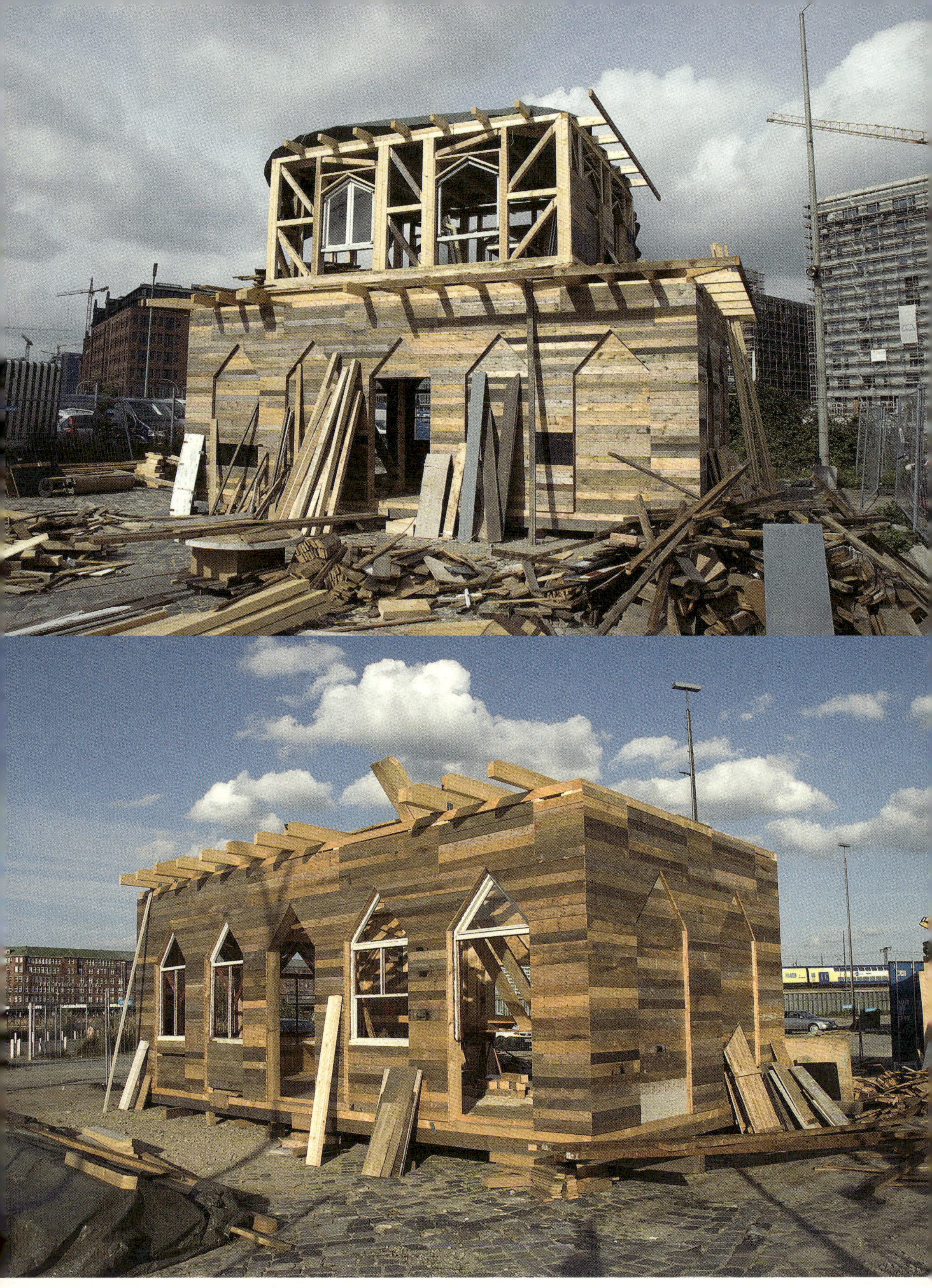

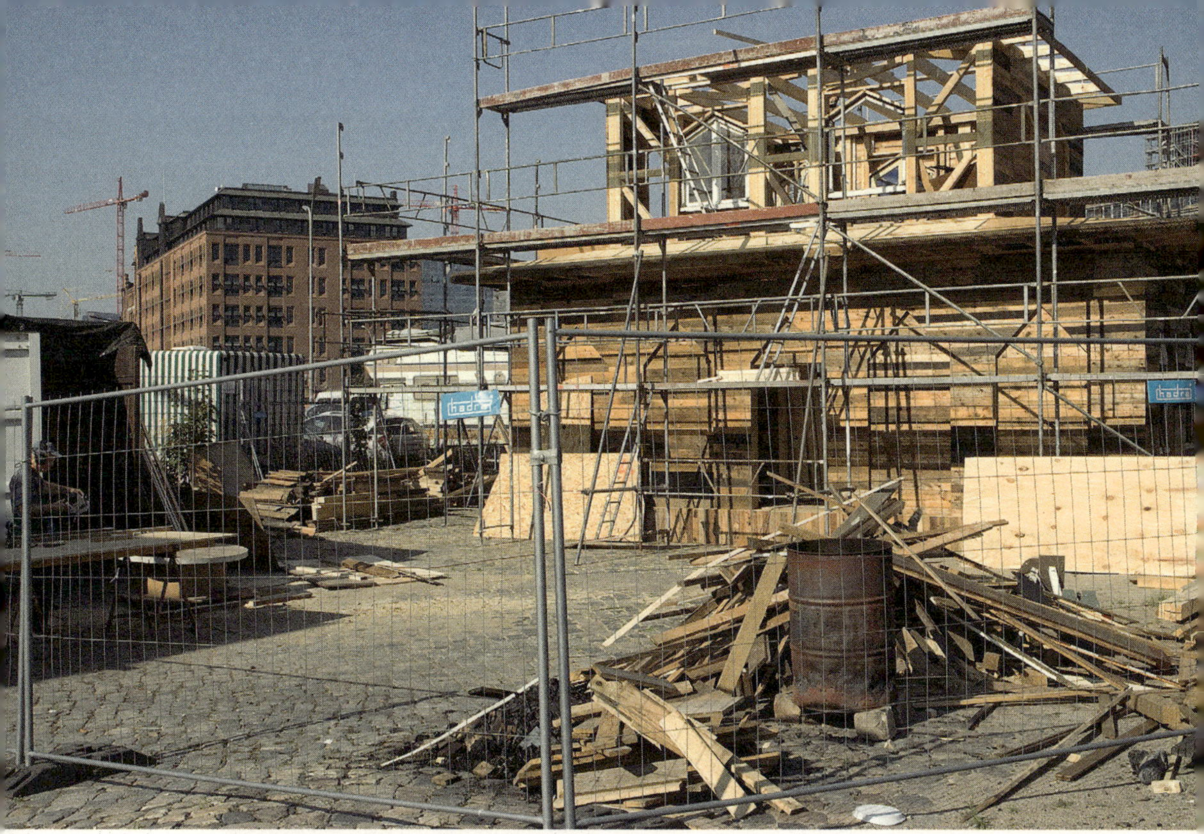

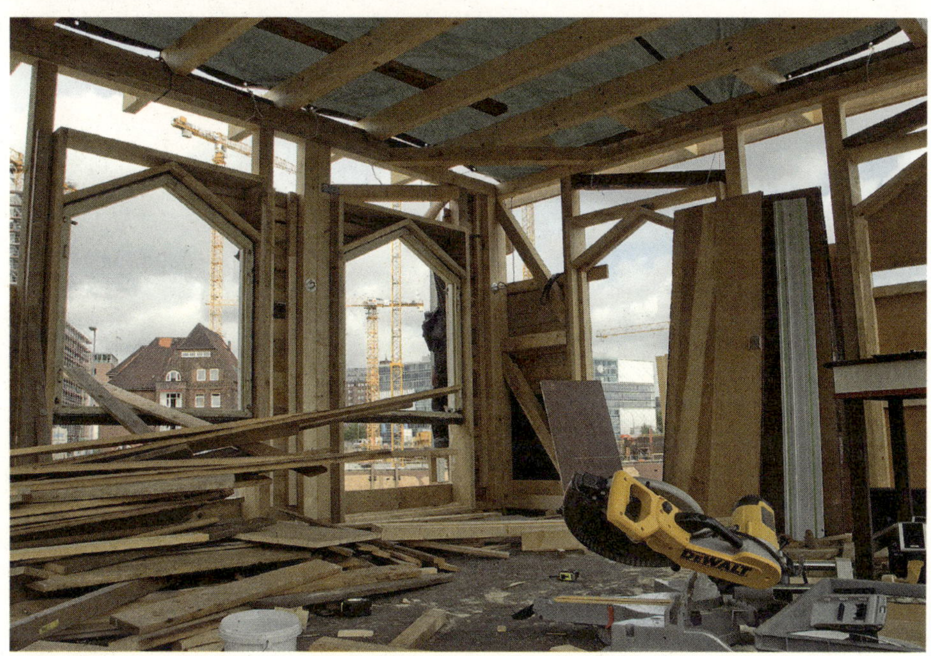

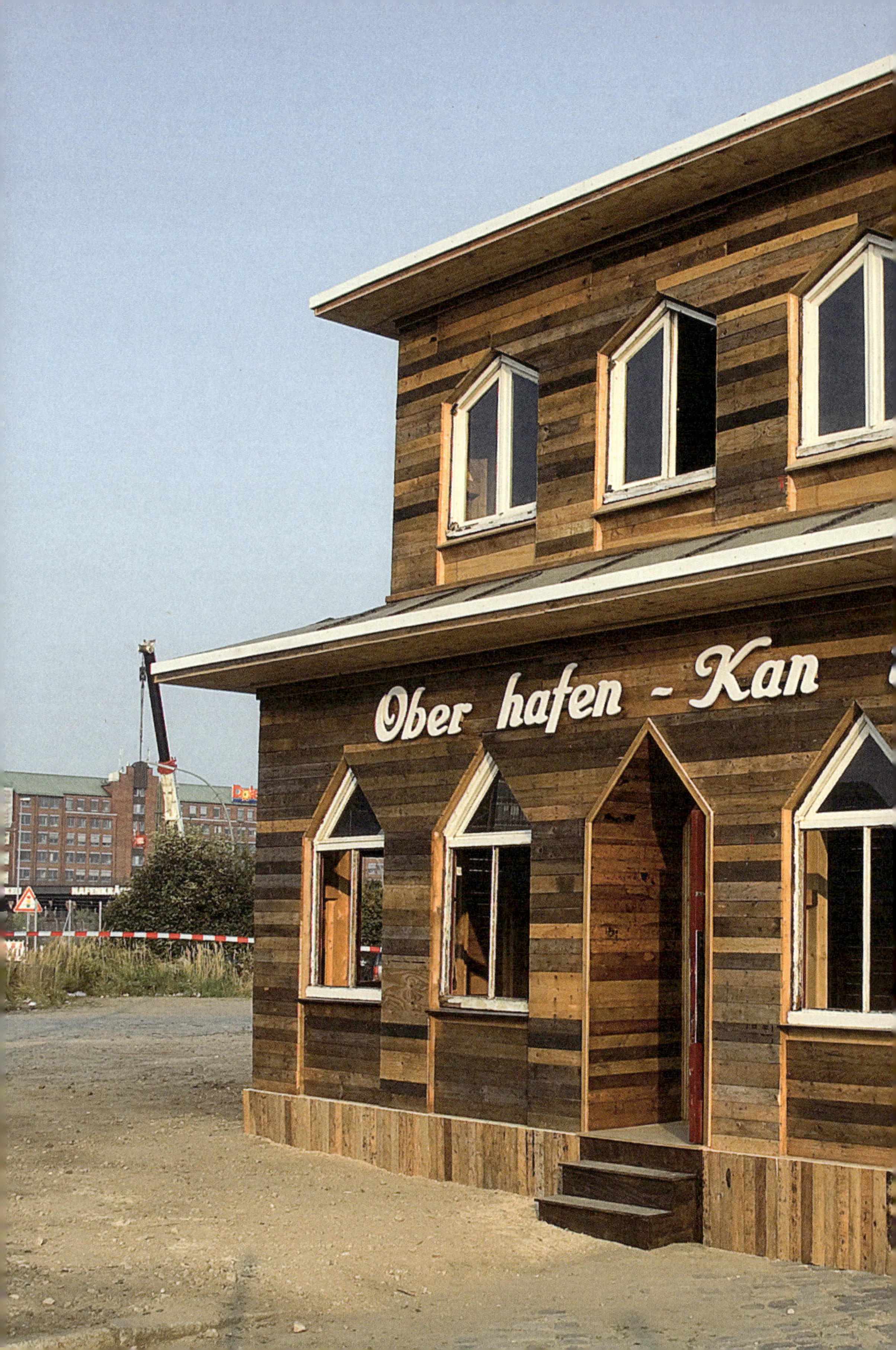

Ober hafen - Kan

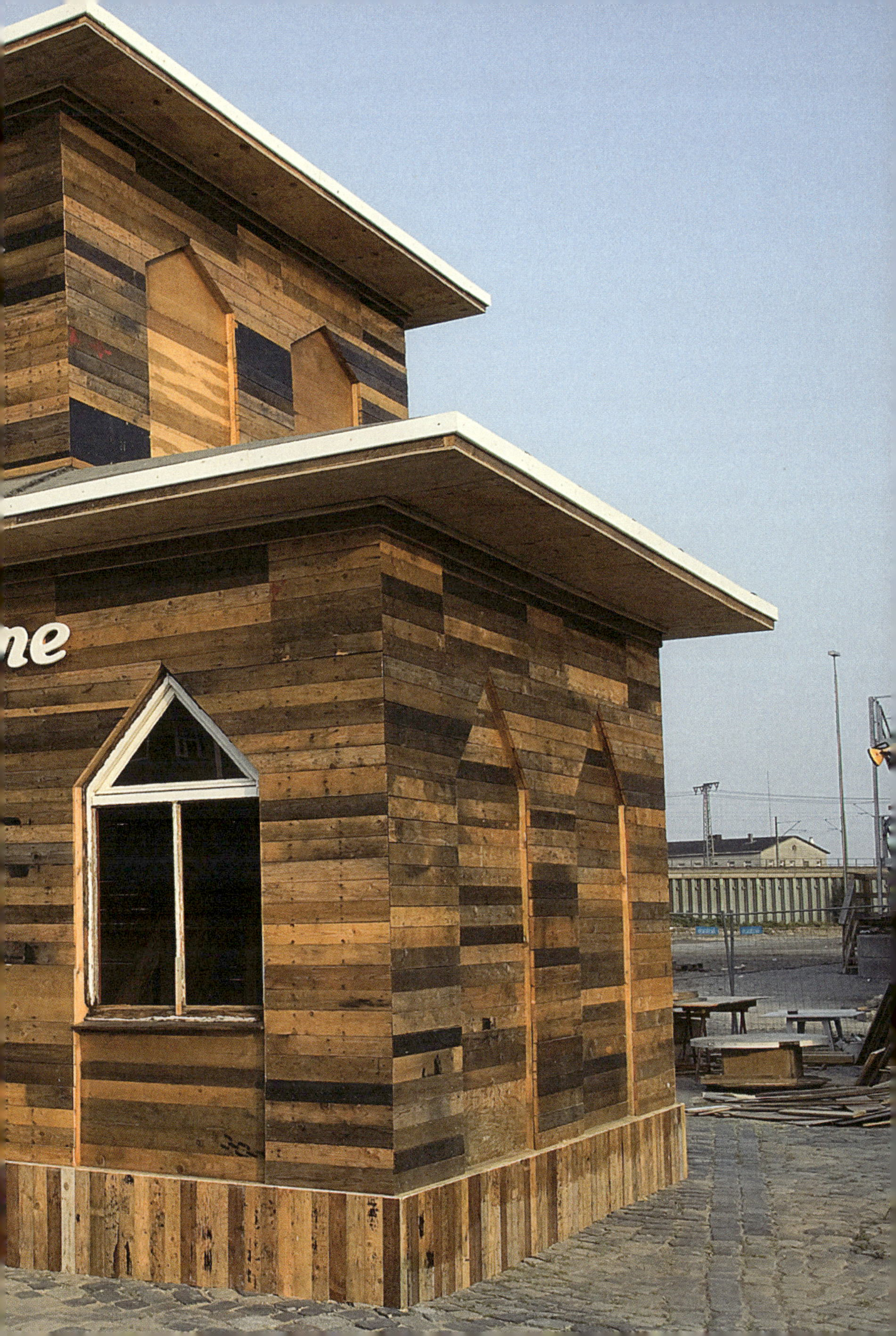

ne

Dies ist ein Text über Thorsten Passfeld. Er soll Ihnen den Menschen näher bringen, ihn hinter dem ganzen Holz hervorholen. Zwar wird auch die Kunst Erwähnung finden (schließlich ist er ein Künstler), aber stellen Sie sich lieber vor, Thorsten Passfeld wäre Fliesenleger. Oder Konditor. (Er backt hervorragend.) Etwas in dieser Art. (Das würde ihm selbst auch gut gefallen.) Im Alltag definieren wir andere Menschen unentwegt. Weil uns das Sicherheit gibt. (Wir selber aber lassen uns nur ungern definieren.) Nun, mir

Meine Zeit mit Thorsten Passfeld

behagt es nicht, in diesem Text eine spezielle Lesart von Thorsten Passfeld zu geben. Das liegt auch an meinem Unvermögen. Ich bin nur ein Freund. Zufällig schreibe ich. Thorsten Passfeld ist zu vielseitig für mich. Da fällt mir Max Ernst ein, dessen Kunst ich sehr schätze. (Ich denke hauptsächlich an Max Ernst, wenn ich an Kunst denke). »Haha«, lacht da Thorsten Passfeld, »Max wer?« Stimmt ja, dass der Ernst keine Musik gemacht hat. Und keine Trickfilme. Keine Comics. Passfeld hingegen schon. Obwohl er dann vor einigen Jahren durch seine Holzbauten, -bilder, -skulpturen und -möbel bekannt geworden ist. Durch die Nachahmung der Wirklichkeit aus Holz.

Dabei hatte es in einem Chaos aus Kunst begonnen. Vor all dem Holz, Mitte der 1990er, veranstaltete Passfeld gemeinsam mit Viktor Marek Veranstaltungen mit dem Titel ‚Materialschlacht'. Das waren Happenings mit Liedern, Witzen, Geschichten und selbstaufgenommenen Hörspiel-Kassetten. Sehr aufwändig, sehr spontan, sehr abwechslungsreich. Wie ein Kindergeburtstag auf Speed. Dort habe ich ihn zum ersten Mal gesehen. 1995 in der Taubenstraße, einer Seitenstraße der Hamburger Reeperbahn. Ein Jahr später trat Passfeld bei Michael Weins und mir im LAOLAclub auf.[1] Passfelds Bruder wohnte in der WG von Michael Weins, da hatte ihn Weins ein allererstes Mal beim Familienbesuch an der Tür getroffen. Jung, blaß und schüchtern. Ab 1997 war Passfeld einer von sieben Liv-Ullmännern.[2] Spätestens als Passfeld und ich angetrunken über Leipziger Asphalt kugelten, waren wir Freunde, und ich durfte ihn beim Vornamen nennen. Ein Moment aus diesen Jahren hat sich besonders tief in mir eingegraben: Wie wir Ullmänner untätig in Noltensmeiers VW-Bus von einem zum nächsten Auftrittsort kutschiert wurden, müde, genervt, gelangweilt, während Thorsten stoisch eine hölzerne Apfelsinenkiste in winzige Stückchen zerlegte, um sie durch ein Rostloch im Bodenblech auf die A7 zu verteilen.

Thorsten machte immer weiter. Wie ein stetig laufender Dieselmotor. Als Apfelsinenkistenzerkleinerer wie als Künstler. Die umschließende Form hieß für eineinhalb Jahre nicht mehr Materialschlacht, sondern Liv-Ullman-Show. Thorsten steuerte Lieder, Geschichten, Trickfilme und das Bühnenbild bei und bedruckte unsere Tour-T-Shirts. Ich staunte. Im Sommer 1999 fuhren Thorsten und ich für 24 Stunden nach Bielefeld, wo wir als Autoren ein Fotoprojekt begleiten sollten. Wie Strom schwirrten wir ziellos durch verregnete Straßen. Aus Verzweiflung kaufte ich einen Cowboyhut, Thorsten suchte nach Schuhen. Seine hatten Löcher. Als der Katalog gedruckt war, fehlte Thorstens Text.

Im folgenden Frühjahr besuchte er mich in Ahrenshoop, wo ich ein Stipendium hatte. Einen Nachmittag betraten wir die örtliche Radierwerkstatt, dann ließen wir uns lieber wieder vom Ostseewind die Frisuren zerzausen.

Thorsten war viel unterwegs und überall produktiv. Obwohl er aufs Reisen verzichten könnte und immer mit dem Gedanken kokettierte, am liebsten zu essen und zu schlafen. Aber wann sollte Thorsten einmal zum Essen, geschweige denn zum Schlafen kommen?

Lange Zeit dachte ich, im Zentrum von Thorstens künstlerischem Universum stünden Bilder. Bilder aus Acryl und Öl. Diese Holzsache wäre nur eine Verlegenheit. Ein Fehler der Natur. Ein Fehler im Lebenslauf. Aber Fehler sind gut für Neues. Gerade für Künstler. Die lieben das Scheitern, die persönliche Katastrophe, den Untergang. Im Winter 2001 jedenfalls froren Thorsten in seinem ungeheizten Atelier die Farben ein.[3] Unmöglich, etwas zu malen. Das Atelier lag voller Holzstücke, aber es gab keinen Ofen. Aus dieser Verzweiflung entstand eine Serie Küchengeräte aus Holzresten, vom Toaster bis zum Kühlschrank, später dann ein lebensgroßer Traktor. Die Maschine Thorsten durfte weder essen noch schlafen. Im Atelier herrschten Minusgrade. Mit dem Traktor begann das Thorsten-Prinzip: Nichts ist für immer. Nach einer Atelierausstellung wurde das Traktorenholz bei den Häusern wiederverwertet. Temporäre Kunst: Auch die Häuser wurden aufgebaut, kulturell bespielt und abgebaut.[4] Und damit der Kreislauf rund blieb, wurden aus Häusern wieder Bilder: Holzbilder. So schön die Kunst sein mag, das beste an Thorstens Atelier war die Tischtennisplatte, an der wir manches Match spielten. Nur der Holzstaub störte.

Wenn ich ein Buch lese, überlege ich oft, hat der Autor das erlebt? Wenn ich ein Bild betrachte, gerade eins von Thorsten, das einem die Unmöglichkeit der Wiederherstellung der Vergangenheit deutlich macht, frage ich mich, wo verbindet sich das Dargestellte mit dem Leben des Künstlers? Wieviel Autobiografisches ist im Bild? Wieviel Autobiografisches verträgt ein Bild überhaupt? Wann wird es zu persönlich, ja peinlich? »Handwerk ist die erste Pflicht des Künstlers«, sagt Thorsten. »Autobiografisches kannst du getrost vergessen.«

Thorsten ist häufiger bei uns zu Besuch. Er kommt immer noch, obwohl ich ihn 2000 beim Renovieren unseres Hauses beinahe mit dem Kopf eines morschen Vorschlaghammers erschlagen hätte. Stundenlang spielt er und unterhält sich mit unseren Kindern in deren Zimmern. Kommt er dann zum Essen herunter, genieße ich es, mit ihm kindisch zu sein, am Tisch zu sitzen und über den winzigsten Anlaß zu lachen. Wir schütten uns aus vor Lachen. Bis meine Familie die Köpfe schüttelt über die albernen Männer. Bei jedem dieser Besuche ist Thorsten seinen Bildern, seinen Skulpturen, seiner

Vergangenheit ausgesetzt: »Würde ich abhängen«, sagt er dann, konsequent das Thorsten-Prinzip vertretend. Immer hat er sich leicht von seinen Kunstwerken getrennt, von Skizzen, Vorarbeiten, Werken. Bilder, die er nicht verkauft hatte, ließ er beim Atelierumzug zurück. Unverkauft können die bloß schlecht sein, ist seine Meinung. Allein ein Bild erinnere ich, das er nicht verkaufen wollte. Da malte er sich in einem schmutzigen, grauen Overall von Neonlicht beschienen. Der Maschinenmensch Thorsten Passfeld. Ich weiß nicht, wo sich das Bild befindet. Es hängt jedensfalls nicht bei ihm in der Wohnung.

Es besteht ein grundsätzlicher Widerspruch in der Erkenntnis, dass das Leben keinen Sinn hat (außer den menschgemachten Versuchen) und wir Menschen dennoch (und Thorsten ganz besonders) versuchen, unsere Zeit sinnvoll zu nutzen und dem Leben eine Ordnung und Struktur zu geben (wenn auch keinen Sinn). Viele von Thorstens Bildern leben für mich von diesem Paradox. Da steht das im Bild Dargestellte gegen den Text/Titel des Bildes. Sein mir liebstes Kunstwerk ist eine Motorsäge aus Holz. Mir kommt es so vor, dass Thorsten schon immer wusste (zumindest seit ich ihn kenne): Auf dieser Welt gibt es weder Eindeutigkeit noch Erlösung. Und dennoch ist da ein Wunsch nach Wahrheit, der in ihm rumort. Wahrheit durch Arbeit. Letztendlich ist es für mich nicht zu sagen, wer oder was Thorsten im Innersten ist.
Jetzt wo ich über meine Zeit mit Thorsten Passfeld geschrieben habe, frage ich mich, wie eine Verbindung zwischen all diesen

Gegebenheiten zustande kam, die wir in unseren Leben bis jetzt durchliefen. All diese Zufälle und einige wenige absichtsvoll herbeigeführte Begegnungen und Ziele. Durch die Schwester meiner Frau ist er nicht nur mein Freund, sondern auch verwandt mit mir. Er ist das Vorbild für meinen siebenjährigen Sohn, der sich von Thorsten eine flugfähige Holzrakete oder zumindest ein Baumhaus wünscht. Wie kam eine solche Verbindung in die Welt? Wie real und belastbar ist sie? Thorsten anwortete darauf einmal sehr prosaisch: »Wenn sich z.B. durch eine Stoffwechselkrankheit unsere Körperchemie änderte, das heißt wir anders riechen würden, dann würden wir nicht mehr befreundet sein, weil wir uns wohl nicht mehr riechen könnten. Und hätten wir schon damals anders gerochen, wir hätten uns nie kennengelernt.«

Alexander Posch

1) 1996 – 1998 LAOLAclub, ein monatl. Club für Bands und Literatur, den Michael Weins und Alexander Posch veranstalteten.
2) 1997–1999 *Liv Ullmann Show*, monatl. Literatur- und Performanceshow im Molotow, Reeperbahn mit Passfeld, Weins, Posch, Mariola Brillowska, Cenk Bekdemir, Oliver Windgassen, Jürgen Noltensmeier in Hamburg und Leipzig sowie 2 Touren durch Deutschland und die Schweiz.
3) dem SKAM-Atelier in der alten Bowlingbahn am Anfang der Reeperbahn.
4) 2002: *Haus aus Holz* (60qm), Diplomarbeit; 2004: *Hoftheater Vierlinden* (130qm), das unter der Intendanz von Tom Stromberg hinter dem Deutschen Schauspielhaus in Hamburg stand; 2005: *Zum Falschen Freund* (15qm), Hafencity, HH, 2006: *Bahnhofsklo zum letzten Anfang* in der City Nord HH; 2007: *Kirche des guten Willens* (130qm), HH-Wilhelmsburg und seit 2009 steht die ‚Oberhafenkantine‘ aus Holz im Hamburger Freihafen.

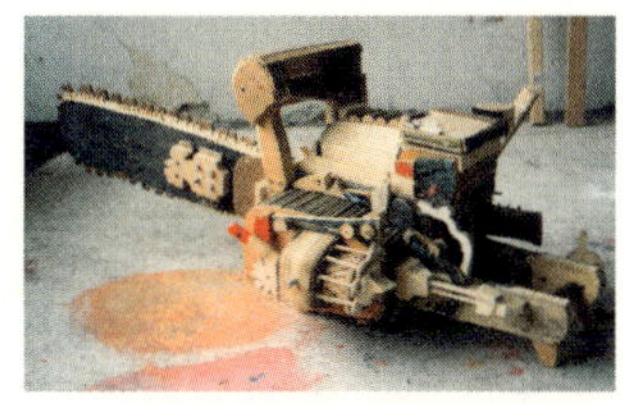

1)

This is a text about Thorsten Passfeld. It is meant to help people understand him better, to draw him out from behind all that wood. I won't be mentioning art as a matter of fact (essentially he is an artist), but imagine instead that Thorsten Passfeld is a floor tiler. Or a pastry chef. (He can bake superbly). Something of that kind. (He would like that too). In everyday life we are constantly defining other people. Because it makes us feel secure. (Yet we don't like being defined ourselves). Well, I wouldn't feel comfortable specify-

My time with Thorsten Passfeld

ing a special way of interpreting Thorsten Passfeld's works. That is due to my incapability. I am only a friend. It just so happens I'm a writer. Thorsten Passfeld is too versatile for me. That makes me think of Max Ernst, whose art I value highly. (I think particularly of Max Ernst when I think about art). "Ha ha", Thorsten Passfeld laughs, "Max who?" It's true that Ernst didn't make music. Or cartoons. He didn't make comics either. Passfeld does though. Although some years ago he became known for his constructions, pictures, sculptures and furniture made of wood. And because he used this material to reconstruct reality.

Though in fact it all began with artistic chaos. Before all that wood, in the mid-nineties, Passfeld organized events entitled *Materialschlacht* (Battle of Material) together with Viktor Marek. These were happenings with songs, jokes, stories and radio plays they recorded themselves on cassettes. Very elaborate,

very spontaneous, very diverse. Like a children's birthday party on speed. I saw him there for the first time. In 1995 in the Taubenstraße, a side street off the Reeperbahn in Hamburg. A year later Passfeld performed at LAOLA-club, run by Michael Weins and I.[1] Passfeld's brother shared an apartment with Michael Weins and Weins had met him for the very first time at the door during a family visit. Pale, young and shy. From 1997 onwards Passfeld was one of seven Liv-Ullmänner.[2] By the time Passfeld and I rolled drunkenly across the tarmac in Leipzig we had become friends and I was allowed to call him by his first name. One moment from this period has engraved itself particularly deep in my memory: How we "Ullmänner" were sitting idly in Noltensmeier's VW-bus, being driven from place to place to perform. Tired, irritated, bored, while Thorsten stoically broke a wooden orange crate into tiny pieces in order to scatter these along the A7 through a rusty hole in the floor panel.

Thorsten kept going. Like a diesel engine that keeps on running. As an orange crate shredder and as an artist. The all-encompassing form that this took for a year-and-a-half was no longer called a battle of materials but the Liv-Ullman-Show. Thorsten contributed songs, stories, cartoons and the stage design, and also printed our tour T-shirts. I was amazed. In the summer of 1999 Thorsten and I drove for 24 hours to Bielefeld, where we were supposed to

accompany a photo project as authors. We buzzed like electricity aimlessly through rainy streets. Out of desperation I bought a cowboy hat, Thorsten was looking for shoes. His ones had holes in them. When the catalogue was printed, Thorsten's text was missing.

The following spring he visited me in Ahrenshoop, where I had a scholarship. One afternoon we went to the local etching studio but then we decided we would rather let the Baltic winds tousle our hair.

Thorsten was frequently on the road and was productive everywhere he went. Although he could easily forgo travelling and always played with the idea of preferring to eat and sleep. But when was Thorsten ever supposed to eat, let alone sleep?

For a long time I thought that pictures were the centre of Thorsten's artistic universe. Pictures painted in acrylic and oil. I thought this thing with wood was just disconcertedness.

A mistake of nature. A mistake in the vita. However, mistakes are good for something new. Especially for artists. They love failure, personal catastrophes, ruin. In any case, in winter 2001 Thorsten's paints froze in his unheated studio.[3] It was impossible to paint anything. The studio was full of pieces of wood but there was no stove. This despondent situation prompted a series of kitchen utilities made of scraps of wood, from a toaster to a fridge, and later a life-size tractor. Thorsten the machine was not permitted to eat or sleep. The temperatures in his studio were below freezing. Together with the tractor, the Thorsten-principle was started: Nothing is forever. Following a studio exhibition the wood used for the tractor was recycled and used to build the houses. Temporary art: The houses were also constructed, became the setting for cultural events, and were dismantled again.[4] And in order that the cycle not be broken the houses were turned back into pictures again: wooden pictures. However beautiful art might be, the best thing about Thorsten's studio was the ping-pong table that we played many a match on. The only bothersome thing was the wood dust.

When I read a book, I often wonder: did the author really experience that? When I look at a picture, particularly one of Thorten's, which makes it clear how impossible it is to recreate the past, I ask myself where the connection between what is represented and the artist's life is. How much autobiographical information is contained in the picture? How much autobiographical information can a picture in fact tolerate? When does it become too personal, even embarrassing? "Craftsmanship is an artist's first obligation", says Thorsten. "You can safely forget about the autobiographical element."

Thorsten often visits us. He still comes, even though in 2000 when we were renovating the house, I almost took his head off with a dodgy sledgehammer. He plays with and talks to our children for hours in their rooms. Then when he comes down to eat I enjoy being childish with him, sitting at the table and laughing at the slightest thing. We tremble with laughter. Until my family shake their heads at these foolish men. During each of these visits, Thorsten is faced with his pictures, his sculptures, his past: "I'd take that one down", he said, true to the Thorsten-principle. He has always parted easily with his art, with sketches, preliminary drafts and works themselves. He left unsold pictures behind when he moved studios. In his opinion, works that are not sold can't be any good. I can only remember one picture that he didn't want to sell. He had painted himself in a dirty, grey overall in the glow of a neon light. The human machine Thorsten Passfeld. I don't know where this picture is. At any rate it is not hanging in his apartment.

It is a contradiction in itself when we realize that life has no meaning (except for human-made attempts) and that in spite of this we humans (and Thorsten in particular) try to make wise use of our time and to give life a system and structure (albeit not a meaning). For me, many of Thorsten's pictures thrive on this paradox. The text/title of the picture contradicts what is shown in the picture. My favourite work of his is a power saw made of wood. It seems to me that Thorsten has always been aware (at least since I have known him) that this world offers neither unambiguity nor redemption. And yet a desire for truth stirs within him. Truth through work. Ultimately it is not for me to say who or what Thorsten is deep down inside.

Now that I have written about my time with Thorsten Passfeld I ask myself how a connection came about between all these circumstances that we have encountered up to this point in our lives. All these coincidences and some less intentional encounters and goals. Through my wife's sister, Thorsten is not only my friend but we are also related. He is a role model for my seven-year-old son who wants Thorsten to give him a wooden rocket that can really fly or at least a tree house. How did such a connection come about in this world? How real and resilient is it? Thorsten once answered this question very prosaically: "If our body chemistry is changed by a metabolic disorder for example, in other words if we smelled different, then we would no longer be friends, because we would not be able to stand each other. And if we had smelled differently back then we would never have got to know one another".

Alexander Posch

1) 1996 – 1998 LAOLAclub, a monthly club for bands and literature organized by Michael Weins and Alexander Posch.

2) 1997-1999 *Liv Ullmann Show,* a monthly literature and performance show in Molotow, on the Reeperbahn in Hamburg with Passfeld, Weins, Posch, Mariola Brillowska, Cenk Bekdemir, Oliver Windgassen, Jürgen Noltensmeier, and also in Leipzig, as well as two tours through Germany and Switzerland.

3) The SKAM-studio in the old bowling alley at the entrance to the Reeperbahn.

4) 2002: *Haus aus Holz* (Wooden house) (60sqm), diploma project; 2004: *Hoftheater Vierlinden* (Vierlinden Theatre Royal) (130qm), created under the directorship of Tom Stromberg and located behind the theatre Deutsches Schauspielhaus in Hamburg; 2005: *Zum Falschen Freund* (to the false friend) (15qm), Hafencity, HH, 2006: *Bahnhofsklo zum letzten Anfang* (Station loo for the last beginning) in the district City Nord HH; 2007: *Kirche des guten Willens* (Church of Goodwill) (130qm), HH-Wilhelmsburg and since 2009 a wooden construction of the *Oberhafenkantine* (Oberhafen Canteen) has been located in the Hamburg free harbour.

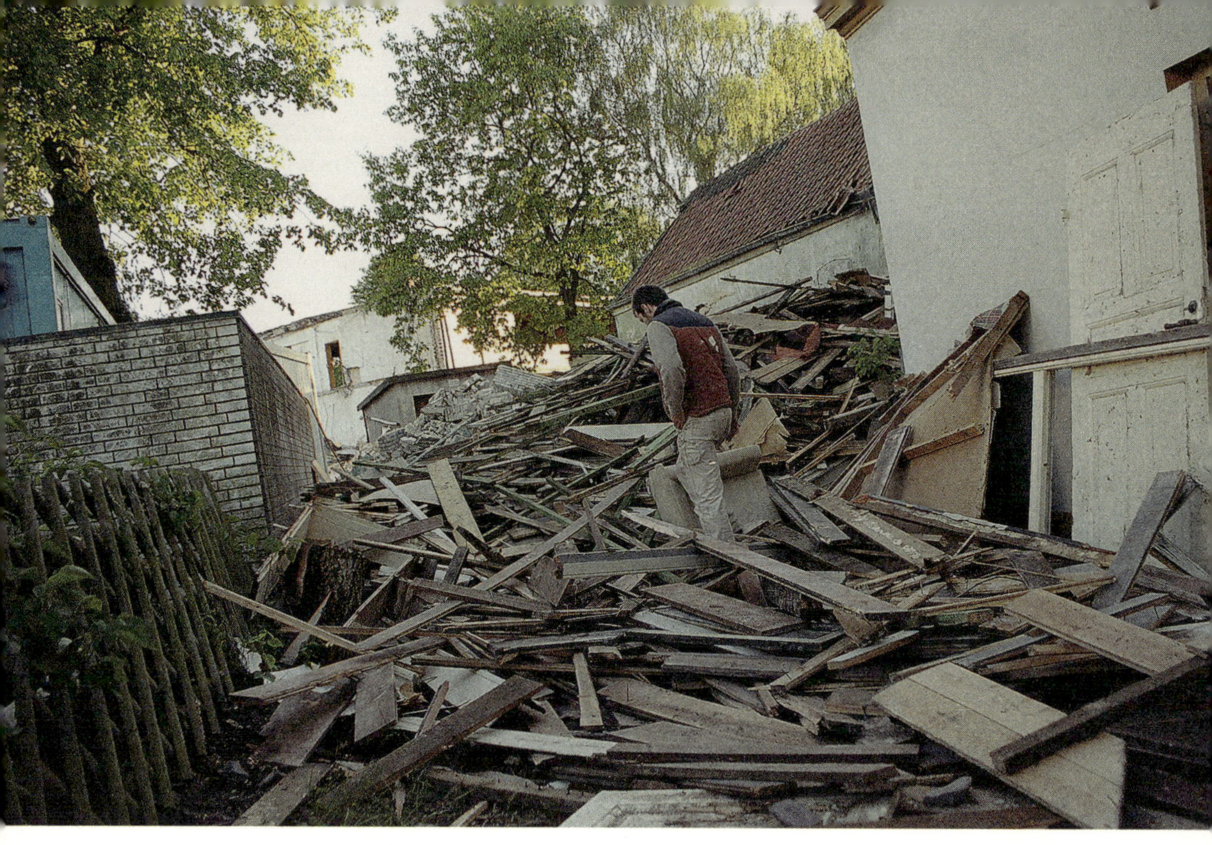

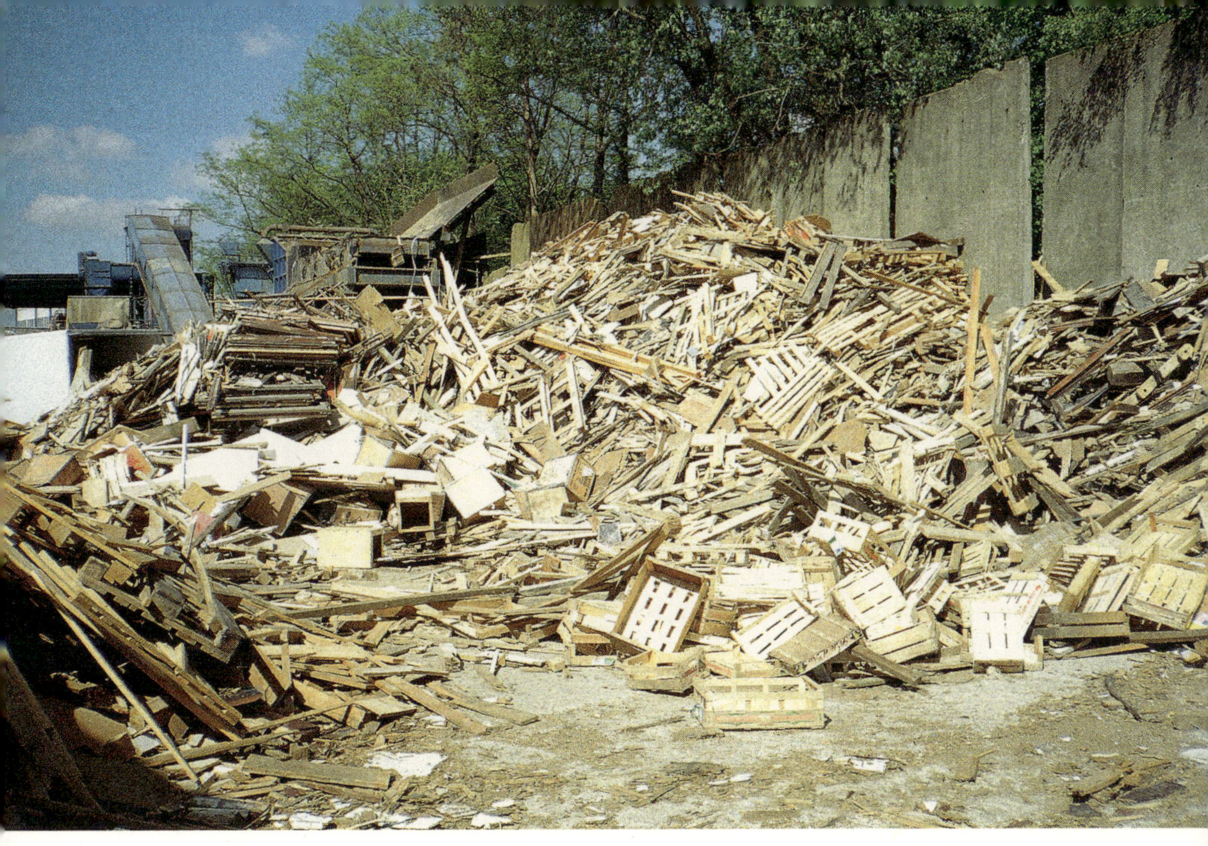

Abbildungsnachweis II / List of Works II

Seite, page 28, 29: Skizzen, sketches
Seite, page 30, 31: Werkstattansicht, März 2010, studio view, March 2010
Seite, page 36: *Referenzgruppe*, 2009
Seite, page 40, 41: *Torpedos der Doofheit*, 2007
Seite, page 42: *Torpedos der Doofheit*
Seite, page 43: *Flieger*, 2008
Seite, page 44, 45: *Flieger*
Seite, page 46: *Traktor*, 2001
Seite, page 47: *Rasenmäher*, 2001
Seite, page 48: *Play with the Big*, Art Basel Miami Beach, 2006
Seite, page 49: *Play with the Big*, Vorproduktion im SKAM, preproduction at SKAM
Seite, page 56, 57: *Haus aus Holz*, St. Pauli Hamburg, Aufbau, setup, 2002
Seite, page 58, 59: *Haus aus Holz*, Außenansicht, exterior view
Seite, page 60 – 69: *Haus aus Holz*, Innenansicht, inside view
Seite, page 70, 71: *Haus aus Holz*, Abriß, demolition
Seite, page 76 – 79: *Hoftheater Vierlinden*, Deutsches Schauspielhaus Hamburg, 2004
Seite, page 80, 81: *Hoftheater Vierlinden*, Premierentag, opening day
Seite, page 82 – 86: *Hoftheater Vierlinden*, Innenansicht, inside view
Seite, page 87: *Hoftheater Vierlinden*, Abriß, demolition
Seite, page 88 oben (top): *Zum Falschen Freund*, Buchholz, 2005
Seite, page 88 unten (bottom), 89 – 93: *Zum Falschen Freund*, Hafencity Hamburg, 2005
Seite, page 94 – 97: *Erholungsheim für schuldbewußte Großstädter*, Altona Hamburg, 2006
Seite, page 98 – 101: *Bahnhofstoilette zum letzten Anfang*, City Nord Hamburg, 2006
Seite, page 102 – 108: *Kirche des guten Willens*, Wilhelmsburg Hamburg, 2007
Seite, page 109 – 110: *Kirche des guten Willens*, Abbau, dismantling
Seite, page 111: *Kirche des guten Willens*, Düsseldorf, 2007
Seite, page 112: *Eine Welt im Keller*, Federzeichnung, pen and ink drawing, 2002
Seite, page 114 – 117: *Oberhafenkantine Replika*, Hafencity Ost Hamburg, Aufbau, setup, 2009
Seite, page 118, 119: *Oberhafenkantine Replika*
Seite, page 124, 125: Holzbeschaffung, wooden aquisition

Lebenslauf / Biography

1975   geboren in Dinslaken | born in Dinslaken
1997–2002   Studium an der Hochschule für bildende Künste(HfbK) in Hamburg
              studied at the Academy of Fine Arts (HfbK), Hamburg

              Passfeld lebt und arbeitet in Hamburg | Passfeld lives and works in Hamburg

Häuser | Houses:

2002   *Haus aus Holz* (60m²), Hamburg
2004   *Hoftheater Vierlinden* (130m²), Deutsches Schauspielhaus Hamburg
2005   *Zum Falschen Freund* (15m²), Kunstverein Buchholz & Hafencity, Baltic Raw Tower, Hamburg
2006   *Heim* (28m²), Ding Dong Art Festival, Hamburg
              Bahnhofstoilette zum letzten Anfang, Skulpturenpark City Nord, Hamburg
              Kapitän Walter Porschels trad. Weinklause, Kunstverein Buchholz
2007   *Kirche des Guten Willens*, Hamburg & Theaterfestival Impulse, Düsseldorf
              (umgeänderte Version des Hauses/ altered version of the house)
2009   *Oberhafenkantine Replika*, Hamburg

Ausstellungen (Auswahl) | Exhibitions (Selection)

              (E) = Einzelausstellung   (G) = Gruppenausstellung   (K) = Katalog
              (E) = Soloexhibition   (G) = Groupexhibition   (K) = Catalogue

1997   *Harmlose große Bilder*, Kaifu Art Center, Hamburg (E)
1998   *Keine großen Werke schaffen*, Hafenklang, Hamburg (E)
1999   *Hengstland*, Fundbureau, Hamburg (E)
2000   *Tagesmaschine* Installation, Produzentengalerie, Kassel (E)
2001   *Final SKAM*, SKAM, Hamburg (G)
2002   *Index 02*, Kunsthaus Hamburg, Hamburg (G)
              Exklusiv 27, Galerie 27, Leipzig
              SKAM plett, SKAM, Hamburg (G)
              Diplomausstellung HfbK, Hamburg (G)
2003   *Falsche Wiese*, Galerie 27, Leipzig (G)
2004   *Turner Toons*, Galerie 27, Leipzig (G)
2005   *Malerei ist doof*, SKAMraum, SKAM, Hamburg (E)
              Frühling, SKAMraum, SKAM, Hamburg (E)
              Nekoaid, Nekojuice, Berlin (E)
2006   *SKAM – Gruppenausstellung*, Raum 2, Mannheim (G)
              Heim, Ding Dong Art Festival, Hamburg (E)
              SKAM Austellung, SKAM, Hamburg (E)
              Play with the Big, Ausstattung und Installation | environment and installation,
              Art Basel Miami Beach
2007   *Kommt jetzt alle rein, bitte*, Feinkunst Krüger, Hamburg (E)
              Torpedos der Doofheit, Galerie Hilger (Wien), Art Cologne, Köln (G, K)
              Und wir gehen lieber im Dunkeln durch die Strassen, Galerie Ölfrüh, Hamburg (E)
2009   *The Power of Trauer*, Feinkunst Krüger, Hamburg (E)

Diese Publikation erscheint anlässlich der Ausstellungen | This publication was produced to accompany the exhibitions:

Du konntest es nicht sein Liebling – 10. 05. 2010 – 09. 07. 2010, LEVY Hamburg
WARM, GROSS, GUT – 12. 11. 2010 – 08. 01. 2011, LEVY Berlin

Thorsten Passfeld – *Ich bin zurück* | *It's me again*
Herausgegeben von | Edited by: Alexander Sairally
Texte | Essays: Sven Amtsberg, Jaques Palminger, Alexander Posch, Ludwig Seyfarth, Tom Stromberg
Redaktion | Editing: Alexander Sairally
Übersetzungen | Translations: Gillian Morris
Fotonachweis | Photo credits: Dirk Masbaum: Cover, Seiten | pages 1 - 31; Nicole Keller: Seiten | pages 14 - 119;
Oliver Fantitsch: Seiten | pages 82 - 86; Willi Passfeld: Seiten | pages 78 oben | top, 79 unten | bottom, 80, 81, 88 oben | top, 111, 124;
Eske Schlüters: Seiten | pages 51 Abb. 1) | ill. 1), Babette Brandenburg: Seiten | pages 109, 110; Marckus Klapper: Seiten | pages 60 - 69;
Thorsten Passfeld: Seiten | pages 36, 40, 42 - 49, 51 Abb. 2) + 3) | ill. 2) + 3), 52, 53, 56 - 59, 70, 71, 76, 77, 78 unten | bottom,
79 oben | top, 87, 88 unten | bottom, 89 - 108, 121 Abb. 1) | ill. 1), 125, Zeichnungen | drawings: Seiten | pages 113, 128
Grafische Gestaltung | Graphic design: Claas Möller, claasbooks.de
Verlag | Publisher: Kerber Verlag

Kerber Verlag, Bielefeld
Windelsbleicher Straße 166, D-33659 Bielefeld
Tel.: +49 521 950 08 10, Fax: +49 521 950 08 88
info@kerberverlag.com, www.kerberverlag.com

US Distribution
D.A.P., Distributed Art Publishers, Inc.
155 Sixth Avenue | 2nd Floor
New York, NY 10013
Tel.: +1 212 627 19 99
Fax: +1 212 627 94 84

Die Deutsche Nationalbibliothek verzeichnet diese Publikation in der Deutschen Nationalbibliografie;
detaillierte bibliografische Daten sind im Internet über http://dnb.d-nb.de abrufbar.
The Deutsche Nationalbibliothek holds a record of this publication in the Deutsche Nationalbibliografie;
detailed bibliographical data can be found under: http://dnb.d-nb.de.

© 2010 Kerber Verlag, Bielefeld | Leipzig | Berlin, Autoren, Herausgeber und Künstler | Authors, Publisher and Artist

ISBN 978-3-86678-408-6, Printed in Germany

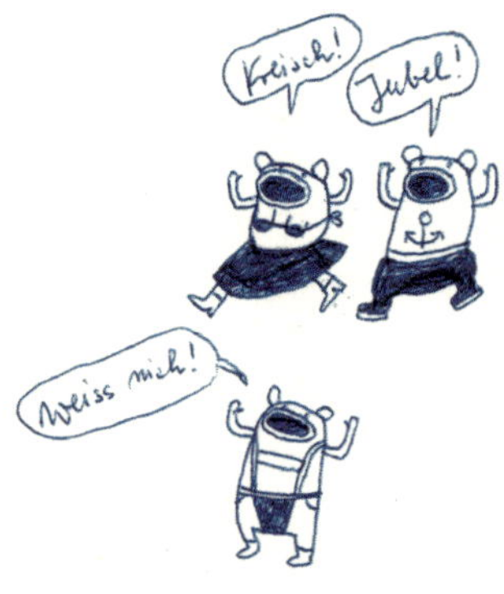

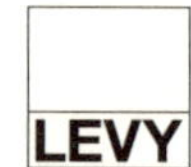

LEVY Hamburg | Osterfeldstrasse 6 | D-22529 Hamburg | T.: + 49 - 40 - 45 91 88 | F.: + 49 - 40 - 44 72 25
LEVY Berlin | Rudi-Dutschke-Str. 26 | D-10969 Berlin | T.: + 49 - 30 - 25 292 221 | F.: + 49 - 30 - 25 292 276
info@levy-galerie.de | www.levy-galerie.de